The Trade Wars of the USA, China, and the EU

The Trade Wars of the USA, China, and the EU

The Global Economy in the Age of Populism

Edited by
Altuğ Günar

LEXINGTON BOOKS
Lanham • Boulder • New York • London

Published by Lexington Books
An imprint of The Rowman & Littlefield Publishing Group, Inc.
4501 Forbes Boulevard, Suite 200, Lanham, Maryland 20706
www.rowman.com

6 Tinworth Street, London SE11 5AL, United Kingdom

British Library Cataloguing in Publication Information Available

Library of Congress Cataloging-in-Publication Data

Names: Günar, Altuğ, 1985- editor.
Title: The trade wars of the USA, China, and the EU : the global economy in the age of populism / edited by Altuğ Günar.
Description: Lanham, Maryland : Lexington Books, 2021. | Includes bibliographical references and index. | Summary: "The book is investigating the developments after the 2008 crisis. The incompatible tone among the populist leaders with a liberal trade system led nations to disintegrate in the fields of economy and to protect their countries under the shadow of populism which is caused trade wars between world-leading economies"—Provided by publisher.
Identifiers: LCCN 2021022609 (print) | LCCN 2021022610 (ebook) | ISBN 9781793631176 (cloth) | ISBN 9781793631183 (ebook)
Subjects: LCSH: International economic relations. | European Union countries—Commerce—China. | China—Commerce—European Union countries. | United States—Commerce—China. | China—Commerce—United States. | Globalization—21st century.
Classification: LCC HF1365 .T723 2021 (print) | LCC HF1365 (ebook) | DDC 337.1/42—dc23
LC record available at https://lccn.loc.gov/2021022609
LC ebook record available at https://lccn.loc.gov/2021022610

Contents

List of Illustrations

List of Tables

Introduction

This study is based on a perspective that has risen all over the world following the 2008 crisis, initially manifesting itself politically and then economically, and calling as the age of populism. Radical parties came to power in the countries that suffered seriously from the 2008 crisis and played a role in the implementation of protectionist policies in countries by giving the message that they take a stand with the populace. The main question of this study (book) is how the concept of populism has become a concept that defines our age and how this concept affects the external economic atmosphere through internal political balances and causes economic tensions between countries. Above all, it is known that capitalism is going through a transformation process seriously. As a result of this transformation process, the system has to rebuild itself and renew all its vehicles while stepping into a new era.

The gap between the financial economy and the real economy gradually increased—after 1980—the nation-states transfer their basic expenses to financial institutions through loans, and the implementation of the financial deregulation process all over the world without slowing down has created a huge financial structure growing uncontrollably. In 2008, the financial welfare process caused by the financial structure has come to an end. This period of prosperity, considered as the success of capitalism, ended up with a devastating system crisis. The crisis that occurred in 2008 indicated that the economic system built after the Second World War came to an end. The system responded with a systemic crisis to get rid of structures that were incompatible with it. In other words, the twentieth-century economic tools and methods of making money had a serious conflict in the face of high technology and new tools and structures that produce added value. This situation emerges as the confrontation between the Silicon Valley and the Wall Street in the United States and the rebuilding of the Wall Street by the Silicon

Valley. As a matter of fact, when the characteristics of the companies operating on the Wall Street are examined, it can be concluded that this company or the companies in the trading markets are big technology giants that have become essential today. A similar situation was experienced again in the 2000s with the "dot.com" crisis and the internet bubble of that period caused the formation of giant technology companies that dominate the world today, see; Amazon, Apple, Google, etc.

This situation also shows itself in the human being who continues his daily life. Industry 4.0 technologies and the marvelous development of artificial intelligence arise as a result of the controlled continuation of human lives. As a matter of fact, this terrifying structure, which acts through data, can manipulate human preferences. Uncontrolled content that people in many parts of the world encounter with social media, such as the Cambridge Analytica scandal, also affects people's economic, political, and individual preferences. This situation, which was one of the consequences of the 2008 crisis, had a much more severe impact on the political structure. The technologically changing content of capitalism has resulted in rulers who accept politically radical discourses and have protectionist perspectives, coming to power or gaining power all over the world. While it is thought that it is impossible to avoid data with technological developments, a period that can be called the age of populism globally has started.

During this transition period, more authoritarian and more radical leaders came to power. The United Kingdom has vetoed twice and decided to leave the European Union (EU) in 2016. President Trump, who came to power in 2016, with his "First USA" policy—Trump Moment—broke the multilateral free trade policy of the United States by waging war on the freedom of the global economic system. Withdrawing from the Trans-Pacific Treaty, first the Pacific and then from the Trans-Atlantic Investment Partnership Treaty—suspended—caused the collapse of economic relations with Europe. These actions of Trump have had repercussions in all countries, and the nationalist logic has been resurrected, clinging to populist rhetoric, and dealing a great blow to the polyphony of the world. At this stage, a mysterious disease that emerged in China began to spread rapidly all over the world.

This study argues that, based on a claim that the 2008 financial and economic crisis led to the rise of the populist leader, the so-called trade war, the world has been going through a process that led to mutual commercial reprisals between the United States, China, and the EU. The current economic sizes of the relevant economic blocks, which have a large share in global trade, are 51.3 trillion dollars in total (US$21.4 trillion, China 14.3 trillion dollars, EU$27 15.6 trillion). The global economic size has been realized as 87.7 trillion dollars with 2019 data for the world. This situation reveals how much the commercial friction between the related blocs has the potential to narrow global trade. The sections of the study have been arranged in a way explaining the state of the global economy in this period and include prominent topics in the global economy.

In the first part of the study, Altuğ Günar touches on the connections between populism and the global economy and trade wars and gives quite striking information on the trade relations and trade wars of economic giants such as the United States, China, and EU, which are accepted as leaders in the world economy. In the second part of the study, Rüya Ataklı Yavuz highlights the role of the World Trade Organization in the process of trade wars by focusing on the role of the World Trade Organization in global trade. In the third part, Samet Zenginoglu tries to evaluate the globalizing economy rather than the Western-centered globalization of the economy in terms of two axes and leading actors. Following Ilhan Aras makes a great evaluation of EU–China economic relations in a historical context. In chapter 5, Süreyya Yiğit sheds light on issues such as the trade deficit, technology transfer, industrial policy, and currency manipulation which President Trump has highlighted as being paramount in dealing with China. Kaan Celikok and Cem Saatcioglu, in the sixth part of the study, underline the importance of the Industry 4.0 technologies with the example of Germany's ecological industrial policy approaches and give deep information about Germany's industrial policy design. In the next part, Omca Altın highlights the importance of energy in global affairs and draws attention to the relations between the EU and Russia. She asserts that accessing energy resources in uninterrupted, reliable ways and at affordable prices is of vital importance for countries. Otherwise, interruptions in energy resources, high dependency on imports, failure to provide affordable access to energy resources, and sudden fluctuations in prices adversely affect the economic and social welfare of societies, thus the global economy, and can lead to serious crises. In chapter 8, Fatma Didin Sönmez presents a theoretical model analyzing the impact of economic integration between developed and developing countries on the economic growth rate, human capital allocation across sectors, and technological change. Technology transfer by trade and foreign investment is the most important positive outcome of economic integration. In her opinion, the role of new technology in enhancing economic growth is widely accepted. However, the diffusion of new technology across the member countries in the integration is not clear. Even if foreign countries producing technology is voluntary to give their innovations, the domestic capacity of countries may be insufficient to use these innovations. Countries that have not human capital skilled enough to use developed countries' technology have to pay a fixed cost. In the next chapter, Çağla Yavuz Özgören elaborates the role and mission of universities evolved toward being more responsible not only to meet the educational need of wider society but also fostering innovation through knowledge transfer activities from university to industry to gain a competitive advantage in a global economy. In addition to that, Özgören not only seeks to provide comprehensive and integrative view on the subject through unpacking dynamics of knowledge transfer mechanisms in university-industry relations but also delineates avenues for future knowledge exchange research, with a particular focus on implications for achieving competitive advantage in a global economy. Eventually, Yusuf Kurtoglu attracts attention to the artificial intelligence technologies. Kurtoglu asserts that in the past two decades, the application of the internet and digital technologies make it possible to collect and availability of big data including images for economic agents. This allowed utilizing the application of creative digital technologies on big data analysis such as machine learning algorithms. Kurtoglu underlines the importance of the artificial technologies on the economic growth, world economy, and the future professions supposed to be created.

It is also important to note that all chapters of this book underwent an external review process. We want to thank all the authors and researchers who are experts in their field for their devotion and diligence and hope to help our readers. We would also like to thank our external reviewers for their expertise and contribution to our book. At the end of our saying, we also offer our endless gratitude to everyone who are the source of motivation for us and our authors for their patience and support during the conduct of these valuable works.

Our respect.

Editor: Assoc. Prof. Altuğ Günar

Chapter 1

World Economy in the Age of Populism

On Trade Wars of the Leaders of World Economy: The US, China, The European Union

Altuğ Günar

INTRODUCTION

Several developments that occurred in 2016 globally have left their mark on the era we live in. The UK's leaving the EU as a result of the United Kingdom European Union membership referendum, commonly referred to as the Brexit referendum, and following this, Trump administration's coming to power in the United States has led global multilateralism to face a serious challenge since the Second World War. The triggering factor of all these developments was the Great Recession of 2008, that is, the capitalist devastation arising from the global financial and economic crisis in 2008. The 2008 financial crisis led all countries around the world to face a serious economic downturn.

Following the 2008 financial crisis, the number and popularity of populist political leaders have increased significantly, first in Europe, then all over the world. After the Second World War, the world has witnessed the rise of populist rhetoric in politics, politically, and culturally, and economically in particular. Populist trends in Europe have emerged in the context of undermining the EU integration process, anti-immigration policies, othering, and antidemocratic practices; besides, coming to the US administration in 2016, Trump, who turned economic nationalism into a foreign policy instrument, has made the United States withdraw from all multilateral agreements. The United States started a trade war that causes great damage to global trade

1

first with the EU and then with China. Trade wars have encouraged populist rhetoric in politics all over the world and the global economy has been under the influence of protectionism.

The key issue of this study is that the 2008 financial crisis has increased populist trends all over the world and destroyed the multilateral global order by triggering trade wars. So indeed, after the 2008 crisis, EU integration has entered a serious existence crisis, and populist leaders, who transform the EU's support to the multilateral global order into a sense of hate on a social basis, have campaigned to convince people that integration is something to be hated. The most concrete outcome of this situation has been "Brexit." Leaders who express themselves as populists have acted with suspicion toward thoughts such as global governance, global economic arrangements, and supranational integration and have begun to use the structures formed by the achievements of democracy to destroy democracy. As protectionism rises in the global economy and trade, the world becomes alienated from itself, collaboration processes suffer, and conflicts increase. This study consists of three chapters. Chapter 1 deals with the concept of populism and discusses its relationship with economic protectionism. Chapter 2 examines the trade wars in a historical context, along with their reasons, and reveals in what way they are similar to today. The third and last chapter, on the other hand, touches on the trade wars between the United States, the EU, and China and tries to explain the current situation from different perspectives.

CONCEPTUAL BACKGROUND: ON POPULISM AND TRADE PROTECTIONISM

Populism is regarded as "one of the main political buzzwords" of the twenty-first century. The term is used to describe left-wing parties in Latin America, but this concept is also preferred to describe dissenting views expressing right-wing trends in Europe. As a matter of fact, when we look at the United States, we see that this concept emerges as an expression used for the US presidents, no matter left or right wing. Using the concept intensely to such a degree leads to a serious contradiction in terms. First of all, it should be revealed that the concept is a term of liberal democracy. In this context, examining the concept theoretically, it can be stated that it is closer to liberal democracy. Indeed, most of the actors identified as populists can exist or continue their existence politically within liberal democracies. Attracting attention, this controversial concept is used to point out different phenomena in many different regions around the world. While populism manifests itself as xenophobia and anti-immigration in Europe, the economic aspect of the concept outweighs in Latin America, and it refers to phenomena such as bad economics, partisan staffing, or "favoritism" (Mudde 2017, 1–2).

When the lexical meaning of the populism is examined, we see that it refers to "a type of politics that claims to represent the opinions and wishes of ordinary people" (Oxford Leaner's Dictionary, 2020). The concept of populist, on the other hand, means a member of a political party claiming to represent the feelings and thoughts, as well as the demands of common people or "a believer in the rights, wisdom, or virtues of the common people." It is stated that the first known use of the concept dates to 1891, being derived from the Latin word "populous" (Merriam-Webster, 2020).

Parties or politicians with a populist political trend base their claim and administration legitimacy on the folk. Therefore, they think that structures created by the nature of the system weaken the public representation. Due to increasingly compromising with the principles of "the rule of law," "an independent judiciary," and "free media," which can be considered as indispensable for today's democratic systems, the political system that wraps itself up in a different structure after a while begins to personalize and it leads to these people shape the system as they wish. While the situation in the political sphere, the superstructure of the system, undergoes such a change, in time, parallel developments occur in economics. Populist leaders desire to gain authority or to establish authority over independent agencies involved in economy administration since they reject restraints on the conduct of economic policy (Rodrik, 2018 196–199).

Today, the concept of populism reflects the spirit of the existing age. As a matter of fact, following the global financial crisis of 2008, political movements which are characterized as populist figures gathered support and strength from far right ideologies. It can be argued that the most specific examples of this situation are the emerging political movements in the countries that suffered from the crisis. Syriza's landslide victory in Greece, the rise of the Podemos Party in Spain is the most explicit sign for this situation. Giving the message that they stand by the common people, the political parties in question left the word that they disapprove the politics made by the elites. However, it is known that both parties get strength from the radical leaning left wing. Consequently, the use of the term populism has led to a big conceptual discussion. This acceleration increased its popularity in the wake of the withdrawal of the UK from the EU in 2016, and, particularly, Donald Trump's election victory as the president of the United States in the same year truly exploded it. The term populism shot to fame with Trump's inauguration in 2017 (Mudde 2018).

One of today's striking paradoxes is the fact that the democracy form adopted after the Second World War appears before the humanity as threatening itself today. The crisis of trust in democratic institutions in Europe is one of the outcomes of the success of the factors that hold together and form democracy. Nationalistic attitudes that manifest themselves concretely and strongly as anti-immigration in Europe has significantly emerged with the rising of Marine Le Pen in France, who brings this trend forward, and his victory in the first round of the election. It is seen that far-right nationalism has gained strength also in Denmark, Sweden, the Netherlands, and Austria. Indeed, it can be explicitly seen that after the 2008 financial crisis, radical trends toward nationalism over identity have increased in Europe. However, radical and antidemocratic trends emerging in Europe shall play a determining role in shaping the future of democracy. Although the concept called populism remains in Europe, the response of European societies to these trends is of vital importance in shaping the future of democracy (Krastev 2011, 11–12, 15).

Studies linking the balance of domestic policy and the policies of global trade have increased after the 1990s. As a matter of fact, along with the 1990s, trends changing the global atmosphere have pushed the world to go through a major transformation. In this regard, national leaders meeting in trade negotiations reflected the situation of their countries in these meetings. Within the relevant period, during the Uruguay Round that led to the creation of the World Trade Organization (WTO), the effects of domestic political developments on global trade were monitored concretely. Domestic politics is not only effective in the context of leaders, groups representing the industry, interest groups, in particular, have been instrumental in resolving the dispute between the United States and Japan in the relevant process. In the 1990s, statist theories were highlighted in political science, and these influenced the foreign trade and economic policy of the states. While statist theories prioritize policies based on national interests and dominated by national interests, they make much less concessions to other political actors or participants, and by not including relevant stakeholders in the process, they become competent in determining international economic policies with an elite decision-making structure (Grossman and Helpman 1995, 676).

The economic globalization continued to develop in a largely unchecked fashion from the end of the Cold War through to the global financial crisis of 2008. In fact, for the United States, to maintain its hegemony was possible in this way. Neither China nor Russia challenged the hegemonic power of the United States, and economic globalization continued to develop without slowing down until 2008. With Donald Trump's presidency in the United States in 2016, the winds have changed. Facing a serious existential crisis in 2016, the EU has also fallen behind its global competitors in the context of technological development and digressed from its role of being the fortress of multilateralism. Predictions that the post–Cold War global order will develop in the context of North America, Europe, and Asia has ended unexpectedly. In this regard, we witnessed the rise of Trump's "America First" illiberal policy in Western and Central Europe, while "Putinesque Revanchisme" has been effective in Eastern Europe and a "Chinese model of authoritarian capitalism" in large parts of Asia. The countries that are unsatisfied with the liberal order let nationalist trends strengthen globally. The world has witnessed in this period a nationalism at levels unprecedented in the life of that order since the Second World War. Strengthening with economic protectionism and restraint measures, the populist rhetoric in a sense also causes culture wars (Higgott 2018, 4–5).

In Europe, populism has turned into a concept that arouses a sense of resentment to agitate societies, which is used to guide audiences toward the targeted goal with a sense of resentment. In this regard, a "thinner" version of populism has manifested itself, at different levels in various countries—especially in EU member countries—as resentment, opposing supranational integration. The political and economic integration process of the EU appears to be one of the reasons for this resentment. Indeed, in the UK, this has undoubtedly made an important claim for Brexit supporters. Likewise, the measures taken to overcome the economic destruction that emerged after the 2008 crisis and the necessities of being in the economic and monetary union have been claims by populists against the EU in Greece, Spain, and Portugal. Moreover, anger against the EU has turned into the belief that immigrants and pro-globalizers in Hungary and Poland pose a threat to national security. In the United States and some Latin American countries, this situation manifested itself as an economic nationalism as opposed to trading (Rewizorski 2020).

The mentioned situation was expressed by the famous economic thinker Karl Polanyi in the 1940s. Polanyi stated that with the integration of global markets, the opening of the global economy, and the growth of the capitalist market, democracies will decline and exemplified that racism increased during the interwar period. However, at this point, Polanyi stated that irregular markets will lead to this situation. Polanyi underlined that if markets are not regulated and taken under control in a way that is replying to society, it will first emerge as a force against the life of people, democracy and then become extreme. Rodrik (2012) expressed this situation as the "Globalization Paradox." Rodrik, in his work on the relationship between Democracy, Global Markets, and States, discussed why these structures cannot coexist.

In the world we live in, a new one is added to the rising inequality every single day. The gradual destabilization of the capitalist system and rising inequality cause us to frequently confront systemic capitalist crises. Socioeconomic inequalities appearing in the social sphere, the pressure of rapid technological change, and deindustrialization concretely destroyed the compromise between liberalism and the system. Indeed, this served the purpose of populist parties and enabled them to develop policies toward the irregularities of modern global capitalism; thus, it increases the power of populist ideas on laborers. Although policies designed in a populist way give results when applied in the short term, they are not preferred because the costs of their implementation in the long term are not sustainable. However, as we have witnessed today, populist leaders, to whom Poland and Hungary can be inferred as examples, integrate nationalist and antidemocratic practices with these tendencies. Polanyi clearly expressed this situation and pointed out that populist and antidemocratic ideas will be strengthened in systems where people are thrown into the lap of the market (Milner 2019, 94).

Another claim that can be associated with populism is the thought related to the fact that the era of neoliberalism is over, and the era of neo-nationalism has just begun. Blyth has explained the situation which he calls "Global Trumpism" in this way and he stated that following the poll defeat of David Cameron in the UK, country's withdrawal from the EU and Trump's inauguration in the United States took place consecutively (Blyth 2016). At the same time, the overt support of the UK Independence Party (UKIP) leaders to Trump and Trump's overt support for the UK's exit from the EU have been announced to the international media during the mutual visits of the parties (BBC 2016; BBC 2016a).

Economic crises give great opportunities for political parties. The most important of these opportunities is to win the election by developing policies to get the votes of the voters who suffer from the economic crisis. In this way, political parties not only win new voters but also protect their existing votes. Therefore, economic crises or external economic shocks have the potential to influence the balance of domestic politics. It can be claimed that there is a relationship in this sense between the rise of populist parties or leaders globally after the 2008 crisis. However, there are many questions that need to be answered regarding the course of the relationship between the crises of capitalism and populism (Ahlquist, Copelovitch, and Walter 2020, 904, 907).

It is a fact that most of those who voted for Trump in the United States are people who live in regions affected by China's membership in the WTO. It is known that there are strong trends within the EU indicating such a trend. It has been stated that in the regions where import competition prevails in the EU, the far-right parties are supported. Likewise, between 1997 and 2009, the tendency to vote for far-right parties increased in Germany in the import competition originating from China (Algan et al. 2018, 4–5).

After the 2008 crisis, measures for protectionism in global trade have increased significantly. Global trade in the twenty-first century is undoubtedly much freer than in the twentieth century. The acceleration of globalization with technological developments and concordant policy changes enabled the factor mobility (free movement of persons, workers, services, and capital) to move freely. This led the post–Cold War global trade rules to become much more flexible and attempts to establish common rules governing global trade have increased. This post–Cold War emerging situation continued until 2008, the 2008 global financial crisis caused the global trade to come under pressure in the context of restrictive rules. The members of the G-20[1] decided that countries refrain from implementing trade-restrictive measures after the 2008 crisis; however, the decision taken could not be implemented. After the 2008 financial crisis, the G-20 governments implemented more than 12,000 trade restrictive-interventionist measures. Besides this, the total number of trade facilitation measures reached 4.500. It can be stated that 70% of the trade interventions implemented after the 2008 crisis were damaging interventions. Even though the failure of the Doha Round of the WTO, whose main function is to deal with the global rules of trade between nations, did not have significant consequences for the global economy, this was the first time for the WTO failing in a global multilateral trade negotiation. The trend of global trade liberalization got a serious blow. But in the spring of 2018, new steel and aluminium tariffs on China levied by the United States have resulted in retaliation levied by various trading partners of the United States on the United States. Chinese retaliation, in particular, led to further pressure on the normal operations of the global trading system, even though it targeted the United States (Shatz and Chandler 2020, 7–8).

The link between populism and economic crises may not always emerge as expected. Thus, even though acceding of populist leaders after the 2008 financial crisis, which also heavily influenced global trade, and increasing protective measures afterward, it is also argued that globalization is the main factor that drives populism. Based on this, Brexit appears as a very explicit example. The social segment supporting Brexit in the UK has been classified as populist, and they shared common fears and concerns, like other prominent populist leaders of Europe. However, most political actors supporting the Brexit process defined the EU as a protective trade bloc that stands out in the global economy. It was thought that after withdrawing from the EU, the UK would gain more profit from the global economy by relieving its commercial responsibilities in EU legislation. This situation indicates that protectionism is not always supported by those who are defined or classified as populists. What populists oppose is the EU's supranational system. They claim that the rules imposed by foreign elites prevented popular sovereignty. Similarly, associating their approach to global trade with these foreign elites, populists are often associated with the protective measures they have developed. The populist movement emerged in the United States in the 1890s sets another example in this direction. The Gold standard caused the United States to suffer an economic shrinkage and bankers, the Gold standard, and financial elite were blamed for this crisis. In 1896, a serious reaction against financial globalization occurred in the

United States. Likewise, US populists opposed the customs tariffs applied. While Republicans were in favor of high tariffs to support the development of the US economy, Democrats and Populists considered import tariffs to be a taxation practice that protected the rich and harmed citizens. Although this clearly shows that there was a more rational perspective on import tariffs at that time, populists did not succeed in their opinions about the Gold standard. Nineteenth-century populists, therefore, supported free trade and they believed that ordinary people should be protected, instead of the country's elites. Most of today's populist leaders want protection for the same reason, namely that globalization benefits the rich and wealthy. In other words, they believe that globalization harms the middle class. The protectionist approach applied by Trump is of course different from the nineteenth century, but in terms of attitudes toward globalization, what has changed in the meantime is just the relationship of the American elite to the world economy (Rodrik, 2020 22–23).

It can be argued that imposing a tariff on imports contributes the country's free trade position and improve its welfare. This situation has been accepted in terms of international trade theory. However, the issue of what kind of results will be given by the sequential implementation of such an application by countries has been discussed in the literature. In fact, even though this was called "Optimum Tariff Theorem," once a country retaliates against tariffs imposed, all parties are bound to lose as compared with the free trade position (Johnson, 1954 142). The concept of economic protectionism has previously threatened international trade regimes. This concept, which emerged in the 1980s, caused the United States to decline globally and caused an increase in the shares of the European Communities (EC) (then) and Japan, which were its competitors in the global economy. The United States has hardly regained its lost trade position in the global economy (Baldwin, 1986). However, whether protectionism policies are necessary for a country is also discussed in the current literature. Protective measures that are effective and strategically determined for countries to reach a certain level of development are implemented in the development stages of the states, and then pro-free trade policies are supported by the relevant countries. Although it is known that protective measures have developed states economically, it is also a fact that the measures for the liberal and free global order are not implemented by the states at first (Çekin and Nuroğlu 2020, 75).

Contrary to the predictions that the economy will deteriorate due to the implementation of protectionist measures, it was pointed out that in some cases protectionist measures have positive results. The prohibitive measures taken against free trade shake the confidence of the country and lead to a decrease in foreign investments. Indeed, such a consequence emerged in the United States in 1930, following the Smoot-Hawley tariff. The consequences of the 1929 "Great Depression" were even worse due to the stated tariff measures. When the economy is faced with the liquidity trap, economic policies cannot be implemented rationally. For this reason, although the implementation of protective measures is not a bad practice for economies facing the liquidity trap, this situation is not considered as a good approach in terms of foreign policy and bilateral relations (Eichengreen 2016).

Nontariff barriers may contribute to eliminate some effects on economy. However, nontariff barriers lead to increase of costs in production and trade. By 2018, nontariff barriers are estimated to be more than twice that of tariffs. Thus, international trade can be strongly affected by this situation, both positively and negatively (OECD 2018, 26).

Protectionist measures on global trade have increased after the 2008 financial crisis. The governments of the G-20 countries have implemented various protectionist measures and imposed restrictive measures on countries by enacting protectionist policies. After the 2008 financial crisis, the following protectionist measures have been implemented until 2015: export incentives, investment measures, nontariff barriers, export tax or restrictions, import countervailing duties, and state aid (Evenett and Fritzs 2017, 40).

ON TRADE WARS

Cambridge dictionary defines trade war term as "a situation in which two or more countries raise import taxes and quotas." Countries often prefer such a practice to try to protect their own economies (Cambridge Dictionary 2020). Today, trade wars suggest economic retaliations imposed by international economic actors such as the United States, China, and the EU, and throughout history, countries have experienced serious tension and even wars over trade. The first example to set in this context is the conflicts between England and the Dutch Republic. The main reason for the maritime conflict between the two countries in the seventeenth and eighteenth centuries was because of trade competition. Global superiority of the Netherlands ended as a result of the war. The two countries became the first instance of trade wars as the Netherlands conducted secret trade agreements and negotiations with the American colonies and triggered an uprising against England. Britain imposed a serious blockade on the Netherlands (Britannica 2020).

The conflicts between 1839 and 1842, and 1856 and 1860, known as "Opium Wars," set another example of trade wars. The triggering factor of two major conflicts between the British and the Chinese governments was the opium trade. The claim of British, representing Western trade in China, on the fact that smuggling opium was made by Western merchants sparked the first war. Profits returned from the sale of opium enabled Western countries to compensate for the losses incurred in the commercial context, but later things had changed, disputes over the sale of opium and failure to improve trade conditions caused conflicts to occur. The Opium Wars negatively affected China. The British increased their global economic dominance with industrialization (Reist 2012, 1).

Another example of trade wars is the conflicts known as the Banana Wars. It was waged to protect the commercial interests of the United States in Cuba, Haiti, and the Dominican Republic and resulted in US intervention in the region between 1898 and 1930 (Crandal 2014, 110). The Smoot-Hawley Act of 1930, the most infamous tariff on record, completely reversed the American trade strategy and provided US domination to shape (Lake 1988, 184). The 1930s witnessed another trade war in terms of global trade. The Anglo-Irish economic war was eventually settled with the "Irish" victory. The bankruptcy of governments and mutual commercial reprisals turned into a great economic war between the two countries. In Ireland, with the "Fianna Fail" party of Eamonn de Valera coming to power in 1932, its first action was the suspension of the land revenues paid to England. The UK reacted rapidly economically to this situation, increased Ireland's agricultural export tax by 68% to 88%. In response to the export decisions taken by the UK, the Irish restricted the imports of coal, cement, sugar, iron, and steel, and machinery from the UK and increased Irish tariffs from 9% to 45% between 1931 and 1936, while also increasing the number of goods entered has also increased coverage at the same time (O'Rouke 1991, 357–358).

The trade war on genetically modified foods has been one of the issues that attracted attention and aroused curiosity within the WTO's solution mechanism. The United States, Canada, and Argentina acted together with the United States in 2003 to initiate the solution process against the EU (European Communities —then—)in the WTO in 2003. The subject has emerged in the context of the effects of genetically modified organisms (GMO) products on human health and has turned into a trade dispute due to the implementation and evaluation of various regulations for the risks of GMO foods. This dispute regarding the risk posed by genetic applications on agricultural products in terms of the future of agriculture has been closely followed in the United States and the EC WTO and made quite detailed defenses. It has been claimed that the ECs slow down the processes regarding the regulation of GMOs or the severe delay of the approvals of these processes and the prohibition of some EC members' GMO products in their own countries violated their responsibilities in the context of the WTO agreements by the EC. The EC claimed that the WTO was not included in the judicial mechanism of the WTO in terms of the subject involving different disciplines, but later it implicitly abandoned this claim. According to the EC, the issue is handled on a very narrow ground for the other party. The United

States handled the issue based on the WTO's Sanitary and Phytosanitary Measures Agreement and pointed out that this agreement should be followed. This agreement regulates the implementation of trade-restricting measures for WTO members in cases that pose a risk to human plant and animal health (Peel, Nelson and Godden 2005, 141–145).

In 2016, the change of administration in the United States, one of the world's leading economic powers, has been effective in changing its global position. As the president of the United States, Trump's "America First" policy has stricken a big blow on the global multilateralism of the United States, at the same time, this policy led to the country's withdrawal from major agreements supporting the global economy. It has been the EU to suffer from this consequence, at first. The "Transatlantic Trade and Investment Partnership"[2] (TTIP) agreement, whose negotiations started with the EU in 2014, was suspended during the Trump period. Following the macroprudential policy imposed against the EU, Trump also made a serious move on the Pacific sphere and withdrew from the Trans-Pacific Partnership (TPP). Trade relations between the twelve countries included in the TPP have taken a different dimension and in this way, the United States ended the era of multinational trade agreements with Trump. The TPP was negotiated under the former president Barack Obama, but never ratified by Congress. Withdrawing from the TPP, Trump, thus, has announced that the United States will only negotiate trade deals with individual allies, and he has taken US trade policy to another dimension (Brookings 2017).

The rapid rise of populist political leaders in recent years in many western democracies, including the United States, has disrupted the global cooperation process and global governance. The short-term protectionist policies suggested by populist political leaders, disregarding their long-term consequences, have remained incapable of paying attention to people's fears and beliefs. In this context, a trend such as opposing global governance systems has emerged. In general, most of the populist leaders disdained international institutions, and they concentrated resources domestically, choosing to strategically disengage from conflicts abroad. After 2016, these trends have showed themselves on a global scale as trade wars, closing of borders, and abrupt disengagement from international issues. In the United States, President Trump's inauguration in 2016 triggered a dangerous trend such as using economic means to pursue foreign policy and to govern global issues. For the purpose of dictating the international interests of the United States, the policy of imposing sanctions through pressure over economic protectionist measures has become a populist practice with Trump, and this sparked the trade wars on a global scale. This process, which is called as trade wars, began in 2018 and the US import tariff tripled in 2019. Naturally, China responded to this situation in the same way with commercial retaliation. As a result, trade wars have caused a serious contraction in trade activities, disruption of the global value chain, uncertainty of policies due to insecurity, and a decrease in global growth figures globally (Mattozzi, Marcos, and Nakaguma 2020, 2).

THE TRADE WARS BETWEEN THE UNITED STATES, CHINA, AND THE EU

Throughout his election campaign, Trump consistently criticized the multilateralism in the global order and the role of the United States in this multilateralism; moreover, he stated that international trade agreements account for the reason why the United States is in its current situation, and the commercial relations the country has entered into with the WTO, North Atlantic Free Trade Area (NAFTA), and other global organizations cost the United States a lot. Trump has clearly expressed that the agreement between the United States and NAFTA was the worst trade deal ever made in the history of the United States; it was a mistake to support China's membership of the WTO in integrating with global trade, and most of the policies to be implemented for free trade shall oblige the United States to implement foreign regulations. Trump remarked that the main reason for United States' trade deficit reaching $1 trillion is the multilateral trade agreements and international trade organizations of which the United States is a member. Uttering remarkably that the United States is subject to international rules, Trump argued that the reason why the United States is losing power is that the country is subject to such practices. Organizations with a multilateral structure such as the WTO have infringed the sovereign right of the United States and tarnished the reputation of the United States. Referring to Abraham Lincoln and George Washington, the founding leaders of the United States, Trump stated that the US trade policy should protect the country and claimed that if the protectionist measures were abandoned, the United States would become impoverished; he also pointed out that the right to sovereignty, which was violated by free trade agreements, should be given back to the United States. Stating that the United States was able to become a great capitalist power with protectionist measures, Trump has identified his own stance with Washington and Lincoln's protectionist policies (Edwards 2018, 183–185).

Bilateral trade between China and the United States has grown extremely rapidly after China's membership in the WTO. Trade figures between China and the United States explicitly show how interdependent the trade relationship between China and the United States is. For the United States, China is a great export channel, source of imports, and one of the leading global trade partners. China's share of total US imports rose from 8.2% in 2001 to 21.6%

in 2017, and in this context, China ranks first in US imports as of 2017. The United States to remove protectionist barriers to China over time has allowed China to access markets globally, outside of the United States. The relation between the United States and China has gained another dimension with the increasing trade deficit. The US trade deficit reached a record level in 2018, with $419.5 billion. Arguing that the main reason for the trade deficit is unfair trade practices, Trump has claimed to act to take the necessary measures individually or mutually (Sukar and Ahmed 2019, 279).

2018 was the year to reach a turning point in the economic relationship with China, by Donald Trump. Following Trump's administration to impose tariffs of 25% on steel and 10% on aluminum, today's last trade war has begun. The Trump administration has continued to impose additional duties on China, and putting a 25% tariff on up to $50 billion of Chinese goods has taken the trade wars between China and the United States to another dimension. In return for this, China retaliated by imposing tariffs on imports from the United States worth an additional $50 billion, and this led the United States to introduce an additional 10% to cover $200 billion worth of Chinese imports. This power struggle in trade between the countries has continued. China announced to increase tariffs on products worth about $60 billion, from 5% to 10%. This went down in history due to being one of the biggest trade wars in the world since the Second World War, the global economic outlook has serious effects on global financial markets (Sheng, Zhao and Zhao 2019, 1–2). As a matter of fact, although the expression of "today's last trade war" is not very accurate, reciprocal retaliations of these economic powers, which cover most of the world economy, have suppressed the global economy.[3]

One of the main reasons for Trump's trade war with China in the context of the "America First" policy is regarded as meeting tax deductions and strengthening the financial position of the country. Thus, it can be stated that the trade wars of the United States served as a fundraising mechanism. China to miss out on this situation in the United States makes negotiations in trade wars less efficient. In 2017 and 2018, during the trade negotiation process, China tried to reduce its trade deficit with the United States, but Trump ignored this. However, the United States' concerns about China such as intellectual property rights, cyberattacks and breaches, and US companies to face discriminatory policies in China appear as the main factors that determine the United States' attitude toward China. Therefore, without settling such disputes, it seems impossible to reach a reconciliation or peace between the two countries (Di, Luft and Zhong 2019, 211).

The trade war between the United States and China is alleged to cause great damage to the Chinese economy. As a matter of fact, in 2018, China has witnessed the lowest growth rate in the past ten years. The United States–China trade war causes significant impact on the automobile and electronics industry. In this context, it seems that it is a necessity for China to seek a deal to end this trade war. Because total vehicle sales of China have dropped by 11.7% from a year earlier, the stated consequence is also observed in all Chinese companies. Alibaba has revised down its full-year revenue, estimated to be 4–6%, the turnover of Chinese brands in the smartphone market has also dropped drastically. In the event of a possible trade deal between the United States and China, the damages witnessed by the global economy due to trade wars are difficult to resolve at a rapid pace. The direct effect of the trade retaliation between the United States and China puts the EU in an economically difficult situation, too. The break of the global supply chain raises serious concerns about the global economy (Jain and Saraswat 2019, 6).

In addition to China, the United States also has serious trade disputes with the EU, another economic partner of hers. These commercial disputes took another dimension with the breakdown of negotiations of the agreement, which is expressed as the biggest trade agreement of the century between the EU and the United States. The main goals of the TTIP, which is expected to be signed between the parties, were determined as "creating jobs", "boosting innovation", "improving competitiveness", and "ensuring long-term growth and prosperity". The partnership, therefore, has set out with the motto of making the best use of available opportunities; moreover, the unite of major commercial parties, creating holistic economic values, and creating a shared vision of Atlantic were determined as the main developments targeted by the agreement. In short, the transatlantic partnership aimed at the creation of a giant multilateral economic growth-oriented trade bloc system (Hamilton and Schwartz 2010, 2).

There were great expectations prior to this agreement to be made between the two parties. Considering that these two major trade blocs are the world's most important economic powers, the possibility of such an agreement to enter into force led to debates. In general, the annual size of the transatlantic commercial activities in the world economy is stated as five trillion dollars, and it is pointed out that it provides fifteen million new job opportunities as employment. Considering that there is a daily trade of 1.7 million dollars between two blocks, it is emphasized that one-third of the goods and services sector worldwide and more than 40% of the service sector are realized between these two blocks. The United States provides three times more product trade to the EU than China and fifteen times more than India. On the other hand, the EU trade block provides the United States with twice as many commercial products as China and seven times more than India. Considering the commercial size of two blocs, the Trans-Atlantic partnership appears to be one of the most leading commercial projects. Examining the profiles of EU and US companies, it is seen that the US and European companies account for 60% of the top R&D companies. When the EU and US trade blocs are considered together, partnership of these two blocs creates a giant bloc with the largest investment in R&D spending around the world, which corresponds to 69% of private R&D spending in the world. In other words, it is thought that the giant trade bloc to be established with the Trans-Atlantic partnership will constitute a structure that has 69% of the world's R&D investments (Hamilton and Schwartz 2010, 2).

The economic crisis affecting the world in general in 2008 also caused millions of dollars of damage to the EU and US trade blocs. Companies having transatlantic economic ties with each other faced the risk of not being able to continue their commercial operations due to the upheaval of current global economic values. For this reason, the EU and the United States aimed to restore the trade volume between these two trade blocs to its former potential with this trade agreement. However, the change of administration in the United States in 2016 has ruined the compromise on this agreement between the EU and the United States.

President Trump withdrew the United States from the TTIP at the end of 2016; thus, the Trump administration has prevented the development of transatlantic trade growth. Indeed, Trump has made it clear that they are against the WTO and other multilateral trade agreements in the context of global trade. Considering the US trade retaliation against China, in addition to the possibility that the "Trumpian" United States will approach the EU, signing a major free trade agreement with the United States appears as a rational option for the EU to eliminate the negative effects of the Brexit process. However, signing of a free trade agreement between the United States and the EU under the Trump administration seems highly unlikely. Examining the situation from a United States–China–EU perspective, it is seen that the aggressive US protectionism vis-à-vis China has caused Chinese export diversion toward Association of Southeast Asian Nations[4] (ASEAN) and the EU (Jungmittgag and Welfens 2020, 260–261).

In the 1900s, the dominant political approach for the United States was the policy of isolationism. The emergence of multilateral agreements in the international arena was possible with the Cobden Chevalier Treaty.[5] Five years after this treaty, the establishment of the International Telegraph Union (today, it's known as International Telecommunication Union) accelerated the globalization process. The world economy has grown well with the dynamics mentioned, while the industrial revolution emerging in the UK has become the economic pillar of globalization. Thanks to its colonies spread all over the world, advanced banking activities, and industrial strength, the UK was able to become the world's largest economic power. However, supporting the international economic order emerged as a must. On the other hand, in the period between the First and Second World War, the intergovernmental organizations that are weak in regulating the global system failed, and in 1930, Smoot-Hawley tariffs were put into effect by the United States. This led to a decrease in the global trade volume. This attitude of the United States caused a serious public reaction at that time. In fact, these tariffs led to imported goods become more expensive, and in addition to reparations, exports of Germany and other European countries have significantly decreased. This situation, on the other hand, caused the real income to reduce and the employment level to decrease. This consequence can be clearly expressed as a dead end. As a matter of fact, in such a situation, the export of the United States to Europe has decreased significantly, too. The situation that emerged between the United States and the EU in 2018 resembles many aspects. But today, there are stronger global organizations that support the global trade system. "Trumpian" United States' trade competition between the EU at first and with China later has resulted in a return to the dynamics of the 1930s, which could pose a great economic danger to the United States. The economic growth of the United States is posted as a guarantee that such a situation will not be experienced. However, it should not be forgotten that although the economic growth of the ASEAN countries was quite high in 1995–1996, a serious crisis occurred in Asia and no signs were perceived before this crisis (Welfens 2019, 151–152).

There is no doubt that continuation of Trump's populism, that is, Trump's isolationism, means enormous damage to the transatlantic and global economy. The withdrawal of the United States from the system where it is the leader may result in jeopardizing the country's global interests in security and other issues. In this way, global costs will increase at a predictable level. Loss of political stability globally will have an impact on global investments, while the global economic size will shrink. The withdrawal of the United States from the world due to economic nationalist policies has the potential to cause serious effects on the Middle East, particularly in Latin American countries. Trump withdrew the United States from the trade deal negotiations with China. This has led to a closer convergence between China and ASEAN and the EU. However, high shipping costs in the EU–China trade relation puts the ASEAN forward. In this case, constructing a network of railway over Russia and accompanying shipping opportunities could bring higher Chinese exports to the EU. At this point, the Russian factor stands out. Differences of opinion between Russia and the EU on Ukraine cause Russia and the EU to fail to find grounds to cooperate. Trump's attitude toward global economic multilateralism and his protectionist policies puts the EU under serious pressure for existence. The Brexit decision sets the most tragic example of the Trump-supported populist approach today. For this reason, when the United States behaves like an enemy for or remains passive toward EU integration, this case leads the EU to face serious crises, too (Welfens 2019, 153–154).

Trade disputes and trade problems between the United States and the EU differ from each other. "In 2018, the United States had an overall $115 billion trade deficit in merchandise and services with the EU, as the merchandise deficit outweighed the services surplus." In this context, Germany, one of the EU member states, accounted for the fourth-largest US bilateral merchandise trade deficit, at $69 billion. Although the Trump administration is against multilateral trade, it is important to reduce the US trade deficit. However, Trump stated that the reason for the trade deficit between the two economic blocs is the policies implemented by the EU. Besides, stating that the policies implemented by the EU in automobile trade also contribute to this situation, Trump points out the different levels of tariffs. According to the EU, mutual trade is in the interests of both sides, and commercial activities carried out by EU companies in the United States contribute significantly to the US economy. Indeed, the Trump administration's unilateral initiation to apply tariffs under the national security-based "Section 232" trade law is regarded as one of the major points of tension in bilateral trade with the EU. In this context, customs duties of 25% and 10%, respectively, have begun to be implemented by the United States for steel and aluminium imports. According to the EU, the United States violates the rules set by the WTO that protect the domestic producer from excessive imports. It has carried out a commercial retaliation by applying unilateral measures to this trade restriction imposed by the United States in the EU. The EU imposed an additional tax of 10% to 25% on US products, around $ 3 billion. Another cause of commercial tension between the parties emerged concerning automobile and automobile parts, and Trump stated that the authority to restrict and enforce imports was revealed, claiming that national security was threatened. In this context, the US trade representative was appointed and revealed that negotiations should be held to investigate the situation with the parties. The EU is regarded as a crucial market for Harley Davidson motorcycles. For this reason, Harley Davidson attracted attention in terms of being the first company aiming to expand its production abroad not to be affected by the trade war between the parties. It raises concerns that the same situation may be the case for automobiles imported from the United States and that the economic consequences may be more severe. Another trade war between the United States and the EU appears in the context of the USA-EU "Boeing-Airbus" that has been going on for fourteen years. This long struggle of the parties resulted in the implementation of trade measures of eleven billion dollars for the United States and twelve billion dollars for the EU, and the parties mutually seriously damaged the civil air transport industries. In addition to this, the United States monitors the EU's activities on data protection, digital trade, and tax evasion. In this context, the United States started an investigation into France regarding the digital services tax (Akhtar 2019).

The first years when the United States began to turn away from the WTO were the eras of the Bush and Obama administrations. Under the Trump administration, the country has only implemented aggressive protectionist measures and found the solution to run its own negotiations bilaterally. However, the course of the Doha Round resulted in the United States drifting away from the WTO. The rise of China, India, and Brazil has led the United States to digress from the multilateralism. The United States has turned to bilateral global trade agreements; however, the blocking of a draft text of the Doha agriculture agreement proposed by the United States and EU by a group of countries, led by Brazil, formed the key catalyst for the United States. The United States, thus, has turned to the strategy of negotiating new bilateral and regional free trade agreements and challenged the rise of China rise in the global economy, and the multilateral system, to protect its geopolitical interests (Hopewell 2020, 8).

Following the Second World War, the United States and EU were the two major economic blocs contributing to the emergence of a multilateral and free global trading system. The Trump administration's skepticism of the commercial and political regulatory role of global organizations poses most threats for the United States. In this context, it may be possible for the United States to withdraw from the WTO. In fact, this situation seriously disturbs other WTO members. However, the EU, like the United States, has the potential to meet at a common point. The United States and EU are actively discussing potential WTO reform, including changes to the present system. However, the Trump administration's skepticism of the EU multilateral nature and the policy of the United States to make bilateral trade agreements with EU member states further increase the tension between the two parties. Since there is no free trade agreement between the United States and EU, both parties trade on WTO's "Most-Favored-Nation" (MFN) terms. Until Trump comes to power, US and EU tariffs were generally low. In 2018, the Trump administration seeks more reasonable trade agreement negotiations with the EU; therefore, President Trump and Jean-Claude Juncker (European Commission President at that time) met and initiated a set of "fairer" and "more balanced" negotiation process. But, due to a lack of consensus between the parties on their scope, the negotiations have not started formally. The differences between the US and EU perspectives were in the fields such as "government procurement," "digital trade," "regulatory cooperation," and "geographical indications" at most. Trump has threatened the EU with increasing tariffs on agriculture, the EU, on the other hand, asserted that it will stop negotiating if it is subject to the "Section 232 tariffs" of the American Trade Law, the Trade Expansion Act of 1962. The United States and the EU each has its own free trade agreements, fourteen trade agreements for the United States and over forty trade agreements for the EU. In the absence of a trade agreement between the United States and the EU, US businesses are disadvantaged in the EU market relative to such trading partners with whom the EU recently concluded free trade agreements. Indeed, the Brexit process presents such a potential for the United States. If Brexit happens, the UK, acting as a trade corridor for US goods, would not access the EU market, and this would harm the commercial interests of the United States (Akhtar 2019).

Considering the current number of cases of the United States, China, and the EU in the WTO dispute settlement mechanism, it is seen that all three blocs have problems on the level of issues that need to be resolved mutually. According to the WTO, there are twenty-three cases brought by the United States against China. On the other hand, there are twenty cases brought by the United States against the EU. It can be seen that the trade disputes brought by the United States for settlement to the WTO covered the whole world. The country which China has the most problems in the WTO is the United States. China brought sixteen cases to the WTO, against the United States. It can be stated that China is the most problem-free country in WTO trade disputes. Of the WTO disputes from the EU perspective, it can be explicitly seen that the country which the EU has the most problems with is the United States. There are thirty-five cases in the WTO brought by the EU against the United States. The number of EU trade disputes pending settlement in the WTO, globally, is higher than China and lower than the United States (World Trade Organization 2020).

CONCLUSION

The concept of populism used in this study is related to the decisions taken by the populist leaders to prevent the liberalization of the global economy as a result of their coming to power. However, it should be noted that with their nation-prioritizing approaches, the leaders of the twenty-first century, who act with the thought that after the Second World War national sovereignty is inviolable, encourage discriminatory and exclusionary approaches in their countries, acting with populist rhetoric not only in terms of international economy but also in domestic and foreign policy decisions. From this perspective, it can be claimed that the EU sets a very good test environment in terms of overcoming the nation-state understanding.

In terms of the crises of capitalism, each crisis is claimed to have changed the spirit of capitalism. The capitalist system takes on a new form by eliminating the irregularities within it, thanks to crises. In this context, the 2008 global financial crisis is important for the way capitalism will evolve in the future. After the 2008 crisis, globalization trend took a major blow, as well as the collapsing of financial structure has damaged the political dialogue in the countries. In countries that suffered from the crisis, the extremist political movements and exclusionary rhetoric have rapidly gained strength, mass-social demonstrations were organized in countries and pro-change calls were made. Therefore, after the 2008 crisis, the rise of populist political leaders has been experienced all over the world. In this respect, the breaking point was Brexit in 2016 and the inauguration of Trump in the United States afterward. Protectionism discourses of the Atlantic have become the routine practice of European leaders, and most of the political leaders have opposed the regulatory organizations existing in the global system, especially the EU. The populist rhetoric, which was perceived in Europe as supranationalism, democratic values, and anti-immigration, came to life in the United States with Trump's economic nationalism practices. Democracy-based structures started to collapse after the 2008 crisis. However, it should be known that the tension between democracy and antidemocratic values shall rebuild the new form of democracy around the world.

In terms of global trade, Trump's moves such as suspending the relations with the EU at first and initiating a trade war with China afterward have strengthened anti-globalization and antidemocracy tendencies around the world. Global trade has come under a protectionism that it has not witnessed since the Second World War; moreover, as global economic growth has shrunk, global supply chains have suffered. Trump has used economic retaliation as a foreign policy instrument to look out for the interests of US foreign policy. The United States opposed not only economic blocs such as the EU and China but global structures that are pioneers of multilateralism all over the world.

Using trade as a means of peace within its own structure, the EU liberalizes the international economy and tries to put it in a certain order. In this way, the EU both imposes its own standards and expands its world trade network. In this respect, there is a firm link between the EU and the globalization process. As globalization deepens, the power of the EU increases and the integration process progresses. But as protectionism increases in the global economy, the economic integration process becomes difficult, and the EU suffers serious political and economic damage. This situation emerged in 2016 after Trump won the elections in the United States. The withdrawal of the United States from the TTIP, agreed in 2014 and expected to be one of the greatest projects of the period, has affected the EU in all respects. Considering the issue in terms of the size of the two economies, it is obvious how great the benefit of such a treaty would be for the global economy and economic development between continents. On the other hand, the "America First" policy adopted by the United States in its economic relations with China not only made the global economy difficult but also caused an incomprehensible situation. The foreign deficit of the United States has increased more than ever before; Trump has begun using trade wars as a tool to improve the financial situation.

The statements made after the election of Biden were in line with these suggestions. After Trump lost the elections, Biden came to power and the whole world was excited about the urgent implementation of US policies to support global multilateralism. Although Biden's declaration "America is Back" at the Munich Security Conference was suspiciously approached by Germany and France, the steps Trump took after leaving the White House and Biden's election as president gave strong signals that it would return. Shortly after Biden took office as president of the United States, quickly; the United States returned to the G-7, rejoined the Paris Climate Agreement and the World Health Organization, extended the duration of the new nuclear agreement with Russia, announced its intention to reengage in the so-called Comprehensive Action Plan with Iran. Withdrawing support for Saudi Arabia, it emphasized human rights and democracy, sanctions were made for the coup in Myanmar, and finally, the United States declared its support against the global effects of COVID-19 (Tepperman, 2021).

It can be assumed that the trade wars between the United States, China, and the EU that have been going on for the past five years are the outcomes of the tension between democracy and capitalism. The unrecoverable economic situation after the crisis has initiated opposition to globalization and multilateralism in all countries. The start of the Brexit process in 2014, and after Trump came to power in the United States in 2016, the global economic and political atmosphere began to disappear under the US-led protectionist measures. The post-Trump United States can regain the role it lost economically and politically globally by reversing the policies accepted as Trump like. Decisions that damage the global role of the United States, such as the United States' withdrawal from multilateral cooperation processes such as the Paris Climate Agreement, should be reversed. It is essential for the post-Trump United States to establish a new economic partnership ground with the EU, to restart its economic and political relations with China in the context of the transpacific, and to put an end to the so-called trade wars.

The structures that hold the capitalist system together or constitute it change over time. However, "the era of uncertainties or populism" happening today stems from the tension the capitalist system has experienced in finding its new form after the 2008 crisis. Conservative and protectionist reactions against global multilateralism after the crisis have led to the rise of protectionism all over the world by attacking democratic values. The whole world has taken on protectionism in the shadow of populist political discourses, and the cooperation promoted by trade has disappeared.

NOTES

1. Argentina, Australia, Brazil, Canada, China, France, Germany, Italy, India, Indonesia, Japan, Mexico Republic of Korea, Russia, Saudi Arabia, South Africa, Turkey, United Kingdom, United States, European Union. For more information, visit: https://ec.europa.eu/info/food-farming-fisheries/farming/international-cooperati on/international-organisations/g20_en

2. The negotiations for the Transatlantic Trade and Investment Partnership (TTIP) started in 2013 and were terminated in 2016, without any conclusion. With the decision taken by the EU Council of Ministers, the regulations regarding TTIP have been invalidated. For further information, see: https://ec.europa.eu/trade/policy/in-focus /ttip/

3. It is useful to be reminded. The GDP of the United States announced by the World Bank today is $21,374,418.88 trillion and China's GDP is $14,342,902.84 trillion. The two economies account for $35 trillion of the total world GDP of $88 trillion. For further information, see: https://data.worldbank.org/indicator/NY.GDP .MKTP.CD

4. The member states: Brunei Darussalam, Cambodia, Indonesia, Lao PDR, Malaysia, Myanmar, Philippines, Singapore, Thailand, Viet Nam. For more information, visit: https://asean.org/asean/asean-member-states/

5. In 1860, with the Cobden Chevalier Treaty, negotiations for trade liberalization between France and Britain began. A series of negotiations that started in 1850 resulted in the signing of the Treaty in 1860. With the agreement, the lowest tariffs in the European continent started to be applied. A. G. Kenwood, A. L. Lougheed, "The Growth of the International Economy 1820–1960: An Introductory Text," Sunny Press, 1971. p. 77.

REFERENCES

Ahlquist, John, Mark Copelovitch and Stefanie Walter. 2020. The Political Consequences of External Economic Shocks: Evidence from Poland. *American Journal of Political Sciences* 64, no.4: 904–920. https://doi.org/10.1111/ajps .12503.

Akhtar. Shayerah Llias. 2019."US-EU Trade and Economic Issues." Accessed 05 October 2020. https://fas.org/sgp/crs/row/IF10931.pdf

Algan, Yann., Sergei Guriev, Elias Papaioannaou and Evgenia Passari. 2018. The European Trust Crisis and the Rise of Populism. European Bank for Reconstruction and Development, Working Paper No. 208.

Association of Southeast Asian Nations. 2020. "ASEAN Member States." Accessed 27 September 2020. https://asean.org/asean/asean-member-states/

Baldwin, E. R. 1986. The New Protectionism: A Response to Shifts in National Economic Power. NBER Working Paper Series, National Bureau of Economic Research, Cambridge, MA.

BBC News. 2016. "Donald Trump: Nigel Farage would be great UK Ambassador." Accessed 22 June 2020. https://www.bbc.com/news/uk-38060434

BBC News. 2016a. "Farage has an 'Extraordinary' Relationship with Trump." Accessed https://www.bbc.com/news/av/uk-politics-38068068

Blyth, Mark. 2016. "Global Trumpism." Accessed 21 June 2020. https://www.for eignaffairs.com/articles/2016-11-15/global-trumpism

Britannica. 2020. "Anglo-Dutch Wars." Accessed 24 August 2020. https://www.bri tannica.com/event/Anglo-Dutch-Wars

Brookings. 2017. "Trump Withdrawal from the Trans-Pacific Partnership." Accessed 02 September 2020. https://www.brookings.edu/blog/unpacked/2017/03/24/trump -withdrawing-from-the-trans-pacific-partnership/

Cambridge Dictionary. 2020. "Trade War." Accessed 23 August 2020. https://diction ary.cambridge.org/dictionary/english/trade-war

Çekin, Semih Emre and Elif Nuroğlu. 2020. The Effect of Trade Wars on International Trade and The Real Economy. *International Journal of Economic and Administrative Studies* 27: 73–90.

Crandall, Russell. 2014. *America's Dirty Wars: Irregular Warfare from 1776 to the War on Terror.* Cambridge: Cambridge University Press.

Di, Dongshng, Gal Luft and Dian Zhong. 2019. Why did Trump Launch a Trade War? A Political Economy Explanation from the Perspective of Financial Constraints. *Economic and Political Studies* 7, no. 2: 203–216.

Edwards, Jason A. 2018. Make America Great Again: Donald Trump and Redefining the US Role in the World. *Communication Quarterly* 66, no. 2: 176–195.

Eichengreen, Barry. 2016. "What's the problem with protectionism?." Accessed 15 August 2020. https://www.theguardian.com/business/2016/jul/15/whats-the-proble m-with-protectionism

European Commission. 2019. "Negotiations and agreements." Accessed 25 September 2020. https://ec.europa.eu/trade/policy/in-focus/ttip/

European Commission. 2020. "Role of the G 20." Accessed 10 August 2020. https:// ec.europa.eu/info/food-farming-fisheries/farming/international-cooperation/interna tional-organisations/g20_en

Evenett, Simon J. and Johannes Fritzs,. 2017. *Will Awe Trump Rules? The 21sat Global Trade Alert Report.* London: CEPR Press.

Grossman, Gene M. and Elhanan Helpman. 1995. Trade Wars and Trade Talk. *Journal of Political Economy* 103, no. 41: 675–708. https://doi.org/10.1086/261999.

Hamilton, Daniel and Pedro Schwartz. 2010. "A Transatlantic Free Trade Area- A Boost to Economic Growth?." Accessed 25 September 2020. http://www.libe ravzw.be/wp-content/uploads/2012/02/transatlantic-free-trade.pdf

Higgott, Richard. 2018. Globalism, Populism and the Limits of Global Economic Governance. *Journal of Inter-Regional Studies: Regional and Global Perspectives* 1, no. 1: 2–23.

Hopewell, Kristen. 2020. Trump & Trade: The Crisis in the Multilateral Trading System. *New Political Economy* 26, no. 2: 1–12. https://doi.org/10.1080/135634 67.2020.1841135.

Jain, Manjura and Saloni Saraswat. 2019. US-China Trade War Chinese Perspective. *Management and Economics Research Journal* 5, no. 4: 1–8.

Johnson, Harry G. 1954. Optimum Tariffs and Retaliation. *The Review of Economic Studies* 21, no. 2: 142–153.

Jungmittgag, Andres and Paul J. J Welfens. 2020. EU-US Trade Post-Trump Perspectives: TTIP Aspects related to Foreign Direct Investment and Innovation. *International Economics and Economic Policy* 2, no. 17: 259–294.

Kenwood, A.G and A. L. Lougheed. 1971. *The Growth of the International Economy 1820–1960: An Introductory Text*. Great Britain: Sunny Press.

Krastev, Ivan. 2011. The age of populism: Reflections on the Self-Enmity of Democracy. *European View* 10, no. 1: 11–16. https://doi.org/10.1007/s12290 -011-0152-8.

Lake, David A. 1988. *Power, Protection, and Free Trade: International Sources of U.S Commercial Strategy 1887–1939*. Ithaca - London: Cornell University Press.

Mattozzi, Andrea, Massimo Morelli and Marcos Y. Nakaguma. 2020. "Populism and War." CEPR DP no. 14501.

Merriam-Webster. 2020. "Populist." Accessed 20 June 2020. https://www.merriam-webster.com/dictionary/populism

Milner, Helen V. 2019. Globalization Populism and the Decline of the Welfare State. *Survival* 61, no. 2: 91–96. https://doi.org/10.1080/00396338.2019.1589087

Mudde, Cass and Cristobal Rovira Kaltwasser. 2017. *Populism A Very Short Introduction*. Great Britain: Oxford University Press.

Mudde, Cass. 2018. "How Populism Became the Concept That Defines Our Age." Accessed 19 June 2020. https://www.theguardian.com/commentisfree/2018/nov /22/populism-concept-defines-our-age.

O'Rourke, Kevin. 1991. Burn Everything British but Their Coal: The Anglo-Irish Economic War of the 1930s. *The Journal of Economic History* 51, no. 2: 357–366.

OECD. 2018. "OECD Economic Outlook." Accessed 20 August 2020. http://www .oecd.org/economy/outlook/General-assessment-of-the-macroeconomic-situation -november-2018-OECD-economic-outlook-chapter.pdf

Oxford Learner's Dictionaries. 2020. "Populism." Accessed 20 June 2020. https://ww w.oxfordlearnersdictionaries.com/definition/english/populism?q=populism

Peel, Jacqueline, Rebecca Nelson and Lee Godden. 2005. GMO Trade Wars: The Submission in the EC- GMO Dispute in the WTO. *Melbourne Journal of International Law* 6, : 141–166.

Reist, Katherine. 2012. "Opium Wars." In *The Encyclopedia of War*, edited by Gordon Martel, 1–5. Blackwell Publishing Ltd.

Rewizorski, Marek. 2020. Backlash Against Globalization and the Shadow of Phobos. *Fudan Journal of the Humanities and Social Sciences* 13, no. 4. https://do i.org/10.1007/s40647-020-00308-0.

Rodrik, Dani. 2012. *Globalization Paradox Why Global Markets States and Democracy Can't Coexist*. Great Britain: Oxford University Press.

Rodrik, Dani. 2018. "Is Populism Necessarily Bad Economics?." *AEA Papers and Proceedings*, 108: 196–199. https://doi.org/10.1257/pandp.20181122.

Rodrik, Dani. 2020. Why Does Globalization Fuel Populism? Economics, Culture and the Rise of Right-Wing Populism. NBER Working Paper Series, National Bureau of Economic Research, Cambridge, MA.

Shatz, Howard J. and Nathan Chandler. 2020. *Global Economic Trends and the Future of Warfare: The Changing Global Environment and It's Implications for the US Air Force*. Rand Corporations.

Sheng, Liugang, Honyan Zhao and Jing Zhao. 2019. Why will Trump lose the Trade War?. *China Economic Journal* 12, no. 2: 137–159.

Sukar, Abdulhamid and Syed Ahmed. 2019. Rise of trade Protectionism: The Case of US-Sino Trade War. *Transnational Corporations Review* 11, no. 4: 279–289.

Tepperman, Jonathan. 2021. "Biden Was Right: America Is Back." Accessed 28 February 2021. https://foreignpolicy.com/2021/02/23/biden-was-right-america-is -back/

The World Bank. 2020. "Data.," Accessed September 10, 2020. https://data.worldba nk.org/indicator/NY.GDP.MKTP.CD

Welfens, Paul J. J. 2019. *The Global Trump: Structural US Populism and Economic Conflicts with Europe and Asia*. Switzerland: Springer Nature.

World Trade Organization. 2020. "Map of Disputes between WTO Members." Accessed 10 October 2020. https://www.wto.org/english/tratop_e/dispu_e/dispu _maps_e.htm.

Chapter 2

From GATT to WTO, Where to Now? The World Economic Order in the Midst of the Trade Wars

Rüya Ataklı Yavuz

INTRODUCTION

Together with the end of the Second World War, various initiatives were taken to remove barriers to world trade and to increase free trade relations. Compared to the prewar era, a fundamentally different world trade area emerged in the post–Second World War era. It can be said that between 1945 and 1975, an important part of the world as a geographical place was opened to open market relations (Kürkçü 2013, 3). During the period in question, the ground has been established for the freer circulation of capital in rich countries. Thanks to the beginning of the capital to circulate with less restriction, the number of countries transitioning to a free market economy, or in other words, capitalism has increased. Thus, the development of capitalism has gained momentum in the countries called as the "Third World" (Büyükbaykal 2004, 19). Besides, unprecedented-scale increases have begun in world trade volume. However, in recent years, trade wars, which continue as imposing surtaxes on imported goods and increasing quotas on export goods for reasons such as the development of the domestic industry through protectionism, creation of new lines of work, enlivening the old lines of work, and other countries to respond to this protectionist approach similarly, spread over vast geography, including the United States and China, Mexico, India, Canada, Russia, and European countries. These trade wars, performed for the protection of the economies of the country, carry serious risks such as slowing down of the world economy and shrinkage of domestic sectors in the long term.

The development of world trade is often studied in the context of globalization today. Pro-globalization classes argue that the increase in world trade increases the welfare level and that the number of people living on the brink of starvation around the world has been constantly decreasing, especially after the 1950s. People opposing globalization, on the other hand, state that free trade policies, which began with the General Agreement on Tariffs and Trade (GATT) in 1947 and continued under the leadership of the World Trade Organization (WTO), get the developed countries richer, while cause the third world countries to be economically and politically disadvantaged. It is an undeniable fact that there should be a structure that functions as a regulatory and supervisory supreme board to ensure the effective functioning of the world trade system despite all differences of opinion and ongoing trade wars. Setting the framework of the point where the developments starting from GATT to WTO have reached today, therefore, forms the main subject of discussion in this study. WTO's role has become more complex and critical at the point where the global trade system has reached today. In this context, we believe that in the long run, the WTO will continue to act as the dominant mediator in the trade disputes and conflicts that may arise between countries and to set the rules of trade in the future. In the light of this idea, the developments from the Customs Tariffs and Trade General Agreement to the WTO will be mentioned first. Then, the development of world trade after WTO will be mentioned. Finally, information about the Doha Round and the latest developments will be given.

FROM THE GENERAL AGREEMENT ON TARIFFS AND TRADE TO THE WORLD TRADE ORGANIZATION

As a result of efforts to liberalize the post–Second World War world trade system, the GATT was signed by twenty-three founding member states on October 30, 1947, and took effect on January 1, 1948. While signing this agreement, the establishment of a world trade system based on certain rules and substantial reduction of all international trade barriers have been the most fundamental purposes. In this context, the deduction of import duties and the elimination of discriminatory practices in trade can also be regarded as other purposes. As a result of the agreement, these 23 founding member states decided to apply tariff concessions for 45,000 items (Gelir İdaresi Başkanlığı 2009).

After the signing of the GATT, a series of global trade negotiations which were held in rounds were performed. Following the signing of the agreement, a total of eight multilateral negotiations were held, including four conferences and four multilateral trade negotiations. These were as follows, respectively: 1947 Geneva Conference, 1949 Annecy Round, 1951 Torquay Round, 1956 Geneva Round, 1960–1961 Dillon Round, 1961–1967 Kennedy Round, 1973–1979 Tokyo Round, and 1986–1993 Uruguay Round. This system has undergone a transformation over the years, and with the decisions taken after the Uruguay Round on December 15, 1993, a signature was put to one of the most significant changes, the creation of the WTO (Karaca 2003, 84–85). The final decision was signed on April 15, 1994, in Marrakesh, Morocco, by the representing ministers of the countries acceding to the Uruguay Round. The WTO officially commenced on January 1, 1995, and replaced the GATT. The establishment of the WTO has been a harbinger of a great transformation for the world economy. The WTO is a continuation of the GATT but more than that. In addition to the subjects covered by GATT, the WTO tries to impose certain rules on the issues that previously concerned countries acceding to international trade but were not emphasized.

The WTO is the only intergovernmental organization that is concerned with the regulation of the international trade between member countries acceding to foreign trade. The basis of the WTO comprises of the agreements negotiated and signed by many of the countries acceding to international trade and approved by the parliaments of these countries (WTO 2020). The agreement establishing the WTO consists of four annexes as follows: The Multilateral Agreements on Trade in Goods (Annex 1), Understanding on Rules and Procedures Governing the Settlement of Disputes (Annex 2), Trade Policy Review Mechanism (Annex 3), and Plurilateral Trade Agreements (Annex 4). As it can be understood from the annexes in question, the WTO is an organization that conducts multilateral studies for the development and liberalization of international trade and the settlement of any dispute that may prevent this development and liberalization. The WTO manages the trade agreements that form the foundation of the organization, signed by member states. Besides, it is WTO's duty to review the national trade policies of the member countries. The WTO also undertakes the function of providing technical cooperation and training to developing countries when necessary. While performing all these functions, the WTO carries out its activities in cooperation with other international organizations. The WTO has 164 members, who realize more than 98% of the world trade volume today (WTO Statistical Review 2020).

POST-WTO WORLD TRADE

In the post–Second World War era, the world has become a different place with the economic, social, and political changes. From initially GATT and then after the WTO, its successor, to the present day, the world trade volume is seen to increase gradually. Particularly in the past fifteen years, bilateral, regional, or unilateral barriers to trade in goods, investments, and services in most WTO member countries and even elsewhere outside the WTO have been greatly reduced (Baldwin 2016, 96). As a result of the WTO's vigorous efforts, today, the tariffs applied in international trade are mostly below 5% and are at zero levels for some goods in import. This is shown as one of the important factors contributing to the increase in world trade volume.

According to export figures published by the WTO, world merchandise exports, which were $58.500 million in 1948, increased to $2.036.136 million in 1980, $6.454.020 million in 2000, $15.306.475 million in 2010, and $18.888.714 million in 2019. As can be seen clearly from here, although the world trade in goods decreased some during the crisis (e.g., world merchandise exports which were $16.497.329 million in 2008 and $12.710.106 million in 2009 due to the shrinkage experienced after the 2008 crisis.), this situation was compensated in a short time, and it followed an exponentially increasing trend over the years (WTO 2020).

DOHA ROUND

The Doha Round, also known as the Doha Development Round, the final round of trade negotiations of the WTO, launched at the Fourth Ministerial Conference of the WTO in Doha, Qatar between November 9 and 14, 2001. The original deadline of the round in question was January 1, 2005.

With the commence of the Doha Round, the studies were begun immediately, and the Trade Negotiations Committee was established on February 1, 2002. All negotiation issues under the Doha Round were handled under separate negotiation groups and all groups are affiliated with this committee. This committee carries out the coordination and monitoring of the negotiations. The Doha Round negotiations are being carried out in many areas on a scale that has never been seen in any negotiating round in GATT/WTO history. In the process of conducting the negotiations, at the fourth meeting of the Trade Negotiations Committee held on October 3–4, 2002, the general tendencies, and differences of opinion of the WTO member countries participating in the Doha Round started to be seen clearly. After this phase, due to the differences in the attitudes and approaches of the member countries, negotiations reached a stalemate (Altay 2003).

As a rule, in the Doha Round negotiations, unanimous consent was required in the possible decisions to be made in trade negotiations. Also, it was not possible to make sub-agreements in parts. Agreements had to be fully accepted, and if even a single country voted negatively or did not join the agreement, it was impossible to reach an agreement. This caused the negotiations to inch along.

Particularly, agriculture was one of the subjects that are emphasized insistently, where no agreement was reached. The Agricultural Trade Negotiations carried out in the Doha Round were mainly aimed at ensuring the continuity of the agricultural liberalization process initiated in the Uruguay Round. In this context, in the Agricultural Negotiations held in the Doha Round, obtaining better access to foreign markets for agricultural products, phasing out agricultural export subsidies, and ensuring fair competition were aimed (Fotourehchi and Şahinöz 2016, 2026). Agriculture was one of the topics that occupy the agenda the most, the reason why the negotiation tour could not be completed, and where the countries acceding to the negotiations cannot find a middle ground. This was the most common issue that pits developed countries against developing countries.

WHERE TO NOW?

In terms of the activities it has carried out since its establishment and achieving the goals set forth, the WTO is generally recognized as a successful organization. However, in recent years, the deviations and failures in the initially anticipated negotiation end date of the Doha Round, the latest WTO negotiation, have led to dissatisfaction with both the member countries and the WTO itself. In total, twenty countries, including China and Russia, have been participating in the negotiation talks since 2001, but the round has not been finalized (Baldwin 2016, 96).

If the goals set in the Doha Round in 2001 had been achieved without deviation and if the round could have been finalized in 2005, as planned, it was thought that any country acceding to the negotiations would benefit mutually. But, at this point today, the world economy is very different from its former state in 2001; therefore, the goals envisaged in the Doha Round no longer derive a profit for everyone. Issues such as especially China's rise in the world economy, international investments to steer for offshore accounts rather than profitable areas, and the great demand for multilateralism instead of unilateralism have made the negotiating items no longer appealing to many countries (Baldwin 2016, 113).

In 2008, WTO member states almost reached an agreement on methods for progressing the Doha negotiations but failed to obtain a result. Today, negotiations seem to have stopped permanently. Recently, the rise of populist and introverted politics in several developed countries presumably contributed to a general feeling of dissatisfaction (Irish 2019, 38).

When the Doha Round begins, the United States and the EU, which usually take the leading role in WTO negotiations, had promised developing countries a trade agreement that would promote their development but not require them to reduce their import barriers to the same extent as industrialized countries. However, since the beginning of the Doha Round, the developing countries, especially China, start to export more goods than they import drew the reaction of the United States and other developed countries.

The United States and other developed countries asked for developing countries to reduce their import barriers and cut agricultural domestic subsidies. Particularly, developing and less developed WTO member countries want the negotiation clauses to be implemented to remove the barriers to the initially promised exports of agricultural products and labor-intensive merchandise, while they expected the United States, Japan, and the EU to take steps on domestic subsidies and export subsidies. The United States and the EU behaved timidly to reduce agricultural subsidies, in particular.

While the United States is opposed to regulation in domestic subsidies in real terms, it does not find it favorable to further tariff discount in agriculture in the EU. The fact that the United States tries to carry out liberalization and protectionist approaches together but failed to clarify which it would concentrate on, and the fact that EU continues its preferential trade policy with its former colonies of Africa, the Caribbean, and the Pacific countries without damaging its internal system too much gave the impression that neither of the major actors was very keen to take action on this issue (Fotourehchi and Şahinöz 2016, 2031). Besides, the United States, which has a certain weight in the world trade system, does not yet see the level of liberalization provided in various negotiation areas sufficient. Therefore, it has made additional demands from rising economies such as China, India, and Brazil. Arguing that especially Brazil, China, and India have become more competitive by taking advantage of the liberal trade environment created as a result of the WTO's efforts and thus become rising economies, the United States asked for the countries in question to make more concessions to agricultural and non-agricultural products (TOBB 2010, 16). China and India, on the other hand, continued to remain unresponsive to these demands and insist on sticking to the initial principles.

Besides, another reason why the Doha process could not be completed was the fact that negative political factors in the United States, EU, India, and other countries have come together. For example, elections held in India in 2009 like Brazil's new protectionist approach toward rapidly increasing imports from China and the increase in exchange rate likely contributed to the failure of the negotiations in 2008 (Gantz 2011, 323). In summary, stalemates occur in the multilateral system at the points where conflicts of interest of developed and developing countries begin.

As a result of the efforts made, negotiations on agriculture, one of the most discussed issues, started to bring results only after fourteen years. During the Doha Round negotiations, instead of reducing the practices that harm reciprocal trade mentioned in the Agricultural Agreement, the goal of *removing them completely* has been adopted (Parıltı 2019, 1888).

Considering all of these, it is very difficult to establish a holistic system where all countries will benefit jointly. However, arrangements and efforts to achieve such a system would mean taking steps for the best possible setup of the system. Hence, ensuring the continuity of the multilateral approach despite all kinds of setbacks and disputes is important for everyone.

CONCLUSION

The number of bilateral, regional, and multilateral trade agreements that are thought to contribute to the development of world trade, in which countries make various concessions to each other and hope to gain high benefits in return, is gradually increasing today. Since such agreements include many issues such as services trade, public procurement, improving investment opportunities, protection of intellectual and industrial property rights, as well as trade in goods, they are broader than the traditional free trade agreements between countries. However, this makes the global trading system more complex rather than facilitating its operation. Therefore, the need for a more comprehensive upper-observer structure, like the WTO, has started to be felt stronger than before. The role of WTO in the global trade system has become more complex and critical today. Although the WTO failed to complete the Doha Round, the final round of negotiations, it already has a more compre-hensive structure than these bilateral, regional, and multilateral trade agree-ments, which are very popular today. In recent years, the WTO has come under serious pressure. While negotiations on the Doha Round agenda have been stalled by agricultural subsidies and disputes over intellectual property rights, member states are increasingly turning to bilateral and regional free trade agreements to boost their commercial interests. In addition, the recent COVID-19 outbreak in the world has caused a sharp decline in international trade and created uncertainty about the future of global supply chains.

The proliferation of complex intersecting problems in international trade in recent years has led to the question of whether the WTO serves the main pur-pose of creating a strong basis for international trade. At this point, the WTO is at a critical point where its legitimacy and authority are eroded, and resto-ration is urgently needed. Therefore, it is necessary to reactivate the negotia-tions on trade, revise the rules-based structure of the global trade system, and ensure its modernization. In this context, it is clear that the development of a new work program for the WTO is important for all participating countries.

We believe that as the multilateral approach continues to live under the WTO roof, the WTO will continue to act as the leading mediating role in trade disputes and conflicts, which may arise between countries, and that the WTO will continue to set the rules of trade in the future. In this case, to ensure that the WTO continues to be one of the main actors of the global economic order in the future, both developed countries and developing countries should be in a vigorous effort.

REFERENCES

Altay, Vural. "Dünya Ticaret Örgütü Doha Kalkınma Gündemi Müzakerelerinde Son Durum." Dışişleri Bakanlığı Yayınları, Ekonomik Sorunlar Dergisi, No. 9 (2003), Last Access Date: 19.08.2020 http://www.mfa.gov.tr/uluslararasi-ekonomik-sorunl ar-_mayis-2003_.tr.mfa

Baldwin, Richard. 2016. "The World Trade Organization and The Future of Multilateralism." *Journal of Economic Perspectives,* vol. 30, no. 1 (2016): 95–116.

Büyükbaykal, Ceyda Ilgaz. *Türkiye'de Televizyon Alanında Küresel Yerel Birlikteliği: CNN Türk ve CNBC-e Örneği,* 1. Baskı, İstanbul: İstanbul Üniversitesi İletişim Fakültesi Yayınları, 2004.

Fotourehchi, Zahra; Ahmet Şahinöz. "DTÖ Doha Müzakereleri ve Tarım Politikalarında Yeni Yönelimler." *Itobiad: Journal of the Human & Social Science Researches* vol. 5, no. 7 (2016): 2017–2040.

Gantz, David A. "World Trade Law After Doha: Multilateral, Regional, and National Approaches." *Denver Journal of International Law and Policy* vol. 40, no. 1 (2011): 321–367.

Gelir İdaresi Başkanlığı. "GATT Bilgilendirme Rehberi." 2009. Last Access Date: 25.07.2020 https://www.gib.gov.tr/sites/default/files/uluslararasi_mevzuat/gatt95 .pdf

Irish, Maureen. "The Trade Facilitation Agreement: Is the Doha Development Round Succeeding." *Trade Law and Development* vol. 11, no. 1 (2019): 38–51.

Karaca, Nil. "GATT'tan Dünya Ticaret Örgütü'ne." *Maliye Dergisi* no. 144 (2003): 84–99.

Kürkçü, Dumanlı, Duygu. "Küreselleşme Kavramı ve Küreselleşmeye Yönelik Yaklaşımlar." *The Turkish Online Journal of Design, Art and Communication* vol. 3, no. 2 (2013): 1–11.

Parilti, Hasan. "Çok Taraflı Ticaret Sistemi ve Teşvik Politikaları." *Third Sector Social Economic Review* vol. 54, no. 4 (2019): 1875–1898.

TOBB. "Dünya Ticaret Örgütü: Doha Kalkınma Gündemi Müzakarelerinde Son Durum ve Geleceğe Dönük Beklentiler." 2016. Last Access Date: 06.08.2020 https ://www.tobb.org.tr/DisTicaretMudurlugu/Documents/Duyurular/doha.pdf

WTO. "About WTO." Last Access Date: 27.07.2020. https://www.wto.org/english/ thewto_e/thewto_e.htm.

WTO. "Statistics on Annual Trade." 2020. Last Access Date: 04.08.2020 https://data .wto.org/

WTO. "World Trade Statistical Review." 2020. Last Access Date: 20.02.2021 https:/ /www.wto.org/english/res_e/statis_e/wts2020_e/wts2020_e.pdf

Chapter 3

Globalization of the Economy or the Globalizing Economy?

An Analysis in the Context of the West (USA and EU) – East (China)

Samet Zenginlioğlu

INTRODUCTION

Globalization refers to a phenomenon analyzed from various perspectives and tried to be defined and interpreted. The multidimensional context of the phenomenon under cause, process, and effect titles suggests that discussions need to be reconstructed. Because many innovations or updates in a broad spectrum, including cultural, economic, political, and theoretical dimensions, force us to reevaluate or re-question globalization. It is thought that the East-West axis has importance in this assessment process. The East-West relations and factors of competition have included cultural, theological, economic, and political components since the historical process. Besides, the bipolar system of the Cold War period led boundaries between these two directions/camps to distinct and fault lines to deepen.

Even though international relations theorists have long debated the unipolarity and multipolarity in the post–Cold War period; the rise of Asia with the twenty-first century, and the Chinese factor standing out in this rise resulted in the necessity of analyzing a new axis in terms of international politics. As a matter of fact, the rise of China in the sight of the political economy in return for the Western-centric or Western-oriented construction of globalization in the context of theory and discourse, and the resulting data, made the picture clearer. When the Western world is addressed under the leadership of the United States and the EU, the Eastern world has represented a new dimension under Chinese leadership in the perspective of macroeconomic indicators.

This study was prepared in three sections to evaluate the globalizing economy rather than the Western-centered globalization of the economy, in terms of these two axes and leading actors. In the first section, basic approaches and conceptualizations for the phenomenon of globalization were mentioned, as well as the assessments regarding globalization's Western-centric construction and perception were introduced on the basis of some concepts and discourses. In the second section, by contrast with these assessments, China's rise in the West-East dilemma and some of the arguments/instruments that took place in this rise were analyzed. The third and final section focused on several economic indicators in the dimension of US-EU and China for the purpose of introducing the comparative perspectives.

GLOBALIZATION: WESTERN CENTRIC OR GLOBAL?

The globalization phenomenon has had various impacts specifically in technology from the second half of the twentieth century and in the political economy field following the post–Cold War period. While the cross-border dimension of technology confirms the characterization of the sphere as a village, processes that can be expressed in terms of response/reaction/dependency in the relations in the field of political economy were discussed. For example, it has been inevitable for an economic crisis to reach a global context and to bring multidimensional outcomes along. In addition to these fields (technology and political economy), the factor of culture has undoubtedly gained a new dimension with the globalization process. In fact, global studies on culture have taken place among the frequently discussed issues in the literature (Rieff 1994, 73–81; Berger 1997, 23–29; Ladegaard 2007, 139–163).

Various approaches have been suggested to interpret and explain the globalization phenomenon (Stefanovic 2008, 263–272). These approaches, discussed under three titles which include hyper-globalists, sceptic, and transformationalists, have regarded several contexts ranging from the future of nation-states through the transformations in the globalization-oriented world. In addition to these approaches, various concepts have come up to analyze the several effects and reflections of the process. Samples such as glocalization (Grigorescu and Zaif 2017, 70–74; Roudometof 2016) or grobalization (Ritzer 2020; Ritzer 2003, 193–209) are considered remarkable expansions in this perspective. However, the fact that the construction of these and similar concepts, discourses, and theories that are expressed in the eyes of the process and effects of globalization are of Western origin has brought along the observations and evaluations that globalization exhibits a Western-centric superiority on the axis of liberal values.

Particularly in the post–Cold War period, Fukuyama's thesis "The End of History?," still a controversial theory at present, is one of the primary studies that try to construct and prove this superiority. Besides, global reflections of technology language, the undeniable influence of the United States in the global political economy since Bretton Woods, and Western-oriented/centric discussions in the cultural field have striking arguments in this sense. The debates on the fact that globalization is Americanization in some way (Daghrir 2013, 19–24; Owolabi 2001, 71–92), therefore, are considered as a perspective that explains this framework. The concepts/approaches such as "Coca-Colonization" (Sorensen and Petersen, 2012 597–617), "McDonaldization" (Ritzer 2020a), or "McWorld" (Barber 1996) undoubtedly offer processes that support the relevant perspective.

Although this context raises explanations and analyzes that globalization is West centric, the fact that globalization has gained a global dimension as of the twenty-first century is encountered. For example, the rise of countries like India in technology, the re-emergence of local elements in the cultural field, and the transformation of the local, so to speak, gains importance in this sense. In the political economy field, on the other hand, the rise of Asia and China's economic and commercial progress, in particular, are regarded in this manner (Florini 2011, 23–33; Saunders 2014, 19–55). Therefore, although it is possible to discuss the Western-centric globalization of the economy until the twenty-first century, it is thought that in this century, an economy globalized with the influence of the Asian actors (especially China) should be uttered.

THE WEST-EAST DILEMMA IN THE GLOBAL POLITICAL ECONOMY

Historically, the West-East dilemma has a multidimensional scope. It is possible to trace this scope in a wide spectrum including political, commercial, cultural, and military dimensions. Several factors such as ideational interaction between the West and the East, religious-cultural rivalry, conflicts, and the political reflections of these rivalries and conflicts, commercial relations, and the economic outputs of these relations should be stated in this context. Even the immigration phenomenon represents a different dimension on this axis.

Considering the East-West relations from a political-economic perspective, it is known that the commercial axis influencing this perspective extends to the Silk and Spice roads. In the context of the processes and effects of arriving at new continents in the fifteenth century and afterward, it is possible to see numerous reflections of this commercial axis. As a matter of fact, relations and rivalry between Asia and the West in production, trade, and consumption were then evaluated in a multidimensional scope. This scope can be analyzed in the context of "China's rise" and trade wars, specifically in the post–Cold War period (Steinbock 2018, 515–542; Zhu, Yang and Feng 2018, 423–426).

Factors that could be considered as an advantage, such as population density, low-cost labor, raw material procurement, (renewable) energy, and large product range have resulted in China being evaluated as a rising actor in this respect. Although the foundations of China's policy to open its doors to foreign businesses initiated with the reforms of Deng Xiaoping period in 1978, regarding specifically the post–Cold War period as a milestone, for China, it now becomes possible to mention a structural thought "to reconstruct the system or to be the leader of the system." China's integration into the system is a remarkable factor in this context. Therefore, it is possible to talk about a transformation dominant in the system rather than a transformation that gets involved in the global economic system externally. Thus, China's International Monetary Fund membership in 1989 and the World Trade Organization membership in 2001 should be interpreted in this regard (Kafkasyalı 2012, 103–128). When viewed from the aspects of the free trade agreements and indicators, the fact that two of the ten biggest banks in the world are Chinese, sixty-one Chinese companies take place in the Fortune Global 500, and it has six of the ten largest container ports in the world (Aydın 2019, 1–12) indicate China's commercial rise in this context.

Besides these developments, China's "Belt and Road Initiative" (formerly One Belt One Road) that will add a new dimension to the trade route between China and the West as of 2013 and located on the historical Silk Road route should be paid regard to (Ikiz 2019, 1688–1700). Thanks to creating an economic corridor, the "Belt and Road Initiative" is considered also as a geostrategic and geo-economic move (Cai 2017, 1–22; OECD 2018; Lu et al. 2018). This move, undoubtedly, can be evaluated in the context of the twenty-first-century trade wars. In fact, trade wars between the West and China, in particular, and reflections of protectionism policies give us important clues. Globally, the countries defined as the world's foreign trade giants are China and the United States (Baran 2019, 36). Economic and commercial relations/indicators between the two giants reveal the dimension of rivalry. Although the United States is regarded as a dominant actor in the global economic system, China's presence now reflects an undeniable truth. In fact, China, with the above-mentioned advantages, today functions as a production station for companies around the world (Patnaik 2020). This is among the factors that trigger competition, on the other hand. Besides, China to rank first (Baran 2019, 40) in the list of countries from which the United States imports is also striking from this perspective. When compared the competition between the

United States-EU and China in terms of several economic indicators, it is possible to see the signs of the rise mentioned in this section.

THE UNITED STATES-EU AND CHINA IN THE CONTEXT OF ECONOMIC DATA

The transformation in the context of the West-East in terms of globalization and political economy has reflected in some data. For example, examining table 3.1, it is possible to see these reflections in the growth rates of the gross domestic product (GDP). Analyzing the table from the perspective of the Eurozone, the United States, and China triad as of the 2000s, the relative superiority of Chinese growth rates draws attention. Additionally, it is possible to make a comparison with China for the 2007–2008 global financial crisis, regarded as one of the first major financial crises of the global economy in the twenty-first century that affects both the US and the EU economy. While the United States' GDP growth rate was −0.1 in 2008, this rate was 9.7 for China.

Table 3.1   GDP Growth (Annual %)

	Euro area	United States	China
2000	3.9	4.1	8.5
2001	2.2	1.0	8.3
2002	1.0	1.7	9.1
2003	0.7	2.9	10.0
2004	2.3	3.8	10.1
2005	1.7	3.5	11.4
2006	3.2	2.9	12.7
2007	3.0	1.9	14.2
2008	0.4	−0.1	9.7
2009	−4.5	−2.5	9.4
2010	2.1	2.6	10.6
2011	1.7	1.6	9.6
2012	−0.9	2.2	7.9
2013	−0.3	1.8	7.8
2014	1.4	2.5	7.4
2015	2.1	2.9	7.0
2016	1.9	1.6	6.8
2017	2.5	2.2	6.9
2018	1.9	2.9	6.8
2019	1.3	2.3	6.1

Source: World Development Indicators, 2020.

At this point, the following question may come to mind: Can the fact that China did not affected by this crisis be evaluated as it is not yet fully integrated into the global economic system? When this question is answered departing from the presupposition that the global economy is West oriented only, it seems possible to answer "Yes" due to China's unique economic structure. This answer, on the other hand, appears to contradict the "global-ization of globalization" assertion of the study. However, a second question has to be asked, on the other hand, and this question would be about whether it is possible to consider this and similar crises truly on a global scale. For example, while a Western-oriented crisis is regarded as a global crisis along with its various exposures (Kim and Haque 2002, 37–44), an Eastern-centric economic crisis might be described as an "Asian crisis" only. While the 1997 financial crisis was regarded as the "Asian crisis," the US-centric financial crisis in the 2007–2008 period was accepted as a "global financial crisis" (Helleiner 2011, 67–87). Hence, in addition to the debates on whether to integrate into the global economic system or not, it should also be clearly explained/analyzed whether the crisis is truly global.

With the globalizing economy argument, as well as the GDP growth rates, the focus is on foreign direct investment. Because the process of foreign direct investment is related to the position of the relevant country in the global political economy, as well as its strong domestic economic process, too. In this respect, when the foreign direct investments in table 3.2 are ana-lyzed in terms of actors, it is possible to refer to the relative success of the Eurozone. In addition, comparing the United States and China, it seems that China has average higher data. Therefore, stating that the above-mentioned question of integrating into the global system does not constitute an agenda item for China in this respect would not be wrong.

As well as the relevant data, it is possible to focus on the current account balance in the context of the United States and China. The current account balance indicates important data in terms of macroeconomic indicators, in particular. Here, a scope such as services, export-import, investment, and current transfers balance is expressed. Data of the current account balance in table 3.3 indicate that as of 2000, the United States has negative indicators while China positive indicators. Although there are disruptions on a global scale in the current account balance in the context of import-oriented growth for developing countries, it is considered that such a table on the US scale is disputable.

Besides, considering research and development expenses and making a comparison in the context of the United States-China, the expenditure to GDP ratio for the United States between 2012 and 2015 was 2.7%, while it was 2.8% for 2016 and 2018. For China, on the other hand, these ratios were realized as 1.9%, 2.0%, 2.1%, and 2.2% for 2012, 2013–2014, 2015–2017,

Table 3.2 **Foreign Direct Investment, Net Inflows (of %GDP)**

	Euro area	*United States*	*China*
2000	8.6	3.4	3.5
2001	4.9	1.6	3.5
2002	3.5	1.0	3.6
2003	3.0	1.0	3.5
2004	2.7	1.7	3.5
2005	6.0	1.1	4.6
2006	7.3	2.2	4.5
2007	10.0	2.4	4.4
2008	4.7	2.3	3.7
2009	3.4	1.1	2.6
2010	4.2	1.8	4.0
2011	6.0	1.7	3.7
2012	4.3	1.5	2.8
2013	4.4	1.7	3.0
2014	2.8	1.4	2.6
2015	6.3	2.8	2.2
2016	4.9	2.6	1.6
2017	3.0	1.8	1.3
2018	0.8	1.3	1.7
2019	1.2	1.5	1.1

Source: World Development Indicators, 2020.

and 2018, respectively (World Bank, 2020a). Therefore, these differences between R&D expenditures, which cannot be ignored in terms of production and investment activities in the context of the global economic system, represent another dimension of the competition between the United States and China. Finally, looking at the world's leading countries in goods and services trade, it is possible to see economic growth, foreign investment, current account balance, and R&D expenditures; also the actors' presence in global trade is one of the most important indicators of presence in the global economy. Analyzing the leading actors in global trade (World Bank 2020b), it is seen that the United States ranks first while China second. On the other hand, Germany, one of the leading actors of the EU, ranks third in this list. Thus, the representation of these three actors between the two axes provides an important view in terms of the main argument of the study. In addition to this view in the context of the West-East, it should be stated that the UK, Japan, France, and the Netherlands came after this triad. Although it can be thought that the EU-centric perspective would remain incomplete in terms of the Brexit process, this is regarded significant in terms of clarifying the complex structure in the context of the West-East in political economy.

Table 3.3   Current Account Balance (of %GDP)

	United States	China
2000	−3.9	1.7
2001	−3.7	1.3
2002	−4.1	2.4
2003	−4.5	2.6
2004	−5.2	3.5
2005	−5.7	5.8
2006	−5.8	8.4
2007	−4.9	9.9
2008	−4.6	9.2
2009	−2.6	4.8
2010	−2.9	3.9
2011	−2.9	1.8
2012	−2.6	2.5
2013	−2.1	1.5
2014	−2.1	2.3
2015	−2.2	2.7
2016	−2.3	1.8
2017	−2.3	1.6
2018	−2.4	0.2
2019	−2.3	1.0

Source: World Development Indicators, 2020.

CONCLUSION

This study aimed to make an evaluation or research in terms of the time period we are in the first quarter of the twenty-first century on political-economic grounds. This objective has grounded on the globalizing economy in the context of the West-East with several macroeconomic data, in particular, or on the globalization of the globalization, so to speak. For more than half a century, the globalization phenomenon distinctively constitutes one of the main discussion/analysis areas of social science disciplines. The multidimensional context of the phenomenon has brought about evaluations containing various perspectives. This study, on the other hand, has grounded on the globalizing economy argument rather than the globalization of the West-centric economy. The superiority of Western values in terms of perception, discourse, and theory during and after the Cold War period has brought with it identifications and determinations regarding the conclusion that globalization is of Western origin. At this point, the Western values, norms, and judgments specific to the United States and EU have been regarded as to be linked to globalization processes. However, it has been observed that with the twenty-first century, there has been a transformation in terms of culture, technology, and political culture.

Departing from the idea that culture and technology-oriented analysis of this transformation field should constitute the focal problem of a different study, this study focused on the transformation in terms of the political economy, in particular. Considering the competition factors and actors in the political economy field, we see Asia and more specifically China, which has a non-ignorable increase trend against the West. China's competitive power in the comparison areas of macroeconomic indicators, as well as its active steps in the field named trade wars, have also attracted attention at this point. In particular, it is possible to evaluate the "One Belt One Road" project in this context. Therefore, it is thought that evaluating the globalization–economy relation in terms of political economy with only West-centric facts, events, and data would bring incomplete or incorrect evaluations along. We, therefore, introduced the analysis of the competition in the context of the West-East in the second section and data confirming this competition in the third section.

At the stage reached in terms of the basic assertion of the study, in other words, in the first quarter of the twenty-first century, we think that it would be appropriate to mention two main issues. The first of these is the fact that today, globalization is globalizing—such that, this fact includes the notion that the United States and the EU are not the sole authority in terms of factors such as management/design in the economy. As a matter of fact, in addition to the China case, discussed in this study, also the presence and influence of actors such as India and Japan have the characteristics of being a determinant. Second, it is possible to discuss the decentralization of globalization. This argument, on the other hand, is directly interested and related to the globalization of "globalization" statement and reflects the opinion that globalization follows a course appropriate to its nature. Therefore, it is thought that in the medium term, the reflections in the field of political economy would become more evident in the context of the West-East.

REFERENCES

Aydın, Figen. 2019. "Çin Yükselişi'nin Ekonomik Perspektifi ve Gelecek Tahminlerinin Orta Asya'ya Yansımaları." *Uluslararası Afro-Avrasya Araştırmaları Dergisi* 4, no. 8: 1–12.

Baran, Tülay. 2019. "Dünyada Gümrük ve Ticaret Savaşları: Türk Vergi Kapasitesine Etkisinin Analizi." *Gümrük Ticaret Dergisi* 6, no. 18: 28–53.

Barber, Benjamin R. 1996. *Jihad vs. McWorld: How Globalism and Tribalism are Reshaping the World.* New York: Ballantine Books.

44   *Samet Zenginlioğlu*

Berger, Peter L. 1997. "Four Faces of Global Culture." *The National Interest*, no. 49: 23–29.

Cai, Peter. 2017. "Understanding China's Belt and Road Initiative." *Lowy Institute for International Policy*, 1–22.

Daghrir, Wassim. 2013. "Globalization as Americanization? Beyond the Conspiracy Theory." *IOSR Journal of Applied Physics* 5, no. 2: 19–24.

Florini, Ann. 2011. "Rising Asian Power and Changing Global Governance." *International Studies Review*, 13: 24–33.

Grigorescu, Adriana, and Zaif, Alexandra. 2017. "The Concept of Glocalization and its Incorporation in Global Brands' Marketing Strategies." *International Journal of Business and Management Invention* 6, no. 1: 70–74.

Helleiner, Eric. 2011. "Understanding the 2007–2008 Global Financial Crisis: Lessons for Scholars of International Political Economy." *Annual Review of Political Science* 14: 67–87.

İkiz, Ahmet. 2019. "Tek Kuşak Tek Yol Projesi ve Türkiye'ye Olası Etkileri." *Elektronik Sosyal Bilimler Dergisi* 18, no. 72: 1688–1700.

Kafkasyalı, Muhammet Savaş. 2012. "Küresel Üstünlük Mücadelesi ve Çin'in Yükselişi: Muhayyilenin Ontolojik Sınırları." *Atatürk Üniversitesi Sosyal Bilimler Enstitüsü Dergisi* 16, 1: 103–128.

Kim, Suk H. and Haque, Mahfuzul. 2002. "The Asian Financial Crisis of 1997: Causes and Policy Responses." *Multinational Business Review* 10: 37–44.

Ladegaard, Hans J. 2007. "Global Culture -Myth or Reality? Perceptions of "National Cultures" in Global Corporation." *Journal of Intercultural Communication Research* 36, no. 2: 139–163.

Lu, Hui., Charlene Rohr, Marco Hafner. and Anna Knack. 2018. *China Belt and Road Initiative*. RAND Europe. https://www.rand.org/pubs/research_reports/RR2625.html.

OECD. 2018. *China's Belt and Road Initiative in the Global Trade, Investment and Finance Landscape*. OECD. https://www.oecd.org/finance/Chinas-Belt-and-Road-Initiative-in-the-global-trade-investment-and-finance-landscape.pdf.

Owolabi, Kolawole A. 2001. "Globalization, Americanization and Western Imperialism." *Journal of Social Development in Africa* 16, no. 2: 71–92.

Patnaik, İla. 2020. "Dünya Ticaretinde Hakim Trendler." In *Küresel Trendler*, Edited by Dilek Demirbaş vd., Ankara: Ekin Basım Yayın Dağıtım.

Rieff, David. 1994. "A Global Culture?." *World Policy Journal* 10, no. 4: 73–81.

Ritzer, George. 2020. *Küresel Dünya*. Translated by Melih Pekdemir, İstanbul: Ayrıntı Yayınları.

Ritzer, George. 2003. "Rethinking Globalization: Glocalization/Grobalization and Something/Nothing." *Sociological Theory* 21, no. 3: 193–209.

Ritzer, George. 2020a. *Toplumun McDonaldlaştırılması, Çağdaş Toplum Yaşamının Değişen Karakteri Üzerine Bir İnceleme*. Translated by. Akın Emre Pilgir, İstanbul: Ayrıntı Yayınları.

Roudometof, Victor. 2016. *Glocalization: A Critical Introduction*, London and New York: Routledge.

Saunders, Phillip C. 2014. "China's Rising Power, the U.S. Rebalance to Asia, and Implications for U.S.-China Relations." *Issues & Studies*, no. 3: 19–55.

Sorensen, Nils Arne and Petersen, Klaus. 2012. "Corporate Capitalism or Coca-Colonization? Economic Interests, Cultural Concerns, Tax Policies and Coca-Cola in Denmark from 1945 to early 1960s." *Contemporary European History* 21, no. 4: 597–617.

Stefanovic, Zoran, 2008. "Globalization: Theoretical Perspectives, Impacts and Institutional Response of the Economy." *Economics and Organization* 5, no. 3: 263–272.

Steinbock, Dan. 2018. "U.S.-China Trade War and Its Global Impacts." *China Quarterly of International Strategic Studies* 4, no. 4: 515–542.

World Bank. 2020a. "World Development Indicators," Accessed October 19, 2020, https://databank.worldbank.org/source/world-development-indicators.

World Bank. 2020b. "World Trade Statistical Review 2019," Accessed October 19, 2020, https://www.wto.org/english/res_e/statis_e/wts2019_e/wts19_toc_e.htm.

Zhu, Zeyan, Yang, Yaotang and Feng, Shuqi. 2018. "Trade War Between China and US." *Advances in Social Science Education and Humanities Research* 206: 423–426.

Chapter 4

China and European Union Economic Relations

Building a Partnership[1]

İlhan Aras

INTRODUCTION

EU and China have been rising powers in the second half of the twentieth century. EU–China relations officially started in 1975. In the following years, the EU wanted to improve its relations with China to establish a close relationship with an economic power. Both opportunities and challenges coexisted in this relationship. However, the basis of the relationship has always been economic issues.

Political problems continue between the parties on many issues, from the arms embargo to human rights. Despite these political problems, EU–China economic relations continue to improve. Trade agreements between the parties and China's increasing investments in Europe show that the future of economic relations will proceed in a similar way. In other words, the similarity between the economic giants of China and the EU and their close trade relationship will continue in the future.

In this context, the study deals with only the economic dimension of EU–China relations. First, the economic relations before 1975 will be discussed in the study. In the next chapter, the development of economic relations since 1975 is presented on the basis of data and related literature. Besides, intense relations and investments of the parties especially after 2000 will be mentioned.

ECONOMIC RELATIONS BEFORE 1975

The first important agreements between China and the EU show that the relations have developed on the trade axis since 1945. During this period, while the United States considered China as an enemy, European countries continued to trade with China (Borght and Zhang 2010, 70). Until the 1960s, although the Chinese market was insignificant in the exports of Western European countries, there was an increase in trade between the parties in the following years.

The political and ideological imperatives of the Cold War period accelerated the development of economic and commercial relations between the parties (Casarini, 2006 9). Therefore, the break-in Sino–Soviet relations in 1963 can be regarded as an important turning point in China–Europe trade relations. In the spring of 1963, China's vice minister of foreign trade Lu Hsung-chang visited Britain, Switzerland, and the Netherlands. In 1964, exhibitions and fairs were organized in China by the French and the British (Bressi 1972, 827).

As can be seen from table 4.1, the break of relations with the Soviet Union also caused a big decrease in trade. In addition, with the development of relations with Western Europe, there has been a continuous increase in trade between the parties.

Trade between the Community and China was limited until the 1970s for some reasons. First, Mao's policy of a self-contained country did not encourage trade with countries outside the communist bloc. In addition, China did not have foreign currency for foreign trade and China did not have products to export (Strange 1998, 59–60). In this context, China, which has improved its trade with the Common Market, has tended to focus on different trade opportunities (Broadbent 1976, 191–192).

From table 4.2, it is seen that China's exports to the European Economic Community (EEC) 9 member states increased from 7.5% in 1971 to 24% in 1972.

From 1972 to 1974, China's trade with Western Europe increased by more than 25%. The most important country in this trade was the Federal Republic

Table 4.1   China's Trade with the Soviet Union and Western Europe

Year	% of Total	% of Soviet Trade	Europe
1950	37.1	35.6	9.8
1955	71.0	49.7	8.7
1960	64.7	41.2	15.9
1965	29.4	10.7	17.8
1970	19.5	1.0	24.0
1975	10.0	0.5	30.0

Source: (Broadbent 1976, 193).

Table 4.2   China's Trade with the EEC (in US$ million)

	Years	Belgium-Luxembourg	Denmark	France	Ireland	Italy	Netherlands	United Kingdom	West Germany	Total EEC Nine	World	EEC Nine (%)
China's Imports	1972	11	9	59	-	79	10	78	165	411	2.777	15
	1971	7	2	112	1	62	17	68	137	407	2.247	18
	1970	22	4	81	-	58	22	107	168	462	2.183	21
China's Exports	1972	23	9	103	3	84	45	89	106	464	2.929	16
	1971	17	11	71	3	64	35	76	95	373	2.364	16
	1970	11	11	70	2	63	27	80	84	348	2.063	17
China's Balance	1972	+12	+1	+45	+3	+6	+35	+11	-59	+53	+152	-
	1971	+10	+9	-41	+1	+2	+18	+8	-41	-34	+117	-
	1970	-12	+7	-11	+2	+5	+5	-26	-83	-114	+120	-
Total	1972	35	18	162	3	163	55	167	271	875	5.706	15
	1971	25	14	183	4	127	53	144	232	781	4.611	17
	1970	33	14	151	2	121	49	187	252	809	4.246	19

Source: (China Association Annual Report (London), 1973; Current Scene, X: 10, (1972); Japanese Foreign Ministry estimates in Tokyo. See Wilson 1973, 656.)

of Germany. In 1973, China's export to Federal Germany exceeded 27%, while its import from Federal Germany was 33%. In 1975, the share of EEC in China's trade was 30%. Thus, China's third-largest trade partner was the Community. On the other hand, after the United States, Japan, and Hong Kong, the Federal Republic of Germany was China's fourth-largest trade partner (Broadbent 1976, 191–192).

China–Italy relations are generally based on economic issues. Italy wanted to play a leading role in the trade negotiations between Western Europe and China. Beijing and Rome negotiated a trade agreement in May 1971. In this process, China's request to trade in Italian and Chinese currencies was accepted by Italy. Thus, China became the first socialist country whose money could be exchanged for a Western country. However, these offers from China and Italy were rejected by the Community, and the agreement later signed included normal provisions (Bressi 1972, 842).

Among the products that China sells to Europe, there is a wide range of raw materials for modern production. Textile, canned food, ceramics, etc. products can be given as examples. China has bought products such as machinery, transportation equipment, special steel products, and nonferrous metals from Europe (Wilson 1973, 656–657).

RELATIONS AFTER 1975

In 1974, the Community discussed commercial relations including China and decided to make European Community Treaties instead of the terminated commercial agreements of the member states. This situation is in line with the Treaty of Rome and the Common Trade Policy. In this context, the draft agreements were sent to the relevant countries, including China. It is possible to evaluate Commissioner Christopher Soames's visit to China in May 1975 within the scope of the Common Trade Policy of the Community (Laursen 2011, 9).

While the trade volume between China and the EU was 2.5 billion dollars in 1975, when political relations were established between the parties, it was 6.4 billion dollars when the Trade Agreement was signed in 1978 (Kovačević and Bojić 2016, 64). Table 4.3 shows China's trade with some European countries during the EEC–China relations period.

A Trade Agreement was signed between the parties on May 2, 1978. Thus, the EU–China Joint Committee was established and its first meeting was held in Brussels fifteen months later. The first agreement between the parties was in the field of textile trade on July 18, 1979 (Filippini, 2009 228). The 1978 EC-China Trade Agreement is the first agreement the EC made

Table 4.3   China-EEC Trade Relations

	Total Trade (£ m.)	
Country	*1974*	*1975*
Federal Republic of Germany	325	420
France	173	300
United Kingdom	165	173
Benelux	144	185
Italy	115	140
Denmark	24*	50
Ireland	8*	12
*Estimated		

Source: (Broadbent 1976, 193).

with an economy outside of the market. The EC Trade Commissioner also supported the establishment of strong trade ties with China (Vichitsoratsatra 2009, 70–71).

In the 1980s, China was an interesting place for Western European businessmen. China has also increased its commercial ties with Western Europe. Until 1987, trade between China and Western Europe totaled 13 billion dollars. In the same period, China's imports from Western Europe increased by 169%. This amount constitutes 15% of China's total foreign trade and 1% of EC's total trade (Shambaugh 1992, 109). It is seen that China's share in the trade of Eastern European countries was realized at a small rate during the same periods. These rates ranged from 0.2% in Bulgaria to 4% in Romania. In addition, this ratio was less than 1% in Hungary and Czechoslovakia in 1985 and 2% in Poland (Sobell 1987, 107).

As a result of the development of China–Europe economic relations, trade between China and the EEC increased from 2.4 billion dollars in 1975 to 5.6 billion dollars in 1984; thus the annual increase between 1975 and 1985 was 15%. In addition, until the end of 1984, direct investments from the EEC in China exceeded 800 million dollars (Shouyuan 1986, 1173). Trade between the EEC countries and China surpassed China-USA trade for the first time in 1983. In 1985, China-EEC trade, which was 8 billion dollars, surpassed the US–China trade, which was 7.2 billion dollars, for the second time. Thus, in 1985, the EEC replaced the United States as China's third-largest trading partner after Japan and Hong Kong (Shouyuan 1986, 1164, footnote 1).

In May 1985, the Agreement on Trade and Economic Cooperation was signed between the EC and China. The 1985 agreement established the basic legal framework in EU–China relations. The agreement is more comprehensive than economic and commercial cooperation as it provides a framework for cooperation in the fields of industry, mining, energy, transportation,

Table 4.4   EU Imports and Exports from and to China, 1979–1996

Year	Exports	Imports	Total volume	Trade Balance
1979	2.882	1.847	4.729	+1.035
1980	2.412	2.628	5.040	−0.216
1981	2.255	2.544	4.799	−0.289
1982	2.150	2.437	4.587	−0.287
1983	2.573	2.485	5.058	+0.088
1984	2.929	2.639	5.568	+0.290
1985	5.484	2.971	8.455	+2.513
1986	6.403	4.106	10.509	+2.297
1987	6.430	5.945	12.375	+0.485
1988	6.772	7.719	14.491	−0.947
1989	6.901	9.159	16.060	−2.258
1990	6.711	12.312	19.023	−5.601
1991	6.935	16.902	23.837	−9.967
1992	8.659	19.460	28.119	−10.801
1993	13.452	20.753	34.205	−7.301
1994	16.246	27.644	43.890	−11.398
1995	19.237	32.333	51.570	−13.096
1996	19.407	34.608	53.015	−16.201

Source: (IMF, The Financial Statistical Yearbook; See Hu, Watkins 1999, 155).

communication, and technology. Within the scope of this cooperation, a Science and Technology Agreement was signed in 1999 (Griese 2006, 546, footnote 2).

During the Deng period, technology transfer, attracting foreign investment and enhancing bilateral trade in economic and trade relations between the EU and China were three important goals (Lirong 2012, 18). As can be seen from table 4.4, China became a country importing from the EU in the relevant period.

According to table 4.4, in the period of 1979–1996, while the exports of the EU to China increased approximately seven times, imports from China increased almost twenty times in the same period. For this reason, it is seen that there is a situation in favor of China in the trade between the parties, especially since the 1990s.

In table 4.5, it is seen that China's exports to the EU and imports from the EU in the 1982–1996 period were generally balanced, and there was no significant increase. In addition, the first half of the 1990s was a period when China's exports to the EU exceeded imports from the EU. The situation that China's exports to the EU are more than imports from the EU continued in the post-2000 period.

The gap between imports and exports was closed in the early 1990s, and imports and exports went hand in hand until the second half of the 1900s. In

Table 4.5   China's Imports and Exports from and to the EU, 1982–1996

Year	Exports (US$ billions)	Imports (US$ billions)	Total trade (US$ billions)	Balance (US$ billions)
1982	2.188	2.588	4.776	−0.400
1983	2.428	3.395	5.823	−0.968
1984	2.220	3.525	5.745	−1.305
1985	2.193	5.562	7.755	−3.369
1986	2.652	5.919	8.571	−3.267
1987	3.619	5.734	9.353	−2.115
1988	4.280	5.915	6.343	−1.635
1989	4.347	6.120	10.467	−1.773
1990	5.070	4.830	9.900	+0.240
1991	6.740	8.400	15.140	−1.660
1992	7.627	9.806	17.433	−2.179
1993	14.407	11.652	26.059	+2.755
1994	16.938	14.580	31.518	+2.358
1995	19.096	21.254	40.350	−2.158
1996	19.826	19.867	39.693	−0.041

Source: (Almanac of China's Foreign Economic Relations and Trade, China National Economy Publishing House; See Hu, Watkins 1999, 159).

the following period, with the increase in China's exports to the EC, a new era was entered in the trade between the parties. Due to the break-in EU–China relations, the economic relationship that started to change in the 1990s and was dominated by China's exports has been permanent in the 2000s (Leal-Arcas 2010, 237–238). In the process, EU has always had an important share in China's trade.

China's share in EU exports has increased gradually since 1995, this share reached 10% in 2005 from 1% in 1981. In addition, the increase after the mid-1990s is also noteworthy. Besides, while there was no significant increase in the EU's exports to China, there was an increase in its imports to China. In this case, it doubled its foreign trade deficit within five years (Leal-Arcas 2010, 237–238).

AFTER 2000

In the post-2000 period, the approach of the EU toward China was carried out more distantly on the grounds that China did not provide sufficient support for the development of the EU–China economic partnership. According to the EU, a balanced partnership with China cannot be established as China always gains more benefits in its economic relations. Therefore, the increasing trade deficit in economic relations has also been an important issue in EU–China relations. In 2001, the EU, which supported China's WTO membership (Eglin 1997, 489–508), aimed to access the Chinese market in better conditions with this support, but the expectations of the EU could not be fully realized. China has made progress only in certain areas, such as removing tariff barriers, and has not made comprehensive progress. It is also estimated that the barriers to investment and trade in China cause a trade loss of 21,400 million Euros to EU companies every year (Bustillo 2012, 365–366).

The EU has been the party with high import in trade with China, and this trade deficit has increased more than five times in the 1999–2010 period. In the said period, there was a decrease in the EU trade balance only in 2009, and in all the remaining years, EU imports from China were more than exports to China.

The number of companies that have contributed significantly to the development of trade between the EU and China has gradually increased. By the end of 2007, the number of EU companies operating in China reached 27,000 (Saili and Lin 2012, 142).

As the trade between China and the EU increased significantly, the EU took the first place in China's trade in 2007. While the share of the United States in China's total exports was 21.1% in 2003, the share of the EU was 16.5%, in 2007 the share of the EU increased to 20.1%, and the share of the United States was 19.1% (Saili and Lin 2012, 149).

Germany has been the leading country among the EU's economic powers in the relations of EU countries with China. The large difference between Germany and other countries (France, UK, Italy) shows once again Germany's power within the EU. Germany exported three or four times more than these countries (Eurostat; Freeman, 2017 192).

Xi Jinping made the following comments on the economic relationship between Europe and China at the conference at the European College in Bruges on April 1, 2014:

> We need to build a bridge of growth and prosperity linking the two big markets of China and Europe. China and the EU are the two most important economies in the world, accounting for one third of the global economy. We must uphold open markets, speed up negotiations on investment agreements, proactively explore the possibility of a free trade area, and strive to achieve the ambitious goal of bringing bilateral trade to US$1 trillion-worth by 2020. We should also look to combine China-EU cooperation with the initiative of developing the Silk Road Economic Belt, so as to integrate the market of Asia and Europe, energize the people, businesses, capital and technologies of Asia and Europe, and make China and the EU the twin engines for global economic growth. (Jinping, 2014 307–308)

Table 4.6　EU Member States' Imports from China: 2002–2015 (Million Euro)

Member States	2002	2005	2010	2015
Austria	1.162	2.119	3.366	5.266
Belgium	4.746	8.552	12.635	14.684
Bulgaria	145	567	493	966
Croatia	271	704	1.085	524
Cyprus	164	193	340	238
Czechia	1.991	1.676	6.929	10.538
Denmark	1.474	2.884	4.674	5.615
Estonia	264	302	336	625
Finland	956	1.953	2.298	1.959
France	8.572	14.479	23.270	27.625
Germany	19.053	35.121	63.032	69.036
Greece	1.028	1.702	2.861	2.551
Hungary	2.208	3.815	6.559	5.574
Ireland	762	1.550	1.890	2.694
Italy	8.306	14.134	28.788	28.158
Latvia	45	105	220	416
Lithuania	193	291	430	725
Luxembourg	73	2.249	1.655	2.436
Malta	65	57	117	212
Netherlands	12.000	25.826	49.475	66.291
Poland	2.197	2.606	6.933	13.083
Portugal	344	568	1.578	1.777
Romania	392	1.315	2.548	2.887
Slovakia	366	407	2.014	2.720
Slovenia	237	213	934	1.458
Spain	4.757	9.782	15.952	19.797
Sweden	1.822	3.196	5.598	7.412
United Kingdom	16.811	24.626	37.907	55.157
EU28	90.418	161.007	283.931	350.435

Source: (Eurostat, 2020).

As can be seen from table 4.6, imports of EU member states from China have gradually increased over the years. It is possible to list the prominent countries in import as Germany, Netherlands, the UK, Italy, and France. Although the Netherlands is smaller than other countries in terms of population and economy, it is noteworthy that it ranks first among countries importing from China.

In table 4.7, it is seen that the exports made by the member states to China lag behind the imports from China. The countries that export the most to China are Germany, the UK, France, and Italy.

Table 4.7   EU Member State Exports to China: 2002–2015 (Million Euro)

Member States	2002	2005	2010	2015
Austria	1.184	1.592	2.573	3.071
Belgium	2.009	2.711	5.404	6.775
Bulgaria	13	57	187	550
Croatia	2	7	28	70
Cyprus	0.4	11	15	38
Czechia	157	240	918	1.664
Denmark	540	848	1.772	3.588
Estonia	20	33	112	135
Finland	1.226	1.562	2.732	2.536
France	3.708	6.297	11.064	17.912
Germany	14.570	21.165	53.660	71.973
Greece	60	80	316	228
Hungary	163	331	1.177	1.262
Ireland	543	908	1.573	1.649
Italy	4.017	4.603	8.608	10.422
Latvia	3	8	28	108
Lithuania	3	11	27	102
Luxembourg	58	138	132	230
Malta	5	17	60	24
Netherlands	1.573	2.625	5.525	9.577
Poland	219	476	1.232	1.819
Portugal	80	170	233	838
Romania	216	165	308	525
Slovakia	42	102	971	1.020
Slovenia	22	43	106	294
Spain	786	1.523	2.626	4.327
Sweden	1.506	2.028	3.735	4.831
United Kingdom	2.363	3.985	8.319	24.797
EU28	35.101	51.748	113.453	170.376

Source: (Eurostat, 2020).

According to tables 4.8 and 4.9, in 2019, the same member states stand out in both imports from China and exports to China: the Netherlands, Germany, Italy, and France.

MUTUAL INVESTMENTS

Foreign direct investment is becoming increasingly important in EU–China economic relations. European companies have invested hundreds of billions of Euros in China since the 1980s, and these investments have contributed to the transformation of China into a new consumption economy. On the other

Table 4.8 EU-27 Imports of Goods from China, 2019

Member States	EUR Million	% of China in Extra EU-27 Imports
Netherlands	88.414	26,1
Germany	76.772	18,8
Italy	31.665	17,3
France	31.426	15,1
Spain	24.821	16,4
Poland	20.536	25,9
Belgium	16.704	10,9
Czechia	14.806	35,6
Sweden	8.424	17,4
Hungary	7.470	24,9
Denmark	6.253	21,4
Austria	5.606	14,3
Romania	4.537	19,3
Greece	4.061	14,9
Ireland	3.146	5,8
Portugal	2.953	14,0
Slovakia	2.904	17,2
Finland	2.296	11,2
Slovenia	2.016	13,6
Luxembourg	1.509	42,7
Bulgaria	1.484	13,8
Lithuania	929	8,7
Croatia	726	13,6
Estonia	651	16,7
Latvia	511	12,1
Cyprus	410	12,2
Malta	255	8,6

Source: (Eurostat (ext_st_eu27_2019sitc) and Comext DS-018995, 2020).

hand, although China's investments in Europe are limited, it is seen that it has an increasing trend in recent years (Hanemann and Huotari 2017, 3).

Subsidiaries and investments of EU member states in China is also an important issue. In table 4.10, this situation is shown in the period 1979–1996.

China's purchases in European countries have become increasingly common. China has shown more interest in Western European countries such as the UK, Germany, and France. Nearly 60% of purchases in 2017 were in these countries. In addition to these investments, Europe's famous brands continue to be purchased by China. Pizza Express, Travelfusion, Emerald Automotive, Manganese Bronze are examples of these brands. In this context, Germany has been recognized as an important market for Chinese companies. While sixty-eight German companies were bought by the Chinese in 2016, it is noteworthy that this figure doubled compared to the previous

Table 4.9   EU-27 Exports of Goods to China, 2019

Member States	EUR Million	% of China in Extra EU-27 Imports
Germany	96.283	15,2
France	20.959	8,5
Netherlands	13.906	6,3
Italy	12.993	5,5
Ireland	8.207	8,6
Belgium	7.108	5,1
Spain	6.799	5,6
Sweden	6.763	9,9
Denmark	4.837	10,2
Austria	4.611	9,0
Finland	3.548	12,0
Poland	2.651	4,3
Czechia	2.146	5,9
Slovakia	1.690	10,5
Hungary	1.456	6,1
Greece	892	5,5
Bulgaria	814	7,8
Romania	612	3,3
Portugal	604	3,4
Slovenia	435	3,9
Lithuania	277	2,1
Luxembourg	198	6,7
Estonia	173	3,8
Latvia	159	3,0
Croatia	108	2,1
Malta	36	2,9
Cyprus	34	1,9

Source: (Eurostat (ext_st_eu27_2019sitc) and Comext DS-018995, 2020).

year. The purchase of the German Kuka company, which is one of the most important robot manufacturers in the world, by China for 4.7 billion dollars has been China's most important investment in Germany, among other acquisitions (Sputnik 2017).

China invested more in Western Europe than in Eastern Europe especially the UK and Germany have been the countries that received the most investments from China. The countries that received the most and the least investment were England and Latvia (Hanemann and Huotari 2017, 10).

From table 4.11, it is seen that foreign direct investments from the EU to China have gradually increased, and there has been a rapid rise especially in the 2000s.

The initiation of negotiations on the EU–China Investment Agreement in 2013 is also an important development. The purpose of the agreement

Table 4.10   Sector Distribution of EU Subsidiaries in China (1979–1996)

Sector Categories	European Investment US $ Million	%
Agriculture, forestry, and fishing	94.74	2.10
Mining	38.55	0.86
Manufacturing	3.758.22	83.47
Food	346.25	7.69
Textiles and clothing	184.52	4.10
Paper and wood products	192.39	4.27
Chemicals, rubber, and plastics	892.53	19.82
Leather	23.42	0.52
Non-metallic minerals	361.10	8.02
Basic metals	160.34	3.56
Metal products, machinery, and equipment	484.54	10.76
Electrical and electronic industries	483.86	10.75
Transport equipment	597.36	13.27
Toys, measuring equipment, and related industries	31.92	0.71
Services and trade	610.91	13.57
Transport and communication	316.48	7.03
Construction	52.03	1.16
Finance, insurance, and real estate	168.04	3.73
Other services	74.36	1.65
Total	4.502.43	100

Source: (MOFTEC database of FIEs in China (1983–1998), See Bulcke, Zhang, Esteves 2003, 62).

Table 4.11   EU Direct Investment in China, 1979–2007

Year	Total Number of FDI Projects	EU Projects	Percentage of Total (%)
1979–1985	6.797	134	1.97
1986	1.498	32	2.14
1987	2.346	42	1.79
1988	5.945	87	1.46
1989	5.779	78	1.35
1990	7.273	82	1.13
1991	12.978	163	1.26
1992	48.764	763	1.56
1996	83.437	1.726	2.07
1997	21.001	1.040	4.95
1998	19.799	1.002	5.06
1999	16.918	894	5.28
2000	22.347	1.130	5.06
2001	26.140	1.214	4.64
2002	34.171	1.486	4.35
2003	41.081	2.074	5.06
2004	43.658	2.423	5.55
2005	43.988	2.846	6.47
2006	41.485	2.738	6.60

Source: (Compiled from Statistical Yearbook of China External Trade and the China Investment Guide website, See Saili, Lin 2012, 143).

is to ensure long-term access of both parties to each other's markets and to protect the investments and investors of both parties. The EU–China 2020 Strategic Agenda for Cooperation is considered the basis of the EU's relations with China as the EU–China Investment Agreement. In the negotiations that started in 2013 for the Investment Agreement, the following were aimed:

i. improve investment for European and Chinese investors by creating investment rights and guaranteeing nondiscrimination
ii. improve transparency, licensing, and authorization procedures
iii. provide a high and balanced level of protection for investors and investments, and;
iv. put in place rules on environmental and labor-related aspects of foreign investment (European Commission 2020)

Looking at the 2010–2016 period, China's investments in the EU started to increase especially in the post-2010 period, and in the post-2013 period, these investments increased much faster than in previous years. The investments of the EU in China, on the other hand, have generally been at the same levels, especially in the post-2012 period, and they have a decreasing trend (Hanemann and Huotari 2017, 5).

In the period 2000–2016, especially advanced technology, service, and infrastructure issues have been prominent issues in China's investments in the EU. In addition, France, Germany, and the UK had the biggest share in China's investments. These three countries received investments from China from 41.7% in 2008 to 59% in 2016 (Hanemann and Huotari 2017, 7–8).

Table 4.12 shows some of China's investments in EU member states. It is seen that commercial relations are established in different fields and in various amounts, from mining to banking, from food to energy.

Despite the EU–China trade and mutual economic relationship, there are some obstacles to trade and investment between the parties. These obstacles are shown in table 4.13.

Table 4.12 A Selection of Mergers and Acquisitions by Chinese Investors in the EU

Activity	Buyer and Seller, Country	Date	Amount (US $mil) (%)
Mining	Zijin Mining Group—Monterrico Metals, UK	2007	186
	Zijin Mining Group—Ridge Mining, UK	2006	15.9 (%29.9)
	China Guangdong Nuclear Power—Kalahari Minerals	2012	1.000
Food	Chalkis—Le Cabanon/Conserves de Provence, France	2004	(%55, then %100)
	CIC—Diageo, UK	2009	370 (%1.10)
Automotive	Fuyao Glass Industry Gp—Fürmotec GmbH, Germany	2007	N/A
	Geely—Volvo, Sweden	2010	1.800 (%100)
	Weichai Power—Moteurs Baudouin, France	2009	6 (%100)
	Nanjing Automotive—MG Rover, UK	2005	85 (%100)
	Huaxiang—Lawrence Automotive, UK	2007	46
	Huaxiang Electronics Co—HIB Trim Part Solution, Germany	2013	38
	Qinjiang Group—Benelli, Italy	2005	N/A
Chemicals	China National Blue Star Group—Adisseo, France	2005	N/A (%100)
	China National Blue Star Group—Rhodia Silicone Division, France	2006	N/A (%100)
	China National Bluestar Group Corporation—Fibres Worldwide, UK	2007	N/A (%100)
	Shanghai Dongbao Biopharmaceutical—Ferring's Malmö Factory, Sweden	2006	
Consumer Electronics	TCL—Schneider Electronics, Germany	2002	11 (%100)
	TCL—Thomson, France	2003	N/A
	Nam Taï Electronics—Stepmind, France	2004	7.75
	Lenovo—Medion, Germany	2011	800 (%100)
Household Appliances	Haier—Meneghetti Refrigerator, Italy	2001	8

(Continued)

Table 4.12 A Selection of Mergers and Acquisitions by Chinese Investors in the EU (Continued)

Activity	Buyer and Seller, Country	Date	Amount (US $mil) (%)
Machinery and Metal Products	LiuGong Machinery—Huta Stalowa Wola (HSW), Poland	2012	N/A (%100)
	SHIG Weichai—Ferretti, Italy	2012	507 (%75)
	Sany—Putzmeister, Germany	2012	500 (%100)
	Shenyang Machine Tool Group—Schiess, Germany	2004	(%100)
	Shenyang Heavy Machinery Group (SHMG)—NFM Technologies, France	2008	27 (70%)
	Huapeng Trading—Welz Gas Cylinder, Germany	2003	1.5 (%100)
	Shanghai ZQ Tools Group—Lutz Maschinenbau, Germany	2003	N/A
	SGSB Group—Dürrkopp Adler, Germany	2004	38 (%100)
	Dalian Machine—Zimmermann, Germany	2005	N/A (%70)
	Harbin Measuring and Cutting—Kelch GmbH, Germany	2005	N/A
	China National Building Material Group—Rotortechnik, Germany	2007	12 (%100)
	Beijing No1 Machine Tool—Waldrich Coburg (Herkules), Germany	2005	N/A
Textiles	Sail Star Shanghai—Boewe Textile Cleaning, Germany	2003	N/A
Research	Suntar Membrane Technology—Hoechst, Germany	2005	N/A (%50)
Energy	Three Gorges Project Corporation—Energias de Portugal, Portugal	2011	3.500 (%21)
	CIC—GDF Suez Exploration and Production Business, France	2011	3.200 (%30)
	Sinopec—Talisman Energy, UK	2012	1.500 (%49)
	PetroChina—Ineos Refining, UK	2011	1.000 (%50)
Banking	China Development Bank—Barclays, UK	2007	3.000 (%3.1)
Utilities	CIC—Apax Partners, UK	2010	960 (%2.3)
	CIC—Thames Water, UK	2012	(%8.7)
	Cosco—Cargo Terminal Piraeus, Greece	2008	
Telecommunication	CIC—Eutelsat Communications, France	2012	485 (%7)
Logistics	LinkGlobal Logistics—Parchim Airport, Germany	2007	50 (%100)
Leisure	Fosun—Club Méditerranée, France	2010	N/A (%7.1)

Source: (Nicolas 2014, 107–108).

Table 4.13 Trade and Investment Barriers between EU and China

Types	EU Actions on China's Goods/Capital	China Actions on EU Goods/Capital
Tariff Barriers	-Discriminatory Duties -Anti-dumping Duties -Anti-subsidy Duties	-Relatively higher tariffs rate (under WTO rules) -Anti-dumping Duties
Nontariff Barriers	-Technical Barriers: Green or environmental protection standards (e.g., Foods, Textile, electronic equipment such as Freezer, Air-conditions) -Export Restrictions(especially on Hi-tech products to keep intellectual property and keep advantages in the future) -Arms sale ban (due to political considerations) -Dumping -Subsidies (especially on agricultural products) -Anti-dumping investigations -Anti-subsidy investigations	Subsidies and Exports Tax Rebates -Quotas and License Regulation -Nontransparent Trade Rules -Exchange regulation -Anti-dumping investigations -Anti-subsidy investigations (on potato starch in 2011, this is the first time to do an anti-subsidy investigation on EU products) -Dumping (especially currency dumping and social dumping)
Capital Mobility Barriers	-Foreign Investment Restrictions and National Security Review on foreign investors' merger actions	-Foreign Investment Regulation (Guidance Catalogue, Regulations) and National Security Review on foreign investors merger actions (launched *in Feb. 2011*) -Nontransparent regulations

Source: (Lu, Yan and Deng 2014, 19).

CONCLUSION

China–EU relations have been continuing intensely since 1975. Economic issues are at the center of the relations between the EU and China, as important actors of the global economy. Although the two sides have disputes over political issues such as Taiwan, the arms embargo or human rights, it is important that economic relations are not affected by these problems.

It is also possible to see the effects of China's rising economic power on EU–China economic relations. China's increasing investments in European countries and its increasing importance in the European market are remarkable. It is seen that the EU and China have become each other's most important trading partners, especially in the post-2000 period.

From the second half of the 1990s, a new era began when China's exports were more than the EU. Therefore, imports from EU member states have been higher. The EU became China's most important trade partner in 2007. Germany has been the country with the most intensive economic relations with China. In addition, investments from China to the EU have exceeded those from the EU to China.

It is possible to foresee that the future of EU–China relations will not be affected by the political problems between the parties and that China will have a more dominant role in this relationship. In addition, another reason that will strengthen the EU–China economic relations will be the problems in the US–China relations. The problems in US–China relations in the period after Trump has shown to China that the EU is an important economic partner that does not have political problems. Therefore, in the future, as in the past, EU countries want to increase their trade with China since they do not see China as an economic rival like the United States, and China continues to increase its investments in European countries.

NOTE

1. This chapter was updated and developed from the book entitled "İlhan Aras, *Avrupa Birliği ve Çin: Ekonomik ve Siyasi İlişkiler [European Union and China: Economic and Political Relations]*, (Ankara: Detay Yayıncılık, 2018), 91-121."

REFERENCES

Borght, Kim Van Der., and Lei Zhang. 2010. "Pragmatism Rules Legal Foundation of China and European Union Relations." *International Trade Law & Regulation* 16, no. 3: 69–76.

Bressi, Giovanni. 1972. "China and Western Europe," *Asian Survey* 12, no. 10: 819–845.

Broadbent, K. P. 1976. "China and the EEC: The Politics of a New Trade Relationship." *The World Today* 32, no. 5: 190–198.

Bulcke, Daniël Van den, Haiyan Zhang and Maria Do Céu Esteves. 2013. *European Union Direct Investment in China Characteristics, Challenges and Perspectives*, London and New York: Routledge.

Bustillo, Ricardo and Andoni Maiza. 2012. "An analysis of the economic integration of China and the European Union: the role of European trade policy." *Asia Pacific Business Review* 18, no. 3: 355–372.

Casarini, Nicola. 2006. "The evolution of the EU-China Relationship: from Constructive Engagement to Strategic Partnership." The European Union Institute for Security Studies, Occasional Paper, no 64. https://www.iss.europa.eu/sites/def ault/files/EUISSFiles/occ64.pdf

Eglin, Michaela. 1997. "China's Entry into the WTO with a Little Help from the EU." *International Affairs* 73, no. 3: 489–508.

European Commission. 2020. "China." Accessed March 10, 2020, http://ec.europa
.eu/trade/policy/countries-and-regions/countries/china/

Eurostat. 2020. https://ec.europa.eu/eurostat/home

Eurostat (ext_st_eu27_2019sitc) and Comext DS-018995. 2020. https://ec.europa.eu
/eurostat/home

Filippini. Carlo. 2009. "Trade and Investment in the Relations Between the European
Union and the People's Republic of China." *European Studies* 27: 225–240.

Freeman, Duncan. 2017. "Redistributing the EU-China economic relationship: the
role of domestic change in China." *Asia Europe Journal* 15, no. 2: 187–198.

Griese, Olaf. 2006. "EU-China relations-an assessment by the communications of the
European Union." *Asia Europe Journal* 4, 4: 545–553.

Hanemann, Thilo and Mikko Huotari. 2017. "Record Flows and Growing Imbalances:
Chinese Investment in Europe in 2016." Rhod Zium Group, MERICS Paper on
China no. 3.

Hu, Xiaoling and David Watkins. 1999. "The Evolution of Trade Relationships
between China and the EU since the 1980s." *European Business Review* 99, no.
3: 154–161.

Jinping, Xi. 2014. *The Governance of China*. Beijing: Foreign Languages Press.

Kovačević, Slaviša and Dijana Bojić. 2016. "The Influence of Rapid Growth of China
to Exchange Relations with the EU." *Proceedings of The Faculty of Economics in
East Sarajevo* 12: 57–67.

Laursen, Finn. 2011. "The EU's Strategic Partnerships: The Case of EU-China
Relations." Dalhousie EUCE Occasional Paper No. 10 Accessed December 27,
2020, https://finnlaursen.com/downloads/papersByFinn/EUSA%20Boston%202011
.pdf

Leal-Arcas, Rafael. 2010. "European Union-China Trade Relations," *Trade, Law and
Development* 2, no. 2: 224–251.

Lirong, Liu. 2012. "The Evolution of China's EU Policy: from Mao's Intermediate
Zone to a Strategic Partnership based on Non-shared Values." *Journal of European
Integration History* 18, no. 1: 11–24.

Lu, Zheng, Tianqin Yan and Xiang Deng. 2014. "EU-China Economic Relations:
Interactions and Barriers." *Review of European Studies* 6, no. 4: 12–30.

Nicolas, Françoise. 2014. "China's Direct İnvestment in the European Union:
Challenges and Policy Responses." *China Economic Journal* 7, no. 1: 103–125.

Saili, Liu and Zhou Lin. 2012. *China's External Economic Relations*. Honolulu:
Enrich Professional Publishing.

Shambaugh, David. 1992. "China and Europe.", *Annals of the American Academy of
Political and Social Science* 519, no. 1: 101–114.

Shouyuan, Shen. 1986. "Sino-European Relations in the Global Context: Increased
Parallels in an Increasingly Plural World." *Asian Survey* 26, no. 11: 1164–1183.

Sobell, Vladimir. 1987. "The Reconciliation Between China and Eastern Europe."
The Washington Quarterly 10, no. 2: 99–113.

Sputnik. 2017. "Türkiye, "Avrupa'nın yeni 'sahibi': Pekin'i AB'de büyük yatırımlar
yapmaya iten nedenler." Accessed August 7, 2020. https://sptnkne.ws/f8TH

Strange, Roger. 1998. "EU trade policy towards China.", In *Trade and Investment in China: The European experience*, edited by R. Strange, J.Slater, L. Wang. London and New York: Routledge.

Vichitsoratsatra, Natee. 2009. "The EU and China in the Context of Inter-regionalism," *European Studies* 27: 65–82.

Wilson, Dick. 1973. "China and the European Community," *The China Quarterly* 56: 647–666.

Chapter 5

Trump vs China

The United States – China Trade Relationship

Süreyya Yiğit

INTRODUCTION

A dominant pole's relationship with an aspiring pole in the international system is undoubtedly one based upon competition. The leading state wishes to maintain its status and the challenger wants to depose it as soon as possible. Their bilateral relationship certainly has an important political dimension but not always a deep economic relationship. The purpose of this chapter is to investigate the trading relationship between the established polar power, namely the United States and the aspiring polar power, China. We shall examine closely the change in tone and policies undertaken by the Trump administration and evaluate its effects on the bilateral relationship.

The preeminent economic issue at the top of the international agenda for the past two years has been the deteriorating United States–China relationship. Historically, this relationship was unimportant in terms of trade for Washington. With the implementation of Deng Xiaoping's economic reforms, the Chinese economy began its dramatic economic ascent and the goal of establishing a presence on the international stage. Needless to say, this development came to be reflected in trading relations with the United States. The end of the Cold War witnessed a China which was politically highly authoritarian but with a relaxed attitude regarding its economy. Year by year, and decade by decade, the trading relationship came to signify that China had arrived on the international stage as a giant economic actor enjoying a sizeable trade surplus with the United States.

During the final months of his administration, President Obama sought to maintain a neutral tone concerning president-elect Trump's statements concerning the relationship with China. Historically, the bilateral relationship which witnessed the reestablishment of diplomatic relations in 1979, five essential issues highlighted the central areas of cooperation and conflict:

  i) Security issues;
 ii) Relations with Taiwan;
iii) Economic issues, which include the United States debt, the trade and investment relationship, China's commitments to the World Trade Organization (WTO), intellectual property, and the negotiation of the Bilateral Investment Agreement;
 iv) Cooperation issues against climate change;
  v) Promotion of democracy and human rights.

OBAMA ERA

During his term of office, the Obama administration maintained diplomatic relations with China in a constructive sense without too much friction on sensitive issues such as Taiwan or the Chinese political system. One of the most emblematic cases in the disputes between China and the United States occurred in 2014 during Obama's visit to Japan, where the president reaffirmed the commitment of the military alliance between both countries (Green and Szechenyi 2014, 19). The background to this related to the dispute with China over the Diaoyu Islands, a situation that caused distress in the Ministry of Foreign Affairs of China, which responded by declaring that the United States should pursue a responsible attitude and not take sides in matters of territorial sovereignty within the region (Zhao 2018, 369–389).

The meeting between President Obama and the Dalai Lama in June 2016 provoked further anger of the Foreign Ministry in Beijing, which requested the Obama administration to respect Chinese sovereignty over the Tibet region (Oxford Analytica, 2016). Similarly, after the decision of the International Court of Justice on the maritime territorial dispute between China and six neighboring countries in July 2016, the State Department asked Beijing to comply with its obligations on international law—referring to the court ruling—to which the Chinese government categorically declared that it would not yield in the vindication of its historical rights (Song 2016, 247–261).

The announcement of the construction of an anti-missile shield in South Korea during the same month provoked a strong reaction from the Chinese Foreign Ministry, stating that the installation of this defense system would "seriously" damage the military balance in the region (Swaine 2017, 1–15). Near the very end of his mandate, in September 2016, during the Summit of the Group of the twenty in Hangzhou, Obama once again warned that there could be consequences for Chinese policy in the face of its territorial conflict with neighboring countries (D'souza 2016).

It is important to note that, during this Summit, China and the United States presented their ratification of the Paris Agreement, demonstrating good faith between both countries and their commitment to the fight against climate change. However, Donald Trump, then still a candidate, repudiated the agreement and called on his team to find a way out of it quickly. In fact, as president, Trump referred to climate change as a "Chinese hoax" (Eilperin 2016, 12).

A few days after the presidential election, President Obama held a bilateral meeting with his Chinese counterpart Xi Jinping within the framework of the Asia Economic Cooperation Forum in Lima. During the meeting, the two leaders called for close cooperation between the two countries in the face of what President Xi Jinping described as a "hinge moment" in the relationship and said he hoped that it would be a smooth transition (Lo, 2018). In the same vein, President Obama indicated that the constructive relationship between the two had benefits for the international community. This meeting was the last between the two Presidents—who in total met nine times and embodying a call to continue cooperation between the two most important economies of the world.

During the eight years of Obama's presidency, balancing the relationship of the United States with the countries of the Asia Pacific region was of utmost importance. To achieve this balance, Obama marked four main pillars:

i. Positioning 60% of the US fleet in the Asia Pacific
ii. Improving dialogue with countries that had territorial disputes with China
iii. Negotiating the Trans-Pacific Economic Partnership Agreement (TPP) as a counterweight to the growing presence of China in commercial and strategic matters
iv. Keeping all communication channels with China open

President Trump once in office reversed course and the United States left the TPP, very much viewing the rise of China as an economic and military powerhouse, as a threat or at least a strategic challenge for the United States and its allies in Asia (Trump 2017, 23). On the one hand, the acquisition of US sovereign debt by China had reached 1.32 trillion dollars in 2013, resulting in concerns about whether Beijing would have intentions to sell its stake in the debt, which would result in a depreciation of the US currency, although it should be noted that in 2016 Japan surpassed China as the main holder of sovereign debt in dollars (United Nations 2019). In another sense, Chinese investment in its armed forces was 261 billion dollars in 2019, having doubled since 2010, although still well below American spending (Glaser 2020).

The last episode that triggered a verbal confrontation between the two countries before Donald Trump took office was on December 16, 2016, when a Chinese combat ship intercepted a US unmanned amphibious vehicle in a disputed maritime region, which led to a formal protest by the US government (Johnson 2020, 1–11). Although a few days later the vehicle was agreed to be returned to US troops, Donald Trump accused China of committing an "unprecedented act" and "stealing" the vehicle (Sputnik 2016). The aggressive tone of the president-elect, which was also given in the framework of the call of congratulations to Donald Trump by the president of Taiwan, led President Obama to warn the president-elect to hope that in matters of foreign policy, Trump would form a team of advisers who would be prepared and informed (Seib 2016). He also recommended that such decisions on international politics be taken systematically and consistent with national interests.

In 2016, China had experienced a strong decline in manufacturing and construction output, which until then had been the main drivers of its economic growth. There were, however, three other major factors that affected long-run growth, namely labor, productivity, and capital. Added to this, before Trump took office, one could identify three important weaknesses which threatened China's role as the driver of global growth:

i. Fixed asset investment no longer coming from the private sector.
ii. Overcapacity acting as a burden on the government.
iii. Services sector not being competitive enough to make up for lost growth elsewhere.

Background to US Tariff Measures

As a candidate campaigning for the Republican Party's presidential nominee Donald Trump had stated in May 2016, "We can't continue to allow China to rape our country and that's what they're doing. It's the greatest theft in the history of the world" (Kim 2019, 104–122). That statement was one of many that he made on the campaign trail concerning China's trade practices. The US trade deficit in goods that Trump inherited was to reach $811.2 billion in 2017, of which $375.2 billion was with China, which encompassed 46.3% of the total (Jiming and Yangmei 2019).

After winning the presidential election, Trump hosted Xi Jinping in April 2017 at his Florida estate, where they agreed to set up a 100 Day Action Plan to resolve trade differences. The US trade representative was authorized later that month to investigate whether steel/aluminium imports posed a threat to national security. The United States and China agreed to a trade deal in May that would give American firms greater access to China's agriculture, energy, and financial markets. The US trade representative started an investigation into Chinese government policies in August 2017 relating to technology transfer, intellectual property, and innovation. President Trump signed a memorandum in March 2018, which allowed for opening a WTO case against China for their discriminatory licensing practices, restricting investment in key technology sectors, and imposing tariffs on Chinese high technology products such as aerospace and information communication technology. In this move, the United States also imposed a 25% tariff on steel imports as well as a 10% tariff on all aluminum imports (Lu 2018, 83–103).

A month later, China retaliated by imposing tariffs on goods worth US$3 billion which included fruit, wine, and pork. The very next day, the US trade representative published a list of goods worth US$50 billion which would be subject to a potential 25% tariff. The next day China reacted by proposing 25% tariffs be applied on goods worth US$50 billion which included soybeans, automobiles, and chemicals. Later on, in the same month, the US Department of Commerce concluded that ZTE Corporation, a Chinese telecom company, had violated US sanctions, and American companies were banned from doing business with ZTE for seven years (Sutherland 2019).

The United States began trade talks in May 2017 with China in Beijing, demanding that China reduce the trade gap by US$200 billion within two years. The talks ended inconclusively though later on in the month the trade dispute was frozen after China had reportedly agreed to buy more US goods. After a week or so, the United States reimposed its original tariff plans. At the beginning of June, trade talks took place once again in Beijing. The United States agreed that ZTE could continue its operations. In mid-June, the list of products was finalized instructing a 25% tariff on hundreds of products to be implemented on July 6. Another shorter list consisting of other products was also announced to be under consideration. The next day, China revised and expanded its initial tariff list to include a 25% tariff on products valued at US$34 billion. This tariff would also take effect on July 6. Furthermore, China also proposed a second round of 25% tariffs on further products valued at US$16 billion (Unites States Trade Representative 2018).

US–China Tariff War 2018

On July 6, the United States began to collect the 25% tariff and China took retaliatory measures by imposing its own 25% tariff on goods which included agricultural products and cars. Four days later, the US trade representative published a third list imposing a 10% tariff on thousands of Chinese goods worth US$200 billion. On August 2, the United States proposed a 25% rather than a 10% tariff for the third list valued at US$200 billion, which included consumer products, chemical and construction materials, textiles, tools, food, and agricultural products. The US Department of Commerce added dozens of Chinese firms to its export control list as posing a "significant risk" to US national security (Zheng 2018). Responding the next day, China announced additional tariffs ranging from 5 to 25% on thousands of American products worth US$60 billion, which included agricultural products, chemicals, machinery, and medical equipment (Wong and Koty 2018).

On August 7, the United States published tariffs on a final list of US$16 billion worth of Chinese imports facing a 25% tariff to be implemented on August 23. China proposed a reciprocal 25% additional tariff on US$16 billion of US exports to be effective the same day. A week later, China revealed that a formal case concerning damaging China's trade interests had been lodged at the WTO against the United States due to its tariffs on solar panels (Stanway 2018).

After inconclusive talks between the two countries on August 23, the United States implemented the 25% tariff on goods worth US$16 billion which included semiconductors, chemicals, plastics, motorbikes, and electric scooters. China, in turn, responded with a similar 25% tariff on goods including coal, fuel, buses, and medical equipment. Moreover, China also filed another WTO case against the United States' 25% tariffs on Chinese goods. On September 17, the US trade representative published the list of tariffs on US$200 billion worth of Chinese goods with the tariffs being implemented on September 24, at 10% increasing to 25% by January 1, 2019. The next day, China stated a similar tariff on US$60 billion worth of US goods after the latest round of tariffs being implemented on September 24. On September 22, China rejected planned trade talks with the United States; two days later the two countries implemented the third round of tariffs (Kwan, 2020 55–72).

Argentina Truce

December 1, 2018, at the G20 Summit in Argentina, the leaders of the United States and China agreed on a 90-day "truce," during which the parties refrained from raising trade tariffs and other restrictive measures. It was assumed that during this time Beijing and Washington would have to compromise on the main economic issues on which the United States had claims to China—providing easier entry of American capital to the Chinese market, protecting the intellectual property of American companies in China, protecting the American market from, in the American interpretation, cyberattacks and technological espionage by the Chinese. At the beginning of 2019, Beijing and Washington demonstrated their readiness to intensify the economic dialogue by organizing a series of meetings of representatives of a high level (Geithner Meets with Chinese Counterparts for Strategic and Economic Dialogue 2009).

The tactics of the parties' behavior were noticeable during the ninety-day "truce." For Beijing, this concerned a readiness for economic compromises, but the unacceptability of "trade" in basic ideological and political interests. China, on the one hand, was aggressively demonstrating the rigidity and intransigence of its position in the main strategic areas—the right to modernize its armed forces, dominance in the South China Sea and the Indian Ocean, the right to own interpretation of human rights, etc. It was significant in this sense that Beijing began the year 2019 with Xi Jinping's call for the armed forces to "prepare for a comprehensive military struggle from a new starting point. . . . Preparation for war and combat must be deepened to ensure an efficient response in times of emergency" (Lau 2019).

On the other hand, Beijing made it clear that it was ready to make acceptable concessions in the economic sphere. For example, since November 1, 2018, China had reduced import duties on more than 1,500 goods imported into the country. In December 2018, China, in response to the demands of the United States, created the Intellectual Property Rights Court of Appeal, opening the possibility of reaching a final compromise (Zhou 2018).

At the same time, despite growing complexity, the military sphere of bilateral relations was interpreted by Beijing as the main channel of a strategic partnership with Washington under the conditions of trade friction. From May to December 2018, five meetings of the defense ministers of China and the United States took place; as well as in November 2018, joint military exercises of countries on cooperation in rescue at sea were held in Shanghai. Their "two sides" were also present in the American approach. The United States increased pressure on China, criticizing it for "illegal" naval activity, for the ambitious plans announced by Beijing in November 2018 to create a modern rocket and space forces, which once again confirmed the status of China (together with Russia) as the "main military target" of the United States. An additional tension in relations was introduced by the active posture, at the end of 2018, of US–Taiwan military relations (Wuthnow 2019, 133–150).

At the same time, Trump demonstrated that he was ready for trade reconciliation with Beijing, but only on those conditions that met American interests, focusing on the interests of the American taxpayer and voter. At the same time, the US president used a different kind of tactic, resembling more of an exchange broker, transferring it to foreign policy: he aggravated relations with China and "removed" domestic dividends from it, proceeding to a partial normalization of relations and once more trying to remove dividends.

US–China Tariff War 2019

In January, talks began in Beijing and continued in Washington to resolve the trade dispute. In February, President Trump declared that no meeting with Xi could take place before the tariff ceasefire expiring on March 1. On February 22, he extended the deadline for tariffs beyond March 1, without specifying a new date as negotiations continued between the two sides. In March, China having suspended tariffs on US autos and auto parts from January 1 until April 1 extended them without giving a firm date. In April, China announced it will ban Fentanyl as negotiations continued. On May 5, President Trump announced tariffs would increase from 10% to 25% on US$200 billion worth of Chinese products that were initially meant to be implemented on January 1, which had been suspended until March 1, would take place on May 10. Furthermore, the Chinese backsliding on commitments and attempts to "renegotiate" a trade deal led to Trump threatening new tariffs of 25% on a further US$325 billion worth of goods, covering nearly all remaining Chinese products (Sider 2019, 15–26).

On May 10, the United States increased tariffs from 10% to 25%. Three days later China proposed to increase tariffs on US$60 billion worth of US goods on June 1. They included beef, lamb, pork, vegetables, refrigerators, and furniture. A tariff exemption system was established providing for temporary exemption. A few days later, the US Commerce Department banned American companies from selling to Huawei without prior government permission. On June 1, China increased its tariffs on US$60 billion worth of products. Three weeks later the US Commerce Department declared that five new Chinese firms (including a state-owned enterprise) had been added to its list, banning them from buying US parts and components without prior government approval. The next day China published a white paper that denounced the US protectionist measures as unilateral and criticized its backtracking on bilateral trade talks. The white paper was important in terms of highlighting China's stance on trade consultations and strategy to achieve real solutions (Singh 2019, 10805).

Chinese Reaction

Overall, China viewed the US measures as determined to keep China down rather than achieve a deal. In the context of the Chinese understanding and response to the trade war, the State Council Information Office published a white paper on June 2, 2019, which outlined nine specific areas (Hi 2019):

   i. China does not want but is not afraid of a trade war with the United States
  ii. US-imposed tariff measures harm others and are of no benefit to itself

iii. US-provoked trade friction is a peril to the world
iv. US accusations of Chinese IP theft, forced technology transfer are unfounded
v. US trade bullying harms the world
vi. The United States backtracks on commitments in China-US trade consultations
vii. China's sovereignty and dignity must be respected
viii. China is committed to credible consultations based on equality, mutual benefit
ix. US government bears responsibility for the setback in trade consultations with China

One can identify five main themes in the Chinese approach:

i. China is against the trade and economic war unleashed by the United States but is not afraid of the current situation and will respond with dignity. China continues to be ready for negotiations, but only on the condition of mutual respect and observance of agreements. Beijing also seeks to continue negotiations on concluding a Sino-US investment and free trade agreement.
ii. The PRC supports the WTO and opposes protectionism.
iii. The Chinese authorities strictly adhere to the standards of protection of intellectual property rights and will make further efforts to improve the regulation of this sphere in the country.
iv. PRC is impartial to Chinese and foreign companies and will protect their interests.
v. Beijing is committed to openness.

In July, President Trump threatened once more to implement tariffs on another US$325 billion of Chinese goods, despite earlier promises not to after the G20 Summit. On August 1, the day after trade talks had ended in Shanghai, Trump tweeted: "The U.S. will start, on September 1, putting a small additional tariff of 10% on the remaining 300 Billion Dollars of goods and products coming from China into our Country." A few days later, the US Treasury branded China a currency manipulator. The same day the Chinese Ministry of Commerce announced that several companies had suspended buying American agricultural products. On August 13, the US trade representative declared that the imposition of additional tariffs on certain Chinese imports would be delayed until December 15, although a 10% tariff on a variety of Chinese goods would still be implemented on September 1. Ten days later China declared that 5% and 10% tariffs would be imposed in two groups, from September 1 and December 15 on US$75 billion worth of US goods. Trump immediately responded on Twitter, stating that "American companies are hereby ordered to immediately start looking for an alternative to China" (Hi 2019).

On September 1, the United States began to implement tariffs on more than US$125 billion worth of Chinese imports, and China began to impose additional tariffs on some of the US$75 billion goods. On September 13, China announced a list of tariff exemptions mainly for agricultural produce which were followed a week later by an American exemption list focusing on chemicals and machinery. On December 13, the United States and China announced a phase one trade deal had been reached. The deal stipulated that the United States would not implement a 15% tariff on US$160 billion worth of consumer goods intended for December 15, and would also lower the September 1, tariffs from 15% to 7.5% on US$120 billion on Chinese goods. Nevertheless, the 25% tariffs on US$250 billion of Chinese imports would remain. China, in return, would buy at least US$200 billion of goods and services, mostly within the manufacturing, energy, and agriculture sectors over the next twenty-four months and freeze its retaliatory tariffs scheduled for December 15, as well as ensure intellectual property safeguards (Lai 2019, 169–184).

US–China Tariff War 2020

On January 13, the United States removed the charge of currency manipulator for China. Two days later the ninety-six-page phase one trade deal was signed. On February 7, China indicated that it would halve its tariffs on hundreds of goods from 10% to 5%, and on others from 5% to 2.5% which would take place on February 4. Ten days later hundreds of other American goods were exempted from Chinese additional tariffs. On May 12, China publicized a new list of dozens of American products excluded for a year from retaliatory tariffs which would be implemented starting from May 19. In mid-July, China announced in line with its commitments under the trade deal that it was buying billions of dollars' worth of corn and soybeans from the United States (Wilson 2020).

US ACCUSATIONS

To reduce the trade deficit and facilitate access for American companies to China's markets, the United States considered it necessary to liberalize the trade and investment regime of China. In this regard, Beijing had to stop using public policies to protect and promote certain industries and state-owned enterprises. The United States demanded the removal of barriers to access to China's domestic markets, a level playing field, lower import duties, elimination of subsidies to state-owned enterprises, reduction of overcapacity, removal of local data storage requirements, and other restrictions on foreign companies (Noland 2018, 262–278). In addition to the direct effect, the United States hoped that this would speed up reforms in China and China's integration into the world economy and force China to accept to live by the rules of global trade.

China, as a measure to reduce the trade deficit, suggested increasing the export of American goods to China, primarily by lifting restrictions on the export of high-tech products. However, this did not appeal to the United States. The complex of problems related to the protection of intellectual property rights was already one of the most sensitive for the American administration. This issue was made especially acute by the fact that the United States considered this as a potential claim of China to compete in the scientific and technological arena, which has traditionally been regarded as the sphere of US dominance (Brander 2017, 908–921).

The United States accused China of creating conditions for the forced transfer of technology and know-how through various regulatory measures, including through legislative coercion of the creation of joint ventures, direct administrative coercion to transfer patents, as well as requirements for mandatory storage of data on local servers. China, according to the United States, did not take measures against cyber espionage, industrial espionage, counterfeiting of branded products, piracy, and had even encouraged them. The Center for Strategic and International Studies estimated that the United States lost up to $ 600 billion annually as a result of fraud, piracy, and theft of trade secrets (Lewis 2020).

Despite the undoubted benefits of the United States from economic cooperation with China, one can ascertain the growing contradictions in several areas of bilateral cooperation. The official list of US claims toward China was as follows. China should stop demanding that American companies operating in the country transfer their technology to Chinese partners (Kwan, 2020). That underlined the fact that the influx of American investments should not be due to the transfer of the latest American technology to China (Harris, 2017). Also, there should be no restrictions on the terms of licensing by American companies of their technologies in China (Qin 2019). Thus, it became necessary to:

i. stop the practice when US companies trading with China must register their business in China as joint ventures (Lai 2019);
ii. stop industrial espionage against American companies, stop unauthorized cyber penetration into American companies to obtain information about new technologies (Oxnevad 2019);

iii. stop subsidizing Chinese national companies operating in high-tech sectors of the economy, as this gave them unjustified advantages over foreign partners (Wu, Liu, and Ma & Chen 2020);

iv. reduce barriers to US agricultural exports (Hopewell 2019);

v. reduce the large US trade deficit in bilateral trade (Hosain & Hossain 2019);

vi. stop manipulating the national currency, which gave China an advantage in foreign trade (Yoon, Kim, and Kwon & Kim 2018).

Let us consider in more detail the essence of the contradictions between the two countries in the trading and economic field, which became the subject of bilateral negotiations. One of the main concerns of the Trump administration was and remains the problem of trade deficits. Thus, the deficit in trade with China in 2016 amounted to $347 billion, which was the largest trade deficit that the United States had among all other foreign trade partners (Lin 2018, 579–600). Trump believed that such a deficit was a result of unfair trade policies and practices by China. Another interpretation concerned that official trade deficit data with China created a distorted picture of bilateral relations since they did not take into account indirect deliveries of goods by US multi-national corporations. Traditional trade statistics also do not fully reflect the added value created in each country and how it participates in foreign trade.

Another area of controversy concerned intellectual property rights and cybercrime. This problem in the United States was considered one of the main obstacles to doing business with China. In 2013, a study conducted by the American Commission on the Protection of Intellectual Property found that China accounted for 80% ($ 240 billion) of all losses resulting from the theft of intellectual property. The US Customs Service noted that China and Hong Kong accounted for 78% of all counterfeit goods confiscated on the US border. According to FBI Director Vray, "Put plainly, China seems determined to steal its way up the economic ladder, at our expense" (FBI 2019). This problem was constantly discussed by representatives of the United States and China, including at the highest level, but, according to the US administration, no progress had been made in resolving such contradictions. The subject of ongoing discussions in the field of trade between the United States and China focused on the issue of violations by China of intellectual property rights.

The subject of contradictions in bilateral relations was the fact that China, in the opinion of the United States, had not completely switched over to a market economy. According to the Trump administration, the Chinese government in its industrial policy through the benefits provided to Chinese companies created unreasonable advantages for them in interacting with their American counterparts.

The issue of the scale of real Chinese investment in the United States worried the Trump administration in connection with attempts by Chinese companies to gain access to advanced US technology. In August 2018, the United States passed a new law on control over the investment market, which clarified the list of critical technologies that are important for US national security, as well as improving the procedures for the activities of the US Foreign Investments Committee.

Another area of trade controversy, which became an important catalyst for the unfolding trade war between the United States and China, related to the supply of steel and aluminum to the United States. Based on section 232 of the Trade Expansion Act of 1962, which referred to the possible impact of imports on US national security, in March 2018, President Trump announced an increase in import tariffs on steel (25%) and aluminum (on 10%) (Dhar, 2018 12–17). In response, in April 2018, China increased duties on $3 billion worth of products imported from the United States (BBC 2018).

An increasingly serious challenge for the United States remained China's participation in international value chains in the areas of high technology in the fields of information technology, in communications, in the production of telecommunications equipment, where China occupied a leading position in the world as the largest producer and supplier. Therefore, in 2018, the volume of US imports from China of information and communication equipment was $ 157 billion, which amounted to 60% of all imports of this equipment in the United States (Morrison 2019). In this regard, President Trump declared a state of emergency in this area and imposed sanctions on one of the largest Chinese telecommunications companies, Huawei, and eight of its partner contractors.

Understanding the vulnerability of their economies, the Chinese authorities took proactive measures to sustain their economic growth. A variety of measures continued to aid state support for the economy. The State Council of China announced plans to implement infrastructure projects such as broadband in rural areas with a total volume of 22 billion dollars by 2020 (China Power Team 2020). Also, a plan was published to improve the rural economy for the period from 2018 to 2022. The Chinese authorities also planned to increase consumer potential in the areas of tourism, medicine, and education. Affected by US sanctions, the Chinese ZTE rather unexpectedly won a series of tenders for the supply of equipment to three Chinese mobile operators (Gao 2018, 19–26).

CONCLUSION

The United States always maintained that it was interested in China fulfilling all its commitments. In practice, this has been quite difficult to achieve, especially since many of them have contradicted each other. Therefore, if China, for example, met the US demand to halting the mandatory transfer of technology, creating joint enterprises, limiting the borrowing of intellectual property, this could stimulate outsourcing from the United States on an even larger scale, which would contradict Trump's call to return jobs to America. The goal of Trump to reduce the trade deficit with China by increasing US exports certainly implies an increased interaction with China and thus contradicts another strategic objective—to limit the scientific and technological progress of China.

The strategy pursued by President Trump has been one whereby quite deliberate excessive demands are put forward to China, following his favorite tactic of first raising the stakes, then, judging by the circumstances, giving away a little and, ultimately, gaining victory. President Trump does not only think in economic and strategic categories, of entering a trade and political confrontation with China. His tasks are also tactical to demonstrate the achievement of any specific results in anticipation of future presidential elections. Trump had calculated that his reelection campaign would focus on a powerful economy with a surging buoyant stock market. Hence, the trade negotiations between the United States and China in July 2019 that did not lead to agreements were postponed until October. The relatively good state of the US economy still left the US administration with time to maneuver. China's depreciation in August 2019 of the yuan against the dollar again aggravated the situation in trade relations between the two countries and led to accusations by the United States of currency manipulation (Contractor 2019).

With the presidential election in November nearing, the trade war with China had become a political football with President Trump accusing his Democratic challenger Biden. On September 8, Trump promised: "We will make America into the manufacturing superpower of the world and we'll end reliance on China once and for all, whether it's decoupling or putting in massive tariffs like I've been doing already. We're going to end our reliance on China because we can't rely on China." He went on directly blame his opponent declaring:

> In 2001 Biden said the United States welcomes the emergence of a prosperous integrated China at the global stage because we expect this is going to be a China that plays by the rules. They didn't play by the rules. . . . The World Trade Organization . . . that's why they became a rocket ship. They were flatline for years and years and years and they joined the World Trade Organization. And frankly, they cheated. (Nelson 2020)

The reaction by the opposing party was to reiterate this outburst to be another instance of Trump's economic nationalism and underline the nature of this issue being highlighted as a model of partisan electioneering. In the final analysis, one cannot identify Trump's trade strategy toward China as being conventional nor predictable. Evaluating his statements and actions, evaluating his statements and actions, one could easily assert that Trump has been anything but a statesman, never possessing the details of complicated trading matters, frequently changing his mind and track, ultimately trying desperately to score political points off a policy he never considered the long-term effects of.

The election of Biden as president has raised questions concerning what the approach of the new administration will be toward trade with China. Will the new president continue the policies of his predecessor or change tactic? As of the time of writing, barely a month into his presidency, President Biden has declared that China must be held to account for its economic practices, insisting that each state must play by the same rules and that China's abuses and coercion which undercut the foundations of the international economic system must be resisted.

It is clear to see that the approach Biden takes will be markedly different from his predecessor. Biden should challenge and encourage China to participate in an economic level playing field. The levers at his disposal include the blunt instruments of tariffs but go beyond them. A restrengthened Transatlantic alliance, with a determined focus on providing leadership to global and international institutions to direct attention to China's economic policies, can achieve the desired results. In all likelihood, the new administration will likely use the tariffs imposed by Trump as a bargaining chip to gain concessions from Beijing, underscoring Biden's public strategy concerning the fundamental concerns he has relating to China's coercive and unfair economic practices.

REFERENCES

BBC. 2018. *China Hits Back with Tariffs on US Imports Worth $3bn.* BBC News. Retrieved 7 September 2020, from https://www.bbc.com/news/world-asia-4361 4400.

Brander, J. A., Cui, V., and Vertinsky, I. 2017. China and Intellectual Property Rights: A Challenge to the Rule of Law. *Journal of International Business Studies, 48*(7): 908–921.

China Power Team. 2020. "How Web-connected is China?." Accessed August 30, 2020. https://chinapower.csis.org/web-connectedness/

Contractor, F. J. 2019. Trump Administration Labels China a 'Currency Manipulator': What's Behind the Accusation, and Who's Right?. *Rutgers Business Review, 4*(2): 93–102.

D'Souza, H. 2016. The 2016 G20 Meeting at Hangzhou What happened, what could have Happened and What Should Have Happened at the G20 Summit. Accessed August 29, 2020. https://www.pgurus.com/2016-g20-meeting-hangzhou/

Dhar, B. 2018. Trade Wars of the United States. *Economic and Political Weekly*, *53*(37): 12–17.

Eilperin, J. 2016. "Trump Says 'Nobody Really Knows' If Climate Change Is Real." Accessed August 30, 2020. https://www.washingtonpost.com/news/energy-environ ment/wp/2016/12/11/trump-says-nobody-really-knows-if-climate-change-is-real/

FBI. 2019. "National Security Threat Landscape: The Next Paradigm Shift." Accessed September 08, 2020. https://www.fbi.gov/news/stories/director-addresse s-council-on-foreign-relations-042619

Foreign Policy Bulletin. 2009. "Geithner Meets with Chinese Counterparts for Strategic and Economic Dialogue," *Foreign Policy Bulletin*, *19*(4): 116–131.

Gao, X. 2018. Effective Strategies to Catch Up in the Era of Globalization: Experiences of Local Chinese Telecom Equipment Firms Illustrate Successful Models for Local Firms in Emerging Economies to Catch Up To and Compete with Multinationals. *Research-Technology Management*, *61*(3): 19–26.

Glaser, B., Matthew P. Funaiole and B. Hart. 2020. "Breaking Down China's 2020 Defense Budget." Accessed September 08, 2020. from https://www.csis.org/anal ysis/breaking-down-chinas-2020-defense-budget

Green, M. J. and Szechenyi, N. 2014. G. *Comparative Connections; Honolulu*, *16*(1) (Jan-May 2014): 19–27.

Harris, J. M. 2017. *Writing New Rules for the US-China Investment Relationship*. Council on Foreign Relations, New York.

Hi, Y. 2019. "China Releases White Paper on its Position on Economic and Trade Consultations with the US." Accessed September 08, 2020. http://www.xinhuanet .com/english/2019-06/02/c_138110173.htm

Hopewell, K. 2019. US-China Conflict in Global Trade Governance: The New Politics of Agricultural Subsidies at the WTO. *Review of international political economy*, *26*(2): 207–231.

Hosain, S., & Hossain, S. 2019. US-China Trade War: Was It Really Necessary?. *International Journal of Business and Economics*, *4*(1): 21–32.

Jiming, H., and Yangmei, D. 2019. The China-US Trade Conflict and Its Impact. *US-China Economic Relations: From Conflict to Solutions*-Part II." Accessed September 07, 2020. https://www.piie.com/publications/piie-briefings/u s-china-economic-relations-conflict-solutions-part-ii

Johnson, J. 2020. Artificial Intelligence, Drone Swarming and Escalation Risks in Future Warfare. *The RUSI Journal*, *165*(2): 26–36.

Kwan, C. H. 2020. The China–US trade war: Deep-rooted causes, shifting focus and uncertain prospects. *Asian Economic Policy Review*, *15*(1): 55–72.

Kim, J. U. 2019. "China Threat" Discourses of the Trump Administration: Overblown or Lopsided. *Journal of Conflict and Integration*, *3*(2): 104–122.

Kwan, C. H. 2020. The China–US trade War: Deep-Rooted Causes, Shifting Focus and Uncertain Prospects. *Asian Economic Policy Review*, *15*(1): 55–72.

Lai, E. L. C. 2019. The US-China trade War, the American Public Opinions and its Effects on China. *Economic and Political Studies*, *7*(2): 169–184.

Lau, M. 2019. "Be Ready for Battle, Hardship, Crisis, Xi tells Chinese Army." Accessed September 08, 2020. https://www.scmp.com/news/china/politics/article /2180772/chinese-president-xi-jinping-gives-army-its-first-order-2019

Lewis, J.A. 2020. "Economic Impact of Cybercrime." Accessed September 08, 2020. https://www.csis.org/analysis/economic-impact-cybercrime

Lin, J. Y., and Wang, X. 2018. Trump Economics and China–US trade Imbalances. *Journal of Policy Modeling*, *40*(3): 579–600.

Lo, C. Y. P. 2018. China's Rise and the US Pivot to Asia: The Implications of Trans-Pacific Partnership on the Regional Economic Architecture. In *The Changing East Asian Security Landscape*, 83–103. Springer VS, Wiesbaden.

Lu, F. 2018. China–US Trade Disputes in 2018: An Overview. *China & World Economy*, *26*(5): 83–103.

Morrison, W. 2019, June 23. "U.S.-China Trade Issues." Accessed September 08, 2020.https://webcache.googleusercontent.com/search?q=cache:q31VoBJSia8J:https://fas.org/sgp/crs/row/IF10030.pdf

Nelson, S. 2020, September 08. "Trump Threatens to "decouple" U.S. Economy from China, Accuses Biden of 'Treachery'." Accessed September 08, 2020, https://www.marketwatch.com/story/trump-threatens-to-decouple-u-s-economy-from-china-accuses-biden-of-treachery-11599553852

Noland, M. 2018. US Trade Policy in the Trump Administration. *Asian Economic Policy Review*, *13*(2): 262–278.

Oxford Analytica. 2016. China may'retaliate' against Obama-Dalai Lama meeting. *Emerald Expert Briefings*.

Oxnevad, I. 2019. Corporate Privateering and Economic Counter-Espionage in US Great Power Competition. *Orbis*, *63*(3): 391–405.

Qin, J. Y. 2019. Forced Technology Transfer and the US–China Trade War: Implications for International Economic Law. *Journal of International Economic Law*, *22*(4): 743–762.

Seib, G. F., Solomon, J., and Lee, C. E. 2016. «Barack Obama Warns Donald Trump on North Korea Threat." Accessed....... https://www.wsj.com/articles/trump-faces-north-korean-challenge-1479855286

Sider, K. J. 2019. Sino-American Clash of Hegemony: An Analysis of US-China Trade War. *Open Journal of Political Science*, *10*(1): 15–26.

Singh, G. 2019. China-US Trade War: An Overview. *Management and Economics Research Journal*, *5*: 10805.

Song, Y. H. 2018. The July 2016 Arbitral Award, Interpretation of Article 121 (3) of the UNCLOS, and Selecting Examples of Inconsistent State Practices. *Ocean Development & International Law*, *49*(3): 247–261.

Sputnik. 2016. "Chinese Takeout." Accessed September 08, 2020. https://sputniknews.com/cartoons/201612191048742777-china-us-drone/

Stanway, D. 2018. "China says U.S. Solar Tariffs Violate Trade Rules, Lodges WTO Complaint." Accessed September 08, 2020. https://www.reuters.com/article/us-usa-trade-china-solar-idUSKBN1L001K

Sutherland, E. 2019. The strange case of US v. ZTE: A Prosecution, A Ban, A Fine and A Presidential Intervention. *Digital Policy, Regulation and Governance, 21*(6): 550–573.

Swaine, M. D. 2017. Chinese views on South Korea's deployment of THAAD. *China Leadership Monitor*, *52*(4): 1–15.

Trump, D. J. 2017. "Presidential Memorandum regarding withdrawal of the United States from the Trans-Pacific Partnership negotiations and agreement." Accessed September 08, 2020. https://www.whitehouse.gov/presidential-actions/preside ntial-memorandum-regarding-withdrawal-united-states-trans-pacific-partnership -negotiations-agreement/

United Nations. 2019. "Trends and Major Holders of U.S. Federal Debt," Accessed August 30, 2020. https://www.cepal.org/en/notes/trends-and-major-holders-us-fe deral-debt-charts

United States Trade Representative. 2018. "USTR Finalizes Second Tranche of Tariffs on Chinese Products in Response to China's Unfair Trade Practices." Accessed September 08, 2020. https://ustr.gov/about-us/policy-offices/press-office /press-releases/2018/august/ustr-finalizes-second-tranche

Wilson, J. 2020. "Ahead of the Open: Corn, Soybeans Jump on China Buying Optimism, Declining U.S. Crop Conditions." Accessed September 08, 2020 https:/ /www.profarmer.com/index.php/ahead-open-corn-soybeans-jump-china-buying-o ptimism-declining-us-crop-conditions.

Wu, R., Liu, Z., Ma, C., and Chen, X. 2020. Effect of government R&D subsidies on firms' innovation in China. *Asian Journal of Technology Innovation*, 28(1): 42–59.

Wuthnow, J. 2019. "US Minilateralism in Asia and China's Responses: A New Security Dilemma?. *Journal of Contemporary China*, 28(115): 133–150.

Wong, D., and Chipman Koty, A. 2018. *"The US-China Trade War: A Timeline - ABC Group"* Accessed September 07, 2020, from https://www.theabcgroupllc .com/the-us-china-trade-war-a-timeline/

Yoon, Y. J., Kim, J., Kwon, H. J., and Kim, W. 2018. Trump Administration's Trade Policy Toward China. *KIEP Research Paper, World Economy Brief*, 18-09.

Zheng, S. 2018. "US Brands Dozens of Chinese Firms 'Threat to National Security.'" Accessed September 08, 2020, from https://www.scmp.com/news/china/diplomac y-defence/article/2157932/us-slaps-export-controls-dozens-chinese-firms-over

Zhou, L. 2018. "China Launches Appeal Court for Intellectual Property Right Disputes." Accessed September 08, 2020 https://www.scmp.com/news/china/dip lomacy/article/2179983/china-launches-appeal-court-intellectual-property-right

Chapter 6

Can Industry 4.0 and Ecological Industrial Policy Approaches of Germany Have Widespread Effects?[1]

Kaan Çelikok and Cem Saatçioğlu

INTRODUCTION

Industry, which is seen as the most important power in the growth and development of countries, on the one hand, contributes greatly to the increase in national income; on the other hand, it is the determining factor of international competitiveness.

It is possible to talk about different and successive stages in the industrialization process: the first success of the Industrial Revolution was that it revolutionized cotton garment production, first with those water wheels and then with new machines powered by steam engines. The mechanization of cotton production has increased the productivity of workers first in textiles and then in other industries. The mechanization of cotton production has increased the productivity of workers first in textiles and then in other industries. The pioneers of technological advances in the economy are innovations driven by new entrepreneurs and businessmen who want to apply new ideas (Acemoğlu and Robinson 2018, 37). The Industrial Revolution in Britain between 1780 and 1840 created a new social order and mode of production, and it also established the factory-based order of industrial capitalism. The changes that started in the economic structure in Britain during this period surrounded Europe after a while, and the order under the influence of capitalism brought new behavioral patterns, lifestyles, and production relations with it. Therefore, the Industrial Revolution did not only have an accelerating effect on economic growth but also led to economic development due to economic and social transformation (Hobsbawn 2013, 32–51).

The first Industrial Revolution was realized with the establishment of mechanical production facilities using water and steam. The second Industrial

Revolution means the creation of mass production and the division of labor by using electrical energy. The third Industrial Revolution involves the establishment of electronics and information systems to automate production. Industry 4.0, the fourth Industrial Revolution, outlined at the Hannover Fair in 2011, together with the use of cyber-physical systems and brand new it has created the modes of production (Wahlster 2013, 6).

It is not possible to separate Germany, which constitutes 24.7% of EU gross domestic product (GDP) in 2019 (2019 data),[2] its industrial power and trade policy in coordination with the EU. In this context, it must be known that the European Commission created a new market access strategy in 2007. In 2013, it announced the start of EU-US Transatlantic Trade and Investment Partnership negotiations, which is expected to contribute 100 billion Euros to Europe and the United States in a few years. In 2015, the EU introduced its new trade strategy. The same year, the EU and Canada signed the Comprehensive Economic and Trade Agreement (Bundesministerium für Wirtschaft und Energie, n.d.).

In this context, while discussing *widespread effects* in our study, trade policy, which is the only foreign policy affecting the industry according to the EU's Industrial Policy and Classification of Policies Affecting the Industry Classification (Darmer-Kuyper Classification) in industrial policy,[3] will also be considered in terms of Germany and globally.

Industry 4.0 has significant effects on technological development and international competition, the level of automation in the sectors, the ability to develop new products and services that will accelerate the development of employment, the adaptation of the education system to future skill needs, and the overall economic growth level. With Industry 4.0, the fact that digital technologies become a part of economic and social life requires a sustainable structural change. Although there is an assumption that digitalization will increase productivity and thus economic growth, its macroeconomic effects on production and employment depend on the level of utilization from Industry 4.0 technologies.

Apart from the Industry 4.0 approach, which will increase the efficiency and productivity of Germany in the production process with digitalization, the ecological industrial policy approach is applied to reduce the negative environmental impacts of economic activities in order to provide sustainable industry. In principle, any environmental policy measure is expected to lead to some degree of innovation. Due to the stringency of government regulation, the change in the opportunity costs of pollution may result in increased costs for some factors of production and thus encourage innovation to save on the use of these factors (OECD 2012, 85).

The purpose of this study is to reveal the guiding power of Industry 4.0 and ecological industrial policy approaches to German industrial policy and to emphasize the importance of making widespread effects in the world by evaluating all aspects of these approaches. And for this purpose, the study first mentions the economic structure of Germany that constitutes the industrial power and its role in global trade policies. Then describes Industry 4.0, which is one of the approaches that shape the industrial policy of Germany. Third, the study focuses on the economic, ecological, and social effect of Industry 4.0 following it examines the ecological industrial policy approach of Germany.

GERMANY AS AN INDUSTRIAL POWER AND ITS ROLE IN GLOBAL TRADE POLICIES

Germany has for many years had an open economic system with a strong industrial base. It exports about half of its GDP.[4] The German economy also enjoys social protection, and it is an economy in which the state plays the dominant role. Due to its openness, the German economy has been affected both by the intense competition in the world product markets and by the capital mobility and technology found in the international factor markets. Therefore, the economic decisions taken in Germany are directed toward the country's need to compete in the world economy. This has been a fundamental economic approach for Germany since the end of the Second World War. In addition to regulations for competitiveness, many areas of the German economy, especially practices aimed at protecting individuals available. For example, there is a social security system, health system, nursing care, pension, and social benefits to protect the unemployed (Siebert 2005, 1).

Germany has become an industrial powerhouse and achieved world-class status in science and technology since the late nineteenth century. The fact that there are many industrial branches with competitive advantage has brought Germany, which has established an innovation-oriented economy since then, a strong position in international competition. As of 2019, Germany, which has the largest national economy in the EU with a population of nearly 83 million and a GDP of approximately US$4 trillion, ranks fourth in the world GDP ranking. Germany provides about one-fifth of EU-GDP and about one-fourth of Eurozone production (2019 data).[5] The reason for this economic transformation in Germany, which could transform itself from the *"sick man of Europe"* to an *"economic superstar"* in a short time, focuses on the implementation of the labor market reforms called the "Hartz reforms"[6] of the early 2000s and the trade balance in the Eurozone context. At this point, however, the focus should be on restructuring the labor market and enhancing competitiveness, which helps Germany's exports (Dustmann et al. 2014, 168). The structural strength of the German economy also increases Germany's influence on the EU bodies and the general policies of the EU (Büyükbay 2016, 50).

At this point, the reproach of the US president Donald Trump is understandable. He criticized Germany for its excessive trade surplus and stated that this situation creates a trade disadvantage for the United States.[7] He announced that high tariffs should be imposed on German cars, which is a very important export item for Germany.[8] In addition, Christian Grimme, who is an expert of Munich-based IFO, which is one of the largest economic think tanks in Germany, critically looked at the excessive foreign trade surplus and stated that "Germany's receivables from foreign countries exceeded foreign countries' receivables from Germany," and drew attention to the problem that "the continuation of a high foreign trade surplus may cause problems in case of non-collection and the interest burden of debtor countries." The EU Commission also emphasized that Germany's foreign trade surplus corresponds to 7.4% of the annual economic output. Although it has relatively declined since the record level of 8.9% in 2015, the Commission stated that it is still well above 6%, which is considered a threat to economic stability. The resulting trade disputes, global uncertainties, and the predictions that the automotive industry will be in trouble cause economic activity in Germany to slow down and warnings that Germany may face the threat of recession (Zeit Online 2019).

Although public debates stress that Germany will suffer from globalization and competitive pressure from low-wage countries, all indicators show that Germany has been benefiting from the international division of labor and integration and maintaining its trading power in world markets

Table 6.1   Leading Exporters and Importers in World Merchandise Trade (2019)

Rank	Exporters	Value (Billion Dollars)	Share (%)	Rank	Importers	Value (Billion Dollars)	Share (%)
1	China	2499	13.2	1	United States	2568	13.4
2	United States	1646	8.7	2	China	2077	10.8
3	Germany	1489	7.9	3	Germany	1234	6.4
4	Netherlands	709	3.8	4	Japan	721	3.7
5	Japan	706	3.7	5	UK	692	3.6
6	France	570	3.0	6	France	651	3.4
7	Republic of Korea	542	2.9	7	Netherlands	636	3.3
8	Hong Kong, China	535	2.8	8	Hong Kong, China	578	3.0
9	Italy	533	2.8	9	Republic of Korea	503	2.6
10	UK	469	2.5	10	India	484	2.5

Source: World Trade Organization 2020, 82.

despite competitive pressure from Eastern Europe and China (Frankfurter Allgemcine 2005).

According to table 6.1, Germany, which accounts for about 7.9% of world merchandise exports with exports of 1 trillion 489 billion dollars, ranks third in the world in this field, after China and the United States in 2019. Germany also takes a 6.4% share in the world merchandise import with its import of 1 trillion 234 billion and ranks third after the United States and China in 2019.

INDUSTRY 4.0: AN OVERVIEW

With the increasing globalization and increasing network communication, there is an improvement in the processing speed of the world. Increasing international competition is creating a violent fluctuation in demand for products, partly with high variance and high-cost pressure. This situation has made the action areas of most companies more dynamic, unpredictable, and turbulent. Industry branches are merging, customers are thinking and taking action more actively, and the competitors are taking the attack. Shortened life cycles of products lead to an increase in technology and product innovations. Since the traditional factory layout cannot meet these requirements, factories and the world of production is on the brink of the Fourth Industrial Revolution, also called "Integrated Industry" (Soder 2017, 3).

Industry 4.0 is used to refer to the fourth Industrial Revolution, includes a new level of organization and the direction of the entire value chain through the life cycle of products. This cycle is geared toward increasingly individualized customer requests and is based on ideas from product development, production requests, delivery of a product to the end customer, and recycling including related services. The main basis here is, on the one hand, real-time access to all relevant information through the networks of all institutions involved in the value creation process; on the other hand, the system's ability to derive the optimal flow of value from the data at any point in time. Through Industry 4.0, it is aimed to create dynamic, real-time, optimized, and self-regulating, inter-business-level value creation networks that can be optimized according to different criteria such as cost, availability, and resource consumption through the connection of people, objects, and systems (Hogrebe and Kruse 2017, 149). With the increasing importance of knowledge with Industry 4.0, "smart" factories are developed by reducing the need for raw materials, labor, time, space, capital, and other inputs (Toffler and Toffler 1996, 62). At this point, the German industry is well-suited for industrial digitalization, based on German companies' good standing, especially in networked mechanical engineering and sensor technology, and their unrivaled export power in the high-quality industrial products market (Weber 2016,

67). However, Industry 4.0 will not only require a technological or IT-related approach for companies. Changing technology will also have wide-ranging organizational impacts, enabling the development of new business and corporate models and facilitating greater employee engagement. Germany successfully launched the third Industrial Revolution ("Industry 3.0") in the early 1980s by providing more flexible, automated production through the integration of Programmable Logic Controllers (PLCs) into production technology, while also managing the impact on the workforce with a social partnership-based approach. A strong industrial base, a successful software industry, and know-how in semantic technologies are signs that Germany is well positioned to implement Industry 4.0 (Kagermann, Wahlster, and Helbig 2013, 16–17). However, in addition to the fact that most of the investments are directed toward large companies, the fact that the vast majority of employees are employed by small- and medium-sized enterprises raises question marks on the level of abstraction, complexity, and networking of small- and medium-sized enterprises (Weber 2016, 67).

German industry is an industry with very favorable conditions to benefit from digital transformation. Germany can be a pioneer in the digital transformation process required by Industry 4.0 with approximately 23% of economic output (approximately 16% at the EU level) obtained from the industry quota, knowledge-intensive products taking a significant share in exports, and leadership in the world market in industrial branches. High-level education in the academic and nonacademic field and the establishment of generally well-functioning networks between businesses and science provide a good basis for the continuation of digital competition. However, the important thing for next-generation products to be equipped with smart services, is that companies, which are among the world leaders in their fields, use system information and the data produced by their products (Bundesministerium für Wirtschaft und Energie 2015, 13).

New technologies empowered by digital capabilities will enable companies to be effective and efficient in R&D, marketing, sales, and distribution channels and will provide an advantage over innovative competitors in terms of quality, speed, and price before, during, and after the production process (Schwab 2017, 59–61).

The expectations of the manufacturers from the changes experienced with Industry 4.0 can be explained as follows:

• *Digital Performance Management*: Digital performance management can contribute to digital production due to its minimum resource requirement and simple and fast solutions. The application accelerates existing lean management processes and helps create a digital capability and data-driven structure that underpins more advanced digital technologies.

- *Predictive Maintenance:* Predictive maintenance makes possible an estimated maintenance approach that combines different data sets and uses complex deep learning algorithms, with significant advances in data availability, machine learning technology, and cloud technology. Companies need three components to be successful in predictive maintenance: deep maintenance expertise and knowledge of related care, strong advanced analytical knowledge, and appropriate change management capabilities.
- *Efficiency, Energy, and Product Optimization:* Integration of process control system data with other data such as cost data helps companies optimize efficiency, energy, and products. It appears that manufacturers are making progress by combining existing data with the right software. In addition, companies have to provide the necessary knowledge to create the right algorithms.
- *Advanced Automation:* There is still great potential for almost all companies to increase the use of automation in jobs that require both blue-collar and white-collar workers. In terms of jobs requiring blue collar, it is expected that the use of robots in more complex systems and situations will be adopted in the coming years, the accessibility and potential value of automation will increase with the decrease in the cost of industrial robotics, the widespread use of sensor technology, developments in the field of artificial intelligence. It is known that there is a great potential for optimization in functions such as demand planning and order management in the supply chain process for white-collar workers.
- *Digital Quality Management*: Beginning manufacturers can gain significant advantages in the form of higher efficiency, ability to trace back errors, and cost reduction from recalls with the application of digital documentation systems that help record and store service information (McKinsey&Company 2016, 14–15).

EFFECTS OF INDUSTRY 4.0

Developments in digital transformation and increased connectivity will bring new challenges to organizations as Industry 4.0 will significantly change product and manufacturing systems for designs, processes, operations, and services. Industry 4.0 will also have a significant impact on industry and markets, affect the entire product life cycle, provide a new way of manufacturing and doing business, improve processes and increase the competitiveness of companies in the creation of management styles, future businesses, and new business models (Pereira and Romero 2017, 1212).

The impacts of Industry 4.0 will be examined under three subheadings as economic impacts, ecological impacts, and social impacts:

Economic Effects

It is predicted that Industry 4.0 will make production very flexible and efficient. In addition, resource efficiency and effectiveness will increase. Thanks to Industry 4.0, it will be possible to manufacture individualized products at the cost of a mass-produced product. With Industry 4.0, products that are both small and complex, unlike conventional methods, can be produced cost-effectively. Industry 4.0 also creates resistance to economic crises or deterioration caused by infrastructure failures and increases its capacity for renewal by enabling predictions to be made earlier and much better thanks to Smart Data (Kagermann 2017, 239).

As shown in figure 6.1, the purpose of Industry 4.0 is to maintain Germany's traditionally strong position in production and engineering and to guarantee its investments in machinery and equipment as a result of the digital transformation. Germany's traditionally strong engineering includes automation and factory areas, and the German industry has an important role in the development of Industry 4.0 (Kagermann et al. 2016, 37).

Industry 4.0 is a very important factor for sustainable economic production in Germany. The aim of Industry 4.0 is to be able to produce more quantities with less raw materials and energy. Industry 4.0 will help companies achieve

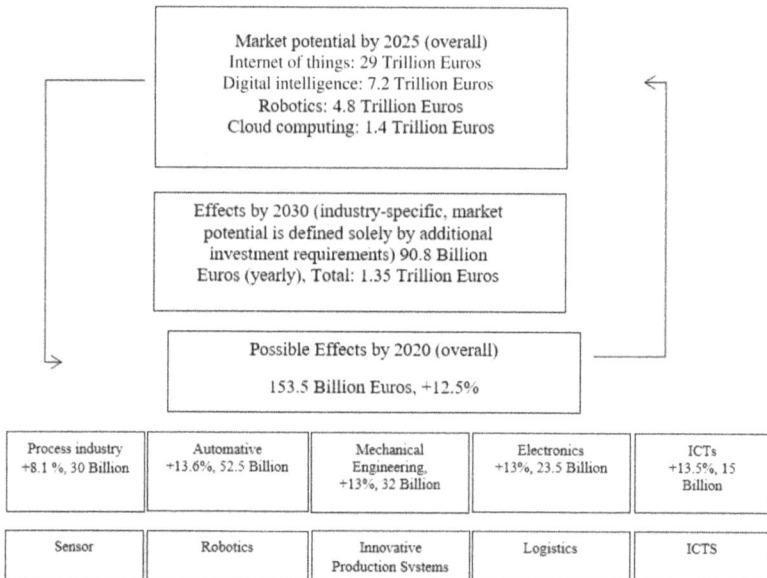

Figure 6.1   Expected Economic Impacts of Industry 4.0. *Source*: Bundesministerium für Wirtschaft und Energie 2015, 8.

an efficient production process with greater production, energy, and resource efficiency (PWC 2014, 19).

Ecological Effects

Intelligent networking through Information and Communications Technology (ICT) ensures more efficient and careful use of resources. For example, in a smart factory, smart processes such as start-stop functions on the machines significantly reduce the factory's energy consumption. Waste is significantly reduced by detecting errors beforehand. Thanks to smart communication networks in logistics, the routes and capacity utilization of road users become more efficient (Kagermann 2017, 240).

Social Effects

With the fourth Industrial Revolution, people's quality of life is increasing. Industry 4.0 provides better job quality as well as securing workers' jobs, reducing resource consumption, and re-industrializing urban areas. ICT will improve work-life balance. With social networks and social media determined and adapted for the jobs in the smart factory, each individual will return to the center of the business world according to his own convenience. On the other hand, employees are less often used as "machine operators"; however, to achieve the right balance between efficiency and flexibility, experienced employees are used in the roles of decision-makers and coordinators. At the same time, the working environment becomes more interdisciplinary, the variety of job content for the individual employee increases, and the duration of vocational training is shortened (Kagermann 2017, 240).

With Industry 4.0, it is obvious that production and service areas driven by robots and computers will eliminate social problems such as worker rights, worker health, working hours, holidays, living conditions, and bring along many social problems as a result of millions of people being unemployed (Arıboğan 2019, 73–74).

Besides, it is undeniable that Industry 4.0 has changed the relationship between consumers and manufacturers by changing the point of view of customers' adaptability to smart product features. On the demand side, customers will increase their awareness of the importance of the acquired and provided information and the quality and reliability of the technical condition of the products. This will affect the real-time collection and analysis of information and, consequently, the customers' new approaches to value creation. This raises the question of how customers will adapt to new technologies linked to products (Roblek, Meško, and Krapež 2016, 7).

ECOLOGICAL INDUSTRIAL POLICY

Many economic activities affect the environment with greenhouse gas emissions, pollution and noise emissions, soil and water consumption, use of limited resources or waste and wastewater generation. The inability of market prices to reflect ecological damages on their own causes markets to fail to reflect the negative effects of economic activities on the environment. In this context, the purpose of creating an ecological industrial policy is to take into account the negative effects of industrial activities on the environment. Therefore, governments are responsible for creating and enforcing rules that absorb the costs of environmental damage. The absorption of external costs provides incentives for producers to avoid negative environmental impacts. Ecological industrial policy must ensure that all environmentally unsustainable behavior is costly to individuals, consumers, and society, through regulatory tools and incentives for more environmentally friendly behavior. Thus, taking into account environmental degradation that exacerbates other impacts will help to correct market outcomes toward a social optimum (Kritikos et al. 2018, 26).

Europe aims to become a world leader in bio-manufacturing, which *is "a form of manufacturing that uses biological systems (e.g., microbial cells, animal or plant cells, enzymes) to produce commercially important molecules for use in the chemical, energy, pharmaceutical, materials, food and agricultural industries"*. In this direction, Europe will develop region-specific raw materials and processes for the production of commercially important molecules, with suitable lands and agriculture that reduce dependence on fossil fuels and promote new environmentally friendly economic activity. Because it is known that an advanced bioeconomy offers a future opportunity where economic growth can be combined with environmental responsibility (European Commission 2018, 26).

Industry plays an important role in overcoming the economic consequences of climate change, increasing resource and energy efficiency, and using renewable energy. The bioeconomy is based on a sustainable economy with bio-based raw materials in industrial processes and therefore from oil in a forward-looking manner. While environmental protection is a cost factor that should not be overlooked, it also offers new market opportunities. The German industry is an international leader, especially in the export of mechanical and installation engineering, measurement, control and regulation technology, and electrical engineering, potential environmental and climate protection products. Therefore, the German industry can, on the one hand, benefit from this development in a special way, and on the other hand, thanks to its know-how, it can make an important contribution to overcoming these challenges. Federal Ministry of Economics and Technology emphasizes the special importance of the industry in implementing the Federal Government's sustainability strategy by establishing a market and technology-oriented framework (Bundesministerium für Wirtschaft und Energie, n.d.). Sustainable industry emerges as one of the fundamental issues in the twenty-first century. The German economy, together with its achievements in macroeconomic indicators, is faced with the necessity to rearrange the structure of the industry in line with sustainable industry targets. The rationale for this imperative is the fact that over time only economies that adapt to the challenges of climate change and the needs for energy and resource efficiency will have a lasting and prosperous future. By 2050, it is predicted that industrial countries will have to reduce their CO_2 emissions by 80–95% compared to the 1990s. It is estimated that the world population will reach nine billion in 2050 and the population growth that will be experienced will make this even more difficult (Machnig 2011, 1).

Ecological industrial policy, called "green industrial policy" has a long history in Germany and a high level of support at the general population level. First, in combating industrial pollution with emission control regulations initiatives date back to the early 1960s. The rise of a politically strong and influential green party began in the early 1980s, primarily based on a heavily antinuclear platform. The relative weight of environmental and energy agendas has changed over time: the former dominated most of the 1980s and early 1990s, then the theme of a necessary transformation or transition of the country's energy system became crucial (Lütkenhorst and Pegels 2014, 5). Germany's Basic Law, amended in 1994, provides a constitutional basis for promoting sustainable development. As a result of national and international commitments, a number of quantitative environmental targets have been adopted. Some of these goals are tracked by the Environmental Barometer included in the Federal Government's annual economic report. Efforts to solidly establish and improve this bill (to include biodiversity, for example) should continue. As part of a wider reform, Germany has strengthened the environmental components of the tax system. Ecological tax reform is an important step in the right direction, although its steering capacity is limited. The reform aims to increase environmental performance and encourage employment. An increase in energy prices, energy density, and in general, it is likely to result in better resource efficiency reductions. The environmental guidance function of eco-taxes should be strengthened, in particular by reviewing the privileges granted. Exceptions for the purpose of promoting competition should be eased. The recently adopted climate protection program is a positive example of an integrated, intersectoral approach (OECD 2012, 11).

According to the proposed motion by the Federal Ministry of Environment in 2006,

- The state should play a leading role in industrial policy by focusing on strategic areas and leading markets.
- Basic criteria should be developed to guide technological development in terms of specific goals and visions.
- A rational regulatory framework should be developed to promote innovation.
- The export potential should be maximized.
- The introduction of innovative technologies to the market must be accelerated through public procurement policy and launch programs.
- The innovation financing structure for companies should be improved.
- Technological projects must be supported to provide market orientation.
- A new institutional dialogue structure should be established at the Federal Government level (including unit cooperation within the "industrial cabinet") (Mikfeld 2011, 3).

Companies operating in global markets within the scope of the environmental economy constitute a large part of the growth outside of Germany. Even if they are not active on the export side, they often compete with international companies in the domestic market. As the growth and development opportunities of the German environmental economy will continue to depend heavily on exports in the future, environmental economy performance must be measured with international standards. Germany's "green export industry," which is strong in innovation, has been successful for many years and is expected to be a pioneer alongside the machinery and automotive industries (Welfens 2011, 23).

CONCLUSION

Germany has designed its industrial policy system with vertical applications in the form of a strong sectoral specialization and a focus on technology-intensive industries through the strong competitive power of companies and supports industrial policy practices with horizontal intervention areas as ecological industrial policy, the accompanying investment-friendly tax policy, future-oriented environmental policy, and Industry 4.0 applications.

While Industry 4.0 vision put forward in Germany is aiming to make "smart production" by developing "smart factories" and in this way maximize the added value obtained in the industry and to guarantee economic growth, it brings environmental and social difficulties that can be evaluated with or external to industrial policies. At this point, issues such as resource efficiency, protection of the environment, demographic change, and the employment problem that will occur and providing better working conditions should be addressed separately.

Germany handles industrial policy applications together with environmental problems and aims to reduce negative externalities on the environment with many regulations, especially ecological tax reforms, in parallel with the EU practices. It wants to make it economically competitive by using tools that encourage employment and innovation.

In this direction, a competition policy in which the laws are adapted to digital markets and the state assumes a watchdog role as in the case of Germany, a trade policy that will open up products and product groups with sectoral specialization, handled together with industrial policy, an innovation policy based on R&D investments, increasing the number of employees in the field of R&D and working more effectively in research institutions, the way for an education policy that includes carrying the current digital agenda, especially Industry 4.0 should be paved in the world.

NOTES

1. This book chapter is extracted from the first author's doctorate dissertation under the supervision of the second author entitled "German-Turkish Industrial Policies within the Framework of the Industrial Policy of the European Union: A Research on the Manufacturing Industry," at Istanbul University Institute of Social Sciences in 2019.

2. Germany constitutes the largest share of EU GDP. Germany is followed by France with 17.4%, Italy with 12.8%, Spain with 8.9%, and the Netherlands with 5.8%. For detailed information, see Eurostat, "Which Member States contributed the most to EU GDP? (%)," accessed May 7, 2020, https://ec.europa.eu/eurostat/web/p roducts-eurostat-news/-/DDN-20200508-1.

3. For details of this classification, see Darmer, Michael, and Laurens Kuyper. 2000. Industry and The European Union: Analysing Policies For Business, Cheltenham: Edward Elgar Publishing: p. 19.

4. This ratio, which has been in an increasing trend since the 1990s, is approximately 47% for 2017.

For detailed information, see The World Bank, "Exports of goods and services (% of GDP)," accessed May 8, 2020, https://data.worldbank.org/indicator/NE.EXP.G NFS.ZS?end=2017&locations=DE&start=1960.

5. As of 2019, Germany's GDP was US$3,861 trillion, the total GDP of the Eurozone was US$13.356 trillion, and the total GDP of the EU was US$15,626 trillion. For detailed information, see The World Bank, "GDP (current US$)," accessed May 8, 2020, https://data.worldbank.org/indicator/NY.GDP.MKTP.CD.

6. The cornerstones of Hartz reforms are "*increasing effectiveness and efficiency of labor market services and policy measures*," "*activating the unemployed*" and "*stimulating employment demand by labor market deregulation*." For detailed information, see: Jacobi, Lena and Jochen Kluve. 2007. "Before and After the Hartz Reforms: The Performance of Active Labour Market Policy in Germany," *Journal for Labour Market Research,* 40 (1): 45–64.

7. Germany had a foreign trade surplus of 224 billion Euros, with 1.328 trillion Euros of exports and 1.104 trillion Euros of imports in 2019. For annual foreign trade data of Germany, see: Statistisches Bundesamt, "Value: Foreign trade (special trade) EUR mn," accessed May 15, 2020, https://www.destatis.de/EN/Themes/Economy/Foreign-Trade/Tables/lrahl01.html.

8. The growth of Germany in the automotive sector, with the exception of the US market, is mostly at increasing levels of motorization in markets in Eastern Europe, Asia, Latin America, and other threshold countries. While Germany exported a total of approximately 4 million vehicles to world markets in 2018, approximately 2.46 million were exported to European markets, while the rest was exported to other markets. In addition, many countries are constantly making regulations to support or even force companies to establish local production facilities. These regulations include high import duties and nontariff trade barriers. All this means that exports from Germany are becoming increasingly difficult. For detailed information, see: Verband der Automobilindustrie (VDA), "Economic Policy and Infrastructure: Trade," accessed June 20, 2019, https://www.vda.de/en/topics/economic-policy-and-infrastructure/trade/importance-oftrade-policy-for-industry-and-for-germany-as-an-industrial-location.html.

REFERENCES

Acemoğlu, Daron, and James A. Robinson. 2018. *Ulusların Düşüşü*. 34th ed. Translated by Faruk Rasim Velioğlu. Istanbul: Dogan Kitap.

Arıboğan, Deniz Ülke. 2019. *Duvar*, 4th ed. İstanbul: İnkilap.

Bundesministerium für Wirtschaft und Energie. 2015. "Industrie 4.0: Volks-und betriebwirtschaftliche Faktoren für den Standartort Deutschland-Eine Studie im Rahmen der Begleitforschung zum Technologieprogramm AUTONOMIK für Industrie 4.0." Accessed June 10, 2019. https://www.bmwi.de/Redaktion/DE/Publikationen/Industrie/industrie-4-0-volks-und-betriebswirtschaftliche-faktoren-deutschland.pdf?__blob=publicationFile&v=6.

Bundesministerium für Wirtschaft und Energie. 2015. "Industrie 4.0 und digitale Wirtschaft: Impulse für Wachstum, Beschäftigung und Innovation." Accessed May 15, 2019. https://www.bmwi.de/Redaktion/DE/Downloads/I/industrie-4-0-und-digitale-wirtschaft.pdf?__blob=publicationFile&v=3.

Bundesministerium für Wirtschaft und Energie. n.d. "Moderne Industriepolitik." Accessed May 14, 2019. https://www.bmwi.de/Redaktion/DE/Dossier/moderne-industriepolitik.html.

Bundesministerium für Wirtschaft und Energie. n.d. "Internationalen Handel stärken und Barrieren abbauen." Accessed September 16, 2020. https://www.bmwi.de/Redaktion/DE/Dossier/handelspolitik.html.

Büyükbay, Can. 2016. *Avrupa Birliği, Almanya ve Türkiye: İlişkilerde Temel Değerler ve Dönüşen Stratejiler*. Istanbul: Istanbul Bilgi Üniversitesi Yayınları.

Darmer, Michael, and Laurens Kuyper. 2000. *Industry and the European Union: Analysing Policies For Business*. Cheltenham: Edward Elgar Publishing.

Dustmann, Christian, Bernd Fitzenberger, Uta Schönberg, and Alexandra Spitz-Oener. 2014. "From Sick Man of Europe to Economic Superstar: Germany's Resurgent Economy." *Journal of Economic Perspectives,* 28 (1): 167–188. http://dx.doi.org/10.1257/jep.28.1.167.

European Commission. 2018. "Re-Finding Industry: Report from the High-Level Strategy Group on Industrial Technologies." Conference Document.

Eurostat. "Which Member States Contributed the Most to EU GDP? (%)." Accessed May 7, 2020. https://ec.europa.eu/eurostat/web/products-eurostat-news/-/DDN-20 200508-1.

Frankfurter Allgemeine. 2005. "Deutschland profitiert von internationaler Arbeitsteilung." Accessed April 20, 2005. https://www.faz.net/aktuell/wirtschaft/2 .1687/aussenhandeldeutschlandprofitiert-von-internationaler-arbeitsteilung-12288 63.html.

Hobsbawn, Eric. 2013. *Sanayi ve İmparatorluk.* Ankara: Dost Kitabevi.

Hogrebe, Frank, and Wilfried Kruse. 2017. "Verwaltung 4.0 als Beitrag zur Wertschöpfung am Standort Deutschland 4.0 – Bedeutung einer weiterentwickelten Wirtschaftsförderung 4.0." In *Industrie 4.0: Herausforderungen, Konzepte und Praxisbeispiele,* edited by Stefan Reinheimer, 147–160. Wiesbaden: Springer Vieweg.

Jacobi, Lena and Jochen Kluve. 2007. "Before and After the Hartz Reforms: The Performance of Active Labour Market Policy in Germany." *Journal for Labour Market Research,* 40 (1): 45–64.

Kagermann, Hennig, Wolfgang Wahlster and Johannes Helbig. 2013. Recommendations for Implementing the Strategic Initiative INDUSTRIE 4.0: Final report of the Industrie 4.0 Working Group. Münich.

Kagermann, Henning, Reiner Anderl, Jürgen Gausemeier, Günther Schuh, Wolfgang Wahlster. 2016. "Industrie 4.0 im globalen Kontext: Strategien der Zusammenarbeit mit internationalen Partnern (acatech STUDIE)." München: Herbert Utz Verlag.

Kagermann, Henning. 2017. "Chancen von Industrie 4.0 nutzen." In *Industrie 4.0 Bd. 4: Allgemeine Grundlagen,* 2. Auflage, edited by Vogel-Heuser, Birgit, Thomas Bauernhansl, and Michael ten Hompel. 235–246. Berlin: Handbuch Springer Vieweg.

Kritikos, Alexander S., Anselm Mattes, Lars Handrich, and Franziska Neumann. 2018. "The Social-Ecological Market Economy in Germany: General characteristics, main features and current challenges of a unique and successful economic system." *Deutsche Gesellschaft für Internationale Zusammenarbeit (GIZ) GmbH,* Accessed May 25, 2019. https://www.reformgestaltung.de/fileadmin/user_upload/ Dokumente/GIZ_Standard_A4_hoch_en_DIW_web.pdf.

Lütkenhorst, Wilfried and Anna Pegels. 2014. "Germany's Green Industrial Policy Stable Policies – Turbulent Markets: The costs and benefits of promoting solar PV and wind energy." German Development Institute: Research Report.

Machnig, Matthias. 2011. "Ecological Industrial Policy as a Key Element of a Sustainable economy In Europe." Friedrich Ebert Stiftung: Perspective.

McKinsey&Company. 2016. "Industry 4.0 after the initial hype: Where manufacturers are finding value and how they can best capture it." McKinsey Digital.

Mikfeld, Benjamin. 2011. "Ecological Industrial Policy: A Strategic Approach for Social Democracy in Germany," Friedrich Ebert Stiftung: International Policy Analysis.

OECD. 2012. "Environmental Performance Reviews: Germany 2012." OECD Publishing. https://dx.doi.org/10.1787/10.1787/9789264169302-en.

Pereira, Ana C., and Fernando Romero. 2017. "A Review of the Meanings and the Implications of the Industry 4.0 Concept." *Procedia Manufacturing,* 13: 1206–1214. https://doi.org/10.1016/j.promfg.2017.09.032.

PWC. 2014. "Industrie 4.0: Chancen und Herausforderungen der vierten industriellen Revolution." Accessed September 12, https://www.strategyand.pwc.com/de/de/st udien/2014/industrie-4-0-chancen/industrie-4-0.pdf.

Roblek, Vasja, Maja Meško, and Alojz Krapež, "A Complex View of Industry 4.0," *SAGE Open,* April 2016. doi:10.1177/2158244016653987.

Schwab, Klaus. 2017. Dördüncü Sanayi Devrimi. Translated by Zülfü Dicleli. Istanbul: Optimist.

Siebert, Horst. 2005. *The German Economy: Beyond the Social Market.* Princeton: Princeton University Press.

Soder, Johann. 2017. "Use Case Production: Von CIM über Lean Production zu Industrie 4.0." In *Handbuch Industrie 4.0 Bd. 1: Produktion,* 2. Auflage, edited by Birgit Vogel-Heuser, Thomas Bauernhansl, Michael ten Hompel, 3–25. Berlin: Springer Vieweg.

Statistisches Bundesamt. "Value: Foreign trade (special trade) EUR mn." Accessed May 15, 2020. https://www.destatis.de/EN/Themes/Economy/ForeignTrade/Table s/lrahl01.html.

The World Bank. "Exports of goods and services (% of GDP)." Accessed May 8, 2020. https://data.worldbank.org/indicator/NE.EXP.GNFS.ZS?end=2017&locatio ns=DE&start=1960.

The World Bank. "GDP (current US$)." Accessed May 8, 2020. https://data.worldba nk.org/indicator/NY.GDP.MKTP.CD.

Toffler, Alvin, and Heidi Toffler. 1996. Yeni Bir Uygarlık Yaratmak, Translated by Zülfü Dicleli. Istanbul: İnkılap.

Verband der Automobilindustrie (VDA). n.d. "Economic Policy and Infrastructure: Trade." Accessed June 20, 2019, https://www.vda.de/en/topics/economic-policy-and-infrastructure/trade/importance-oftrade-policy-for-industry-and-for-germany-as-an-industrial-location.html.

Wahlster, Wolfgang. 2013. "Industrie 4.0: Active Semantic Product Memories for Smart Factories." Linköping: IDA 30 Year Celebration Seminar.

Weber, Enzo. 2016. "Industrie 4.0: Wirkungen auf den Arbeitsmarkt und politische Herausforderungen." *Zeitschrift für Wirtschaftspolitik,* De Gruyter, 65 (1): 66–74. https://doi.org/10.1515/zfwp-2016-0002.

Welfens, Paul J.J. 2011. "Überwindung der Banken- und Finanzkrise: Optionen der Wachstums bzw. Wirtschaftspolitik." In *Zukunftsfähige Wirtschaftspolitik für Deutschland und Europa,* edited by Paul J.J.Welfens, 1–74. Berlin-Heidelberg: Springer-Verlag.

World Trade Organization. 2020. "World Trade Statistical Review." Accessed October 10, 2020 https://www.wto.org/english/res_e/statis_e/wts2020_e/wts2020 chapter06_e.pdf.

Zeit Online. 2019. "Deutschland weiter mit weltgrößtem Exportüberschuss", Accessed February 19, 2019, https://www.zeit.de/wirtschaft/2019-02/leistungsbi lanz-exportueberschuss-deutschland-2018-ifo-institut.

Chapter 7

The Political Economy of the European Union-Russia Energy Relation in the Context of Russia – Ukraine Dispute and its Global Effect

Omca Altın

INTRODUCTION

Energy is a compulsory essential element in the economic development of countries. Especially for sustainable development, also sustainable energy is extremely important. Therefore, sustainable energy relationships, the security of energy supply, and the diversification of energy resources have become the main targets of countries.

The EU is one of the regions with the highest energy consumption in the world. Hence, it has the largest energy markets globally. The EU to be a very poor region in terms of energy resources has made it dependent on Russia, which has an advantage in terms of energy resources. Russia is an extremely important country in the EU's natural gas imports, in particular. However, Russia uses energy as an economic and political tool and causes troubles in the supply of energy by applying different price policies at times. This situation threatens the EU's energy security.

Energy cuts faced by the EU owing to the crises between Russia and Ukraine strained EU–Russia economic and political relations, and the EU has begun to take various steps in the direction of reducing its dependence on Russia for energy and develop new policies. Hence, the EU, whose energy dependence on Russia is increasing day by day, is prospecting for alternative energy resources. Russia, on the other hand, in response to the EU's search for alternative energy sources, made attempts to eliminate the countries of transit to maintain its share in the European market.

The Turkish Stream and Nord Stream 2 pipeline projects developed by Russia particularly in this context led to the reaction of the United States, a liquefied natural gas exporter. Hence, the United States, which wants to be a dominant power in the region and global energy markets by opening to the European market, the largest gas market, but coming up against the EU–Russia energy trade barrier, has followed a global sanction policy against the EU, Russia, also including Russia's international partners to cancel the Nord Stream 2 pipeline project and to hinder the EU–Russia energy trade under the Countering America's Adversaries Through Sanctions Act; this circumstance, thus, has created a global effect. However, although liquefied natural gas is regarded as an opportunity for the EU, which is searching for alternative energy sources, it is not advantageous in terms of price and infrastructure compared to pipe gas. Russia, therefore, will maintain its position to be the key supplier for the EU. Therefore, this study aims to examine the political economy of EU–Russia relations within the scope of the Russia–Ukraine crisis and to evaluate its effects reflected on the global system.

RUSSIA–UKRAINE GAS DISPUTES

Ukraine is dependent on Russian natural gas supply by its location, also a key transit country for EU–Russia natural gas trade. This situation, therefore, constantly makes Ukraine a part of the energy disputes (Siddi 2018, 1553). Between 1991 and 2000, more than 90% of natural gas was transported to Europe through Ukraine (Chyong 2014). Although this rate has decreased with transit corridors diversified by Russia, such as Belarus, Nord Stream, and Blue Stream, almost 15% of the natural gas transported to EU member states is still supplied through Ukraine (Ramesh 2014). Therefore, Russia cutting off the natural gas transmitted to Ukraine would pose serious problems in terms of energy supply to the EU.

All gas supplies passing through Ukrainian territory were cut off by Russia in 2006 for the first time, so the gas transported to the EU through Ukraine was also interrupted. This sudden gas cutoff has been extremely effective in taking some steps for the EU to reduce its dependence on Russian energy, in other words, in the EU's strategy to diversify its energy supply (European Commission, n.d.).

Gaining its independence in 1991, Ukraine has faced some economic and social problems arising from its being a new state, whereas these problems, which increased even more in 2004, ended with the Orange Revolution (Hacıtahiroğlu 2014, 273). The main reason for this trouble between Ukraine and Russia was the pricing dispute between Russia and Ukraine that happened about one year after the change of government in Ukraine follow-ing the Orange Revolution (Chyong 2014).

With Viktor Yushchenko, who came to power after the Orange Revolution, a management understanding that desired to be in harmony with the West in domestic and foreign policies prevailed in Ukraine (Hacıtahiroğlu 2014, 273). Hence, it was claimed that the reason why the gas to Ukraine was cut off by Russia was not only due to economic reasons but also to weaken the legitimacy of Viktor Yushchenko, who pursued a western-oriented policy (Chyong 2014). The decrease of Russia's influence in the region after the election of Yushchenko, who was supported by the EU and the United States, to the presidency underpins this claim (Erkan 2014, 98).

However, it is clearly seen that Russia was also trying to follow a different policy in sales of natural gas to Ukraine. The major reason behind this idea was that Russia previously sold gas to Ukraine at lower prices, and Ukraine transferred gas coming from Russia to Europe both safely and at a reason-able price (Chyong 2014). It was emphasized that in the last Russia–Ukraine dispute, Russia intended to increase gas sales prices (Russia wanted to increase the price of 1,000 cubic meters of gas from about $ 50 to $ 220–230) and strategically made this move to interrupt EU–Ukraine relations (Parfitt 2006). Ukraine's convergence with the EU and the North Atlantic Treaty Organization (NATO) during this period was perceived by Russia as a threat to its national security. According to Russia, the EU and NATO to increase their effectiveness in the region meant that the US interest in the region would also increase. Hence, this situation has been interpreted by Russia as NATO's policy of containment of the Union of Soviet Socialist Republics (USSR) turned into a policy to contain Russia. In short, Russia wants to keep NATO, namely the United States and the EU, as far from its neighborhood as possible; however, these powers continue their desire to be effective in the region. The leading motive for this is the rich resources in the region and the geographical location of the region (Erkan 2014, 98–99). Russia, thus, has used its economic power in the gas market also in the political sphere (Riley 2012, 3). Under these circumstances, Ukraine did not accept Russia's price offer of $220–230 for 1,000 cubic meters of gas and offered to make this price increase gradually. Consequently, Russia has offered to give Ukraine a loan to make its payments easier and to postpone the stated price for three months as another option, but Ukraine did not accept these offers of Russia. Thus, Russia cut off gas to Ukraine for three days. Particularly, Hungary was also affected by this case and experienced a 25% decrease in the gas coming to them through Ukraine (Parfitt 2006). This issue was settled on January 4, 2006. In this case, Ukraine would supply the gas from the Russian-Swiss company RosUkrEnergo, half of which belongs to Gazprom. This company would supply the gas from Russia at a price of $230, which was demanded by Russia, and also from Turkmenistan at a cheaper price, and would sell it to Ukraine at $95 (BBC NEWS 2006).

However, although it seems like a consensus was built, a crisis arose again between Russia and Ukraine in 2009 (Pirani, Stern, and Yafimava 2009), and the reason for this crisis was again the disagreement over the price. Russian Gazprom company demanded $250 per 1,000 cubic meters from Ukraine, but Ukraine rejected this offer and proposed a price of $210. Therewith, emphasizing that the EU member states paid $500 per 1,000 cubic meters of natural gas, the Russian company Gazprom increased its price offer submitted to Ukraine to $418 and reminded Ukraine that the bill for gas deliveries in 2008 valued around $600 million remained unpaid. No agreement could be reached between Russia and Ukraine on prices, and Russia cut off the gas sent to Ukraine in 2009 again (Kramer 2009).

These gas price disputes between Russia and Ukraine between 2006 and 2009 also caused the interruption of the gas flow toward the EU member states and seriously affected the societies and economies of the EU member states (Pirani, Stern, and Yafimava 2009). Following Russia's cutoff of gas to Ukraine in 2009, a ten-year agreement has been signed between Russia and Ukraine, and according to the agreement, Russia agreed to make a 20% discount to Ukraine. Consequently, Ukraine made a decision to transfer natural gas to EU member states also in 2009 at the price it requested in 2008 (Shi 2009, 56). However, also this circumstance was not enough to end the tension between Russia and Ukraine, and Russia continued to use its geopolitical power against Ukraine. The Russia–Ukraine dispute erupted again with the annexation of Crimea by Russia in 2014.

Russia agreed to a 30% drop in the price of natural gas sold to Ukraine in exchange for allowing the Russian Black Sea fleet to stay in Crimea from 2010 until 2042. On the other hand, it was claimed that Russia made a 33% drop in the gas prices sold to Ukraine in return for not signing the EU–Ukraine Association Agreement between the two parties (Chyong 2014). The statement of Viktor Yanukovych, the president of Ukraine who stands out with his pro-Russian policies, that he rejected the pending EU Association Agreement, which paved the way for the EU membership of Ukraine in the long term, further strengthened this claim. Consequently, the Ukrainian people, who want Ukraine to continue its cooperation with the EU, started protests, and following the case becomes worse, Yanukovych left the country. In the elections held after Yanukovych left the country, Petro Poroshenko was elected president on May 25, 2014 (Koçak 2015, 9, 19).

After Yanukovych lost power, Russia, on the other hand, cancelled the gas sales discounts planned to perform. Ukraine, with approximately $5.3 billion outstanding debts, did not accept the gas prices already cancelled by Russia. Thus, no consensus could be reached after the bilateral negotiations.

Russia cut off the gas of Ukraine again and occupied Crimea (Chyong 2014). Afterward, it was stated that Ukraine would pay its debts to Russia gradually, under the guarantee of the EU, and gas prices would be increased to $365 in the first quarter of 2015 (Kirby, 2014).

As it is seen, having used its geopolitical power generating from the fact that Ukraine has adopted a foreign policy conflicting with its interest and did not accept the increases in gas sales prices, throughout history, Russia has preferred to implement a direct energy cutoff to Ukraine. However, Ukraine has responded to Russia with the geopolitical power used by Russia itself and has used its geopolitical power arising from being a transit country by interrupting Russia's gas exports to the EU. In other words, Ukraine has preferred to use its strategic position and the advantage of being a transit country as a tool to prevent EU–Russia energy trade by including the EU in this crisis and to reduce the prices Russia desires to impose on itself (Pirani, Stern, and Yafimava 2009).

THE HISTORY, ECONOMIC, AND POLITICAL IMPORTANCE OF THE EU– RUSSIA ENERGY RELATIONS

Energy trade serves as an important driving force in EU–Russia economic relations. Russia maintains its key supplier position for the EU for energy resources such as oil, natural gas, and coal. Oil and natural gas trade, in particular, has been the basis of relations between European countries and Russia in recent years. In the 1960s, Russia performed its large amounts of oil and gas exports through pipelines to the member states of The Council for Mutual Economic Assistance in Eastern Europe first and then to Western European countries, including NATO and European Community member states. Especially in the late 1960s and also in the early 1970s, Italy, Austria, West Germany, Finland, and France were important customers of Soviet fossil fuel exports (Hogselius 2013; Siddi 2017a).

Following the oil crisis, which occurred between 1973 and 1974 and greatly affected also the global system, Europe's interest in Soviet oil and natural gas increased. In 1983, the USSR commissioned the Transcontinental Export Pipeline, also known as the Urengoy-Uzhgorod pipeline, and transported Siberian gas to Western European markets. After the dissolution of the Soviet Union, the East-West gas trade continued to grow (Siddi 2018, 1554–1555).

Despite losing its feature of being a superpower and going through a serious economic crisis after the dissolution of the Soviet Union, as being Europe's main gas supplier thanks to its energy resources, Russia has both strengthened economically and regained the prestige it lost in the region and globally (Ağır 2016, 26). Of the energy resources imported by the EU in 2015, 37% of natural gas, 29.1% of crude oil, and 29.1% of solid fuels were supplied from Russia. This situation, therefore, has been an important indicator of the EU's dependence on foreign sources in the energy field. In 2016, the EU imported more than half of the energy it consumed (including 72% of the natural gas it consumes, and 85% of the oil it consumes). In particular, considering the decline of domestic fossil fuel production and the phasing out nuclear power in some EU member states, oil and natural gas import dependency is expected to increase gradually in EU member countries, especially in Germany (Siddi 2018, 1554–1555). The increasing dependence on foreign sources is thought to cause serious concern in the natural gas industry. It is estimated that in the long-run, domestic production will decrease further, demand will remain constant or increase (Dickel et al. 2014, 71).

However, although Russia is a key energy supplier for the EU, the EU, on the other hand, is the main investor in the Russian economy, including the energy sector. EU companies have the necessary technological infrastructure to develop Russian seabeds, as well as they also facilitate access to ultimate consumers (Kaveshnikov 2010, 598). The EU, therefore, is a very important market for Russian energy exports. According to the current statistics, sales of crude oil, petroleum products, and natural gas account for about two-thirds of Russia's total export revenue, and most of these exports are made to EU countries (Metelitsa 2014).

While crude oil and petroleum products make up more than half of Russia's export revenues, the share of natural gas is around 15%. Particularly natural gas trade is the main source of disputes and political issues in EU and Russia energy relations. The main reason for this is that EU member states in Central and Eastern Europe such as Estonia, Latvia, Bulgaria, and Slovakia have an insufficient infrastructure in terms of importing gas from other countries and therefore depend on Russia's natural gas. Most EU member states in Central and Eastern European countries have few or no alternatives they can import to replace Russian natural gas, which they mostly use for household heating purposes (Grigas 2013; Siddi 2017b). In other words, its market superiority in the Central and Eastern European natural gas markets makes Russia strong economically and politically (Riley 2012, 3). While particularly these countries are vulnerable to natural gas cuts, their doubts toward Russia are raising gradually, too.

Most of Russia's natural gas exports to the EU are made to Western European countries that have alternative suppliers and strong connections with global natural gas markets, such as Germany, Italy, France, and the UK (Yafimava 2015, 3–4). In other words, these countries, which constitute the largest share in the natural gas imports realized by the EU, are less dependent on Russia (Serpin ve Demirtaş 2017, 64). As well, the long-standing close cooperation of these countries with Russia made them trust Russia more compared to Central and Eastern European countries. Therefore, it has been frequently stated that natural gas trade with Russia by these EU countries does not pose serious energy security and political problem (Yafimava 2015, 3–4). However, following the emergence of tensions between Ukraine and Russia regarding natural gas, the fact that almost half of the gas from Russia to the EU passes through Ukrainian territory (Siddi 2017a, 107), the concerns of these countries about the interruptions in the energy trade with Russia have started to increase, and thus their trust toward Russia to decrease (Dickel et al. 2014, 2).

CHANGING EU–RUSSIA ENERGY RELATIONS IN THE CONTEXT OF RUSSIA–UKRAINE CRISIS AND ITS GLOBAL EFFECT

There have been some tensions in EU–Russia relations especially after the annexation of Crimea by Russia, and the EU has imposed different types of sanctions against Russia. These sanctions imposed by the EU were mostly in the fields of banking, finance, technology, and industry (Koçak 2015, 18–19). Especially import bans on goods from Crimea and inhibitions on trade and investment related to certain economic sectors and infrastructure projects of Russia were among the sanctions imposed by the EU in return for Russia's annexation of Crimea (European Commission 2015). Besides, while the limited access to EU primary and secondary capital markets for certain Russian banks and companies composes the economic sanctions (Cipek 2018, 19), import and export ban on trade in arms, on the other hand, covers the sanctions in the dimension of the military article. Curtailing Russian access to certain technologies that can be used for oil exploration (European Commission 2015) and restrictions on lending or investing in the oil sector appear as sanctions imposed in the field of energy (Furuncu 2019, 11).

However, one of the most striking points is that the EU has not been able to introduce some of the restrictions it imposed on the oil sector in the natural gas sector (Dediu, Czajkowski, and Kiewra 2019). The EU cannot impose any sanctions on Gazprom or other Russian companies in the gas sector (Furuncu 2019, 11). The main reason for this is the EU's dependency on Russia in the field of natural gas. While the EU, which ranks first in energy consumption, has very limited alternatives to energy imports, Russia, aiming to become a global superpower in the energy field, stands out as the only alternative for the EU in the gas import (Erkan 2014, 104). Therefore, some EU member states that are dependent on Russia in the field of oil and natural gas are concerned that Russia will respond by reducing its energy exports, and they oppose firm sanctions (Furuncu 2019, 10). Besides, suspending the financing of new operations, and relieving Russian managers within the European Bank for Reconstruction and Development of their duties and rescheduling of their positions within the bank to the detriment of Russia, and the reassessment of the Russia EU bilateral cooperation with a view to reducing the level of the cooperation was among other EU sanctions (The Council of European Union 2014).

As a result of all these sanctions, strong EU–Russia economic relations have been seriously damaged, and this brought along major disputes (Vara 2014). However, although it suffers economically from the sanctions imposed on it by the EU, Russian did not take a step back on the Crimea question (Motyl 2015).

Since it is directly dependent on Ukraine in gas transfer and to reduce its dependence on Russian gas in consequence of the crises between Ukraine and Russia; the EU, thus, has sought to increase its energy supply diversity with the effect of natural gas flow interruptions and all these tensions with Russia. As the EU seeks to increase its energy supply diversity, Russia, which wants to maintain its share in the European market, has made attempts to eliminate the countries of transit as an alternative to EU projects.

In this context, the EU aimed to realize geopolitically important pipeline projects such as the Nabucco pipeline and the Southern Gas Corridor, which would eliminate Russia and enable it to import gas from other producers in the Caspian region (Siddi 2018, 1558). With the Nabucco project, which emerged in 2002, it was planned to transport gas supplied from the countries in the Caspian region, the Middle East, and Central Asia to Austria through Bulgaria, Romania, and Hungary. It was stated that the amount of energy planned to be transported through this pipeline would be approximately thirty-one billion cubic meters, and the Nabucco project, planned to be commissioned in 2011, was considered to operate in full capacity in 2019. Subsequently, Turkey, Austria, Bulgaria, Hungary, and Romania signed the agreement in 2009 that will form the legal framework for the Nabucco project (Lane 2009, 6–7). In 2010, the project was stated to cost €8 billion. Therefore, it was stated that the Nabucco project would not be realized entirely due to its high cost, and thus, it was decided to continue the Nabucco-West project, which has almost half capacity. At the same time, the Shah Deniz consortium decided to prefer the Trans-Adriatic Pipeline (TAP) and the Nabucco-West project, however, it was later decided to transport the gas to Europe through the TAP project. The gas, which was planned to be transported to Europe with the TAP project, was planned to pass through Turkey first with the Trans-Anatolian Natural Gas Pipeline (TANAP). Through the pipeline project in question, it was aimed to transport almost 16 billion cubic meters of gas, where 6 billion cubic meters to Turkey and 10 billion cubic meters to Europe. The resource aimed to be transported through TANAP was six new resources in the Shah Deniz 2 gas field of Azerbaijan (Bremen 2013, 2–3). Following the failure of the Nabucco project, thanks to the TANAP project, an important step was taken for the Southern Gas Corridor that the EU plans to realize. The gas transported with the TANAP project via the route Turkey-Greece-Albania-Italy was planned to spread to Europe. Thus, the gas that would reach Europe via the Caspian would not be under the control of Russia (Cain, İbramihov, and Bilgin 2012, 19).

In response to all these attempts of the EU to increase its energy supply diversity, Russia, on the other hand, made attempts to market natural gas to China and Japan, yet, in order not to lose its biggest market (Talus 2011, 264), it started to take steps for the projects that will prevent Ukraine from becoming a transit country and ensure uninterrupted gas flow to Europe. Accordingly, Russia put forward the South Stream project right after the EU announced the Nabucco project. With the South Stream project, Russia has aimed to prevent Nabucco and other pipeline projects so that natural gas is not transferred to the European market beyond Russia's control (Baran 2008, 1). In 2012, Russian Gazprom and Bulgarian energy holding EAD signed a mutual agreement for the construction of the South Stream project that will transfer natural gas from Russia to Bulgaria through the Black Sea and from there to Serbia, Hungary, and Austria (Rodova 2012). With this project, Russia, thus, would reduce natural gas transports through Ukraine and would transfer it to Bulgaria (Varol 2013, 212). However, by the European Commission, the South Stream project was requested to be stopped on the grounds that it violates the EU's Third Energy Package and that the intergovernmental agreements signed between Russia and some EU member states do not comply with EU laws (Munteanu and Sarno 2016, 66). In other words, the dispute between the liberal energy policy of the EU toward the market and the Russian energy policy based on monopoly and political control ideas was a cause in demanding the project be stopped (Kaveshnikov 2010, 601). This decision regarding the South Stream project was at the same time one of the sanctions imposed by the EU after the tension experienced after Russia's annexation of Crimea (Marini 2014).

Following the EU's decision for the South Stream project, although it spent many years and made serious investments for this project, Russia reached the conclusion that the project would not provide as much economic advantage as they thought (Sharples 2015, 47). For this reason, after the Third Energy Package negotiations made with the European Commission reached a stalemate, Russia, not taking the risk of losing their investment due to the obstacles they will face from the side of the European Commission, decided to cancel the project. Thereupon, Russia decided to put the Turkish Stream project into action as an alternative to the cancelled South Stream project (Sıvış 2019, 1380).

Showing similarity to the South Stream project, the Turkish Stream project aimed to prevent Ukraine's transit country role by making the routes of gas suppliers even more diverse. At the same time, the Turkish Stream project would enable Russia to gain an advantage over other gas suppliers in the export market and would have also fulfilled the condition of adapting to the Third Energy Package required by the European Commission (Franza 2015, 53). Commercially speaking, Turkey, on the other hand, is the second-largest importer of Russian gas. Considering that the gas demand of Turkey will increase even more in the future, Gazprom wants to strengthen the regional export infrastructure (Demiryol 2015). It was planned to transport natural gas to Turkey through the first line of the Turkish Stream, and to the consumers in Southern and Southern and Southeastern Europe through the second line. The Turkish Stream was expected to have an average gas capacity of 31.5 billion cubic meters per year and includes two lines, the first line, approximately 930 km offshore pipelines, and the second line, shore pipelines to the countries adjacent to the borders of Turkey (Sıvış 2019, 1380). Therefore, the Turkish Stream project would strengthen Turkey's role in European energy security (Furuncu 2019, 17).

Concurrently to the Turkish Stream project, Russia has also commissioned the Nord Stream 2 project that allows Russia to double the gas resources going to Europe by transporting natural gas directly to Germany through the Black Sea (Boersma and Johnson 2018). Therefore, while it would be able to transport natural gas to the eastern parts of Europe through the Turkish Stream project, the north of Europe would supply natural gas through the Nord Stream 2 project. Russia, thus, would continue to have the largest share in the European natural gas market with these projects (Markoviç 2017).

The United States, on the other hand, strongly opposes Russia's Turkish Stream and especially Nord Stream 2 pipeline projects. The United States was explaining the reasons why it opposes Russia's pipeline projects as it violates the rights of Ukraine arising from being a transit country and as these projects would further reduce the possibility of the EU getting rid of its energy dependence on Russia (Gotev 2019). However, the main reason why the United States strongly opposes the Nord Stream 2 pipeline project was the fact that the United States is an LNG exporter (Akhiyadov 2019).

Having recently emerged as a reflection of the liberalization process in natural gas markets, the competitive market structure has brought a global character to regionally fragmented natural gas markets, with the effect of LNG. LNG market, which stands out with the demand of the increasingly competitive environment for more flexible supply resources, began to strengthen its position in the gas markets and has increased the share of LNG trade in the global system. The natural gas market to become much more flexible and to gain a global qualification at the same time has started to be regarded as an important opportunity for the EU, the world's largest importer of natural gas who tries to diversify its gas market in order to reduce its dependence on Russia in terms of energy security (Serpin and Demirtaş 2017,48,49,52, 54).

Hence, the United States, which increased its LNG exports after 2016, desires to be a dominant power both in the region and in the global energy markets by getting into the EU market, the world's largest gas market. Apart from the United States, on the other hand, Qatar and Australia are also among the countries trying to expand their LNG market. These countries, however, are faced with the EU–Russia trade barrier based on long-term agreements and realized through pipelines. The United States, therefore, tries to prevent the passage of Russian gas transported to Europe by putting all kinds of political and economic means of pressure into action against Russia while trying to halt Qatar, the world's largest LNG exporter, from being a rival itself in the European market. Besides, the United States makes effort to create an environment where it can compete with Russia in the European market (Akhiyadov 2019).

In addition to the United States, also Ukraine, Poland, Slovakia, and the Baltic states are other countries that oppose Russia's Nord Stream 2 pipeline project. However, EU member states such as France, the Netherlands, Austria, Italy, and Germany support the Nord Stream 2 pipeline project (Akhiyadov 2019). The main reason why Ukraine and Poland opposed the Nord Stream 2 pipeline project was the fact that gas transit revenues would diminish as a result of the reduction in the amount of transit gas. The reason why the Baltic States, the Central and Eastern European countries oppose the Nord Stream 2 project was the fact that they regard dependency on Russian natural gas in natural gas supply as a threat for themselves. These countries were concerned about the fact that the EU's dependency on Russia for gas supply on such a scale would entirely put the EU under the influence of Russia politically (Demirci 2019).

On the other hand, drawing attention to the gas cutoffs that happened in the past, Germany, the main supporter of the Nord Stream 2 pipeline project, emphasized that wider import channels would increase supply reliability (Maio 2019). Several important factors play a role in Germany's support for the Nord Stream 2 pipeline project. With this project, a significant amount of gas to Baltic States, Central and Eastern Europe would be transported through Germany, and thus, Germany would take control of Eastern Europe. Therefore, Germany would become Europe's energy center (Demirci 2019). However, this has disturbed the United States and the United States, which increases its pressure on Germany, had a falling out with Germany (Şeker 2019).

As is seen, the EU member states also had disputes within themselves related to the Nord Stream 2 pipeline project. However, the most important factor in the future of the Nord Stream 2 pipeline project is the United States. The United States utters threats to impose several sanctions to halt the Nord Stream 2 pipeline project. The United States warns that it may penalize companies participating in the Nord Stream 2 pipeline project, based on the CAATSA Act (Akhiyadov 2019). The United States has warned five companies with which the Nord Stream 2 project's executive firm has signed an agreement and that will provide long-term financing support up to 50% of the total cost of the project under the agreement, consisting of German energy firms Wintershall and Uniper, French firm Engie, British-Dutch oil and gas giant Royal Dutch Shell, and Austria's energy firm OMV (Gazprom n.d), involved in the Russian-led Nord Stream 2 gas pipeline that they could face sanctions if they stick with the project, pursuant to the CAATSA. However, these companies continued the project despite the warning made by the United States (Furuncu 2019, 15).

When the Nord Stream 2 pipeline project reaches its final stage, Denmark and Poland very quickly settled the dispute between them on the demarcation of maritime areas in the Baltic Sea, which poses a problem and lasted for nearly forty years, and the region where the Nord Stream 2 pipeline project would pass was determined to be the restricted economic zone of Denmark. Settlement of the dispute between Denmark and Poland after the negotiations made by the United States, and Denmark to extend the process of giving permission to Gazprom for passing a pipeline through its own restricted economic zone were other important attempts made by the United States to block the Nord Stream 2 pipeline project (Akhiyadov 2019).

On the other hand, ExxonMobil, one of the largest energy companies in the United States, had to stop its joint ventures with Rosneft in 2018 since it could not get permission for the oil exploration project in the Black Sea in April 2017 from the US Department of the Treasury (Gazprom n.d.). Hence, the sanctions imposed by the United States cause large energy companies to pull out of the Russian market by hampering their cooperation and partnerships with Russian energy companies (Furuncu 2019, 15).

The United States also applies pressure on India, which is in communication with Russia for weapon systems such as S-400s, nuclear submarines, and two battleships built, not to purchase Russian weapons (Sen 2019). These sanctions will negatively affect also Turkey, which has partnerships with Russia in the field of energy (Furuncu 2019, 18). The investments of $1 million or more or $5 million or more over a twelve-month period that directly and significantly contribute to increasing Russia's capacity to construct energy export pipelines would be sanctioned under the CAATSA. In other words, construction, modernization, or repair of energy export pipelines would be regarded within the scope of these sanctions (Davispolk 2017). This will significantly hinder the activities of energy companies operating in Turkey in Russia's energy infrastructure and construction fields. At the same time, since it is foreign dependent in terms of energy, Turkey needs to develop collaborations and projects with energy exporters such as Russia for energy security. Therefore, the CAATSA will affect new cooperation and projects that Turkey will develop with Russia in the future in the field of energy and will also prevent different investments targeting Turkish-Russian energy projects. The CAATSA will negatively affect the future of the Turkish Stream project, in particular, and the countries involved in the project. Hence, the CAATSA appears to be the major obstacle for Russia to export gas to Europe with new pipelines in the future and also hinders Turkey's goals of becoming an energy base (Furuncu 2019, 18–19).

On the other hand, the US Congress approved the defense budget for 2020 in the amount of $738 billion, which includes the sanctions targeting Russia and the Nord Stream 2 pipeline project and allocation of $300 million for the needs of the Ukrainian army. Apart from the sanctions against Russia, due to the S-400 missile system bought from Russia, the US 2020 Defense Budget includes imposing serious sanctions on Turkey and Turkey's ban on military cooperation with Russia (BBC NEWS 2019). Hence, the sanctions imposed by the United States create a global impact by threatening not only the EU and Russia but also Russia's international partners.

However, despite all kinds of political and economic sanctions imposed by the United States, while Russia continued the Nord Stream 2 pipeline project, LNG abundance to increase competition on the EU natural gas market distresses Russia. Russia, therefore, revises its long-term natural gas contracts with European countries in order not to lose its largest market, rescinds anti-competitive provisions in the agreements, and makes investment initiatives for LNG to offer much more flexible supply opportunities. All these efforts have been an indication that Russia does not want to lose the leader in the gas competition (Serpin and Demirtaş 2017, 49).

Thanks to its features such as the ability to progress on demand, being an alternative to unexpected shocks experienced, etc., LNG markets are extremely important for energy supply security. In terms of the flexibility it provides to changing market conditions and strengthening the markets, the LNG market acts as a buffer. However, although LNG seems to be an advantage for the EU, which is seeking different resources to reduce its energy dependency on Russia (Karagöl and Kaya 2016, 9), it cannot compete with Russian gas transported through pipelines due to its high cost (Akhiyadov 2019). When viewed from this aspect, beyond resource diversification for the EU, LNG is not regarded as a substitute for pipe gas. Therefore, having an advantage in terms of price albeit the rise of LNG, Russia will continue to maintain its share in the EU natural gas market with the reduction in transition costs of the Turkish Stream and Nord Stream 2 pipelines (Serpin and Demirtaş 2017, 54, 58, 59, 70).

When taken all of these into account, uninterrupted, reliable access to energy resources at affordable prices is very important for countries. Otherwise, cutoffs in energy resources, failure to provide access to energy resources at affordable prices, and sudden changes in prices negatively affect also the global economy. Energy, the main input of many production and consumption activities, is the most important source of economic growth. Energy use drives economic productivity and industrial growth and takes place at the heart of the functioning of any modern economy. Being used as a fuel and raw material source particularly in industrial activities, energy represents less than a tenth of the cost of production, while it is responsible for at least half of industrial growth in a modern economy. Energy resources, therefore, are among the top global trade goods (Asghar 2008: 167). Global energy consumption is expected to increase by 37%, especially by 2035. According to the forecasts, while Russia will continue to be the world's largest energy exporter by meeting 4% of the world's energy demand by 2035, Europe will be the world's largest natural gas importer (Ercümen 2016).

CONCLUSION

Energy is an indispensable element of all goods and service sectors. Because of this feature, energy emerges as a basic requirement for the acquisition and sustainability of economic, social, and political developments of countries. Therefore, uninterrupted, reliable access to energy resources at affordable prices becomes very important for countries. Otherwise, energy cutoffs cause serious crises both regionally and globally.

It is the energy that makes up the basis of EU and Russia relations. The EU, one of the largest consumers in the world in the field of energy, meets a large part of this need, especially natural gas, from Russia, which is very rich in energy resources. However, the EU member states to be seriously dependent on Russia for gas supply, negative effects of energy crisis between Russia and Ukraine in 2006, 2009, and 2014 on the EU states, and the gas cutoffs in EU states that provide Russian gas through Ukraine have jeopardized the EU's energy supply security. The EU, thus, has made attempts to increase its energy supply diversity in order to ensure its energy supply security and to reduce its dependency on Russia. In return for the EU's attempt to increase its diversity of energy supply, Russia, on the other hand, has focused on policies aimed at eliminating transit countries to maintain its share in the European market.

Within the scope of increasing its energy supply diversity, the EU has launched Nabucco and Southern Gas Corridor pipeline projects that will eliminate Russia and allow gas to be imported from other producers in the Caspian region. However, the Nabucco project, which aimed at transmitting the energy to be supplied from the Caspian region countries, the Middle East, and Central Asia through Turkey to the route of Bulgaria-Romania-Hungary-Austria, failed due to its high cost, and then, TAP and TANAP projects were put into action. The gas transported with the TANAP project through Turkey to Greece was planned to reach the route of Greece-Albania-Italy with the TAP project and to spread to Europe therefrom. Thus, the EU tried to prevent Russia's control of gas that will reach Europe from the Caspian region.

In return for these attempts of the EU, Russia, on the other hand, following the announcement of the Nabucco pipeline project, in particular, has taken steps for the South Stream project, which will transport natural gas from Russia to Bulgaria through the Black Sea and to Serbia, Hungary, and Austria and reduce the natural gas transport transmitted through Ukraine.

However, the EU expected Russia, which would get into its markets through this pipeline project, to comply with certain rules and procedures. Due to these difficulties raised by the EU, Russia did not want to risk its investments and decided to cancel the project. Following the cancellation of the South Stream project, The Turkish Stream project, which was basically the same as this project and where it was planned to transport gas to Turkey through the first line and to the consumers in Southern and Southeastern Europe through the second line, has been put into action. Thanks to the Turkish Stream project, Ukraine's role of being a transit country was eliminated, and Turkey's role in European energy security was increased. Concurrently to the Turkish Stream project, Russia has also commissioned the Nord Stream 2 project that allows Russia to double the gas resources going to Europe by transporting natural gas directly to Germany through the Black Sea.

The United States, on the other hand, strongly opposes the Turkish Stream and especially Nord Stream 2 pipeline projects. The main reason why the United States strongly opposes the Nord Stream 2 pipeline project was the fact that the United States is an LNG exporter, and it wants to be a dominant power in the region and global energy markets by getting into the European market, the world's largest gas market. Facing the EU–Russia energy trade barrier, the United States, therefore, is disturbed by this energy relationship between the EU and Russia and imposes all its political and economic sanctions. In order to halt the Nord Stream 2 pipeline project and to prevent EU–Russia energy trade, under the CAATSA, the United States tries to hamper cooperation and partnerships with Russia by making various warnings to both EU member states outside Russia and other countries and companies with which Russia cooperates on energy. The US sanctions threaten not only the EU and Russia but also Russia's international partners. The United States, thus, pursues a global sanctions policy and these sanctions create a global effect.

Despite the political and economic sanctions imposed by the United States, Russia, on the other hand, continues its Nord Stream 2 project at full speed, and as it worries about the fact that LNG would increase competition in the EU natural gas market, it also makes investments in LNG in order not to lose its largest market.

However, although LNG seems to be an advantage for the EU, which is seeking different resources to reduce its energy dependency on Russia, Russia will continue to remain the main supplier for the EU since pipe gas provides an advantage in terms of price and infrastructure compared to LNG. Therefore, LNG is not an option for the EU that is seeking resource diversification as a substitute for pipe gas other than resource diversification.

In this context, accessing energy resources in uninterrupted, reliable ways and at affordable prices is of vital importance for countries. Interruptions in energy resources, sudden fluctuations in prices, and failure to provide access to energy resources at affordable prices will have negative effects on the global economy. Energy, the main input of many production and consumption activities, is the most important source of economic growth. Energy, with a wide usage area, is one of the leading global trade goods. Hence, according to the forecasts, considering that global energy consumption will increase even more in the 2035s; it is an inevitable fact that Russia, rich in energy resources, will continue to be an important energy exporter in the global arena and that Europe, which has a high energy consumption rate and is dependent on foreign countries, will become the world's largest energy importer. In this context, it should increase energy efficiency and savings and establish a supply system where renewable energy sources are at the center in order to reduce the dependence on Russia in the field of energy and to reach uninterrupted, reliable, and affordable energy resources. Besides, it will also be extremely important to implement emergency support mechanisms by integrating the energy infrastructure and energy market among member countries therefore creating a mechanism that will enable all EU members to act together in the energy fields.

REFERENCES

Ağır, Osman. 2016. "Rusya – Ukrayna Krizinin Avrasya Ekonomik Birliği Bağlamında Değerlendirilmesi, *Kahramanmaraş Sütçü İmam Üniversitesi İktisadi ve İdari Bilimler Fakültesi Dergisi* 6, no. 2: 23–42.

Akhiyadov, Mokhmad. 2019. "AB, ABD ve Rusya Üçgeninde Kuzey Akım 2 Doğal Gaz Boru Hattı." *İnsamer*, Accessed March 2, 2020. https://insamer.com/tr/ab-abd-ve-rusya-ucgeninde-kuzey-akim-2-dogal-gaz-boru-hatti_2172.html.

Asghar, Zahid. 2008. "Energy- GDP Relationship: A Casual Analysis for the Five Countries of South Asia." *Applied Econometrics and International Development,* 8–1: 167–180.

Baran, Zeyno. 2008. "Security Aspects of the South Stream Project." *Center For Eurasian Policy Hudson Institute,* Accessed March 15, 2020. https://www.hudson .org/content/researchattachments/attachment/670/baran-south_stream_for_ep.pdf.

BBC NEWS. 2006. "Q&A: Ukraine Gas Row." Accessed April 1, 2020. http://news .bbc.co.uk/2/hi/business/4569846.stm.

BBC NEWS. 2019. "S-400 ve F-35 Krizi: ABD Senatosu'nun Açıkladığı 2020 Savunma Bütçesi Tasarısı, Türkiye'nin F-35 Programına Son Verebilir." Accessed April 22, 2020. https://www.bbc.com/turkce/haberler-dunya-48379417.

Boersma, Tim and Johnson, Corey. 2018. "U.S. Energy Diplomacy." *Columbia Sıpa Centre on Global Energy Policy,* Accessed March 4, 2020. https://energypolicy .columbia.edu/research/report/us-energy-diplomacy.

Bremen, Kusznir, Julia. 2013. "TAP, Nabucco West, and South Stream: The Pipeline Dilemma in the Caspian Sea Basin and Its Consequences for the Development of the Southern Gas Corridor." *Caucasus Analytical Digest* 47: 2–8.

Cain,G., J., Michael, Ibrahimov, Rovshan, Bilgin, Fevzi. 2012. "Linking the Caspian to Europe: Repercussions of the Trans-Anatolian Pipeline." *Rethink Institute,* Accessed March 8, 2020. https://dochot.net/document/linking-the-caspian-to-euro pe-repercussions-of-the-trans-anatolian-pipeline.

Chyong, Chi Kong. 2014. "Why Europe Should Support Reform of the Ukrainian Gas Market or Risk a Cut-Off." *Phosphate Price,* Accessed April 2, 2020. http://pho sphateprice.com/why-europe-should-support-reform-of-the-ukrainian-gas-market -or-risk-a-cut-off/.

Cipek, Tihomir. 2018. "Russia and European Union: What Remains of The Partnership?" *Journal of Balkan and Black Sea Studies,* 1(1): 11–29.

Davispolk. 2017. "Countering America's Adversaries Through Sanctions Act Becomes Laws." Accessed April 19, 2020. https://www.davispolk.com/files/201 7-08-07_the_countering_americas_adversaries_through_sanctions_act_becomes_l aw.pdf.

Dediu Dumitru, Czajkowski Mateusz and Kiewra Janiszewska Ewa. 2019. "How Did the European Natural Gas Market Evolve in 2018." Mckinsey&Company, April 5, 2020. https://www.mckinsey.com/industries/oil-and-gas/our-insights/petroleum -blog/how-did-the-european-natural-gas-market-evolve-in-2018.

Demirci, Cem, Mehmet. 2019. "ABD Kuzey Akım 2 Projesine Neden Karşı Çıkıyor?." *Euronews,* Accessed March 5, 2020. https://tr.euronews.com/2019/12 /30/abd-kuzey-akim-2-projesine-neden-karsi-cikiyor.

Demiryol, Tolga. 2015. "Interdependence, Balancing and Conflict in Russian– Turkish Relations." *In Great Powers and Geopolitics: International Affairs in a Re-balancing World,* edited by Aharon Klieman, 65–86. Switzerland: Springer International Publisher.

Dickel Ralf, Hassanzadeh Elham, Henderson James, Honore Anouk, El-Katiri Laura, Pirani, Simon, Rogers Howard, Stern, and Jonathan Yafımava Katja. 2014. "Reducing European Dependence on Russian Gas: Distinguishing Natural Gas

Security from Geopolitics." *Oxford Institute for Energy Studies*, OIES Paper 92: 1–65.

Ercümen, Aksoy, Merve. 2016. "Dünyanın Enerji Görünümü." *İnsamer*, Accessed April 13, 2020 https://insamer.com/tr/dunyanin-enerji-gorunumu_388.html.

Erkan, Çağlar, Anıl. 2014. "Küresel Doğal Gaz Krizlerine Karşı Enerji Arz Güvenliğinin Sağlanması ve Enerji Arz Güvenliği İçin Kriz Yönetimi." *Sosyal Bilimler Dergisi 4*(7): 87–110.

European Commission. 2015. "Commission Guidance Note on the Implementation of Certain Provisions of Regulation." Accessed April 5, 2020. https://europa.eu/ne wsroom/sites/newsroom/files/docs/body/1_act_part1_v2_en.pdf.

European Commission. n.d. "Energy Security Strategy." Accessed April 3, 2020 https ://ec.europa.eu/energy/en/topics/energy-strategy-and-energy-union/energy-securit ystrateg.

Franza, Luca. 2015. "From South Stream to Turk Stream: Prospect For Rerouting Options and Flows of Russian Gas To Parts of Europe and Turkey." *Clingendael International Energy Programme*, Accessed March 2, 2020. https://www.clingend aelenergy.com/inc/upload/files/CIEP_paper_2015-05_web_1.pdf.

Furuncu, Yunus. 2019. "Rusya Yaptırımlarının Etkileri ve Türkiye Enerji Sektörüne Yansımaları." *Siyaset, Ekonomi ve Toplum Araştırmaları Vakfı*, 298: 7–20.

Gazprom. n.d. "A New Export Gas Pipeline Running from Russia to Europe Across the Baltic Sea," Accessed April 4, 2020. https://www.gazprom.com/projects/no rd-stream2/.

Gotev, Georgi. 2019. "US Readies Sanctions Against Nord Stream 2 and Turkish Stream." *Euroactiv*, Accessed March 2, 2020. https://www.euractiv.com/section/en ergy/news/us-readies-sanctions-against-nord-stream-2-and-turkish-stream/.

Grigas, Agnia. 2013. *The Politics of Energy and Memory between the Baltic States and Russia*. Farnham: Ashgate.

Hacıtahiroğlu, Kürşad. 2014. "Küreselleşmenin Siyasal Etkileri, Göç ve Ukrayna-Rusya Krizi." *Trakya Üniversitesi Sosyal Bilimler Dergisi* 16(2): 259–284.

Hogselius, Per. 2013. *Red Gas: Russia and the Origins of European Energy Dependence*. New York: Palgrave.

Karagöl, Tanas, Erdal ve Kaya, Salihe. 2016. "LNG'nin Dünya Enerji Ticaretindeki Ticaretindeki Yeri." *Siyaset, Ekonomi ve Toplum Araştırmaları Vakfı*, Accessed April 7, 2020. https://setav.org/assets/uploads/2016/12/LNGnin-Dunya-Enerji -Ticaretindeki-Yeri-PDF.pdf.

Kaveshnikov, Nikolay. 2010. "The issue of energy security in relations between Russia and the European Union." *European Security* 19(4): 585–605.

Kirby, Paul. 2014. "Russia's Gas Fight with Ukraine." BBC NEWS, Accessed April 2, 2020. https://www.bbc.com/news/world-europe-29521564.

Koçak, Muhammed. 2015. "Bölgesel Çatışmadan Küresel Krize Doğu Ukrayna." *Siyaset, Ekonomi ve Toplum Araştırmaları Vakfı* 135: 1–29.

Kramer, E., Andrew. 2009. "Russia Cuts Off Gas Deliveries to Ukraine." *The New York Times*, Accessed April 3, 2020. https://www.nytimes.com/2009/01/02/world /europe/02gazprom.html.

Lane, Andrew. 2009. "The Nabucco Gas Pipeline: A Chance for the EU to Push for Change Turkmenistan." *The Quaker Council for European Affairs*, Accessed April 5, 2020. http://www.qcea.org/wp-content/uploads/2011/04/rprt-nabucco-en-dec -2009.pdf.

Maio, De, Giovanna. 2019. "Nord Stream 2: A failed test for EU unity and trans-Atlantic coordination." *Brookings*, Accessed April 2, 2020. https://www.brooking s.edu/blog/order-from-chaos/2019/04/22/nord-stream-2-a-failed-test-for-eu-unity-and-trans-atlantic-coordination/.

Marini, Adelina. 2014. "EU Has Circles Bulgaria on the Geopolitical Napkin." *Euinside*, Accessed March 3, 2020. http://www.euinside.eu/en/analyses/bulgaria-s outh-stream-boyko-borissov-juncker.

Markovic, Filip. 2017. "Energy strategy of Russia in the Western Balkans." *Energy and Environmental Policy Laboratory*, Accessed March 3, 2020. http://energypo licy.unipi.gr/wp-content/uploads/2017/12/Unipi_WP7_Markovi%C4%872017.p df.

Metelistsa Alexander. 2014. "Oil and Natural Gas Sales Accounted for 68% of Russia's Total Export Revenues in 2013." *U.S. Energy Information Administration*. Accessed March 8, 2020. https://www.eia.gov/todayinenergy/detail.php?id=17231.

Motyl, J., Alexander. 2015. "The West Should Arm Ukraine." *Foreign Affairs*, April 5, 2020. https://www.foreignaffairs.com/articles/russia-fsu/2015-02-10/west-sho uld-arm-ukraine.

Munteanu, Daniela and Sarno, Cıro. 2016. "South Stream and Nord Stream 2-Implications for the European Energy Security." *Analise Europeia* 2: 60–96.

Parfitt, Tom. 2006. "Russia Turns Off Supplies to Ukraine in Payment Row, and EU Feels the Chill." *The Guardian*, Accessed April 3, 2020. http://www.theguardian .com/world/2006/jan/02/russia.ukraine.

Pirani, Simon, Jonathan, Stern and Katja, Yafimava. 2009. "The Russo-Ukrainian gas dispute of January 2009: A Comprehensive Assessment." *Oxford Institute for Energy Studies*, Accessed April 3, 2020. https://www.chicagomanualofstyle.org/ tools_citationguide/citation-guide-2.html.

Ramesh, Kaavya. 2014. "The Bear Unsheathes its Energy Weapon: The Russian Gas Cutoff," *Institute for Energy Research*, Accessed April 3, 2020 http://institutefore nergyresearch.org/analysis/bear-unsheathesenergy-weapon-russian-gas-cutoff-u-s -can/.

Riley, Alan. 2012. "Commission v. Gazprom: The antitrust clash of the decade?" *CEPS Policy Brief,* 285: 1–15.

Rodova, Nadia. 2012. "Russia, Bulgaria Sign Final Investment Decision on South Stream Gas Pipeline." *S&P Global Platts*, Accessed March 11, 2020. https://ww w.spglobal.com/platts/en/market-insights/latest-news/natural-gas/111512-russia-b ulgaria-sign-final-investment-decision-on-south-stream-gas-pipeline.

Şeker, Talha, Cafer. 2019. "Avrupa Jeopolitiğinde Rus- Amerikan Rekabeti ve Almanya'nın Yükselişi." *İnsamer*, Accessed April 3, 2020. https://insamer.com/tr /avrupa-jeopolitiginde-rus-amerikan-rekabeti-ve-almanyanin-yukselisi_2530.html.

Sen, Ranjan, Sudhi. 2019. "India May Adopt New Payment Formula to Avoid US Sanctions." *Hindustan Times*, Accessed February 11, 2020. https://www.hindusta

ntimes.com/india-news/india-may-adopt-new-payment-formula-to-avoid-us-sanct ions/story-VGGvOQdM9hHX9jzhwVReQJ.html.

Serpin, Telli, Azime ve Demirtaş, Işıl. 2017. "Jeopolitik ve Jeoekonomik Perspektiften LNG- Boru Hatları Rekabetinin Avrupa Enerji Güvenliği'ne Etkileri." *Balkan Sosyal Bilimler Dergisi*, Special Issue: 48–73.

Sharples, D., Jack. 2015. "South Stream: Gazprom Abandons the Project and Announces a New Gas Pipeline to Turkey." *European Union Foreign Affairs Journal* 1: 41–55.

Shi, Chunyang. 2009. "Perspective on Natural Gas Crisis between Russia and Ukraine." *CCSE Review of European Studies* 1(1): 56–60.

Siddi, Marco. 2017a. "The EU's Gas Relationship with Russia: Solving Current Disputes and Strengthening Energy Security." *Asia Europe Journal* 15: 107–117.

Siddi, Marco. 2017b. "Identities and Vulnerabilities: The Ukraine Crisis and the Securitisation of EU–Russia Gas Trade." *Energy Security in Europe: Divergent Perceptions and Policy Challenges*, edited by Kalcper Szulecki, 251–273, Basingstoke: Palgrave Macmillan.

Siddi, Marco. 2018. "The Role of Power in EU–Russia Energy Relations: The Interplay between Markets and Geopolitics." *Europe-Asia Studies* 70(10): 1552–1571.

Sıvış, Efe (2019). Enerji Politikalarında Denge Arayışı, ABD, Rusya ve Avrupa Birliği Üçgeni: Türk Akım Projesinin Belirli Faktörleri, A*tatürk Üniversitesi Sosyal Bilimler Enstitüsü Dergisi* 23(3): 1373–1388.

Talus, Kim. 2011. "Long-term natural gas contracts and antitrust law in the European Union and the United States." *Journal of World Energy Law and Business* 4(3): 260–315.

The Council of European Union. 2014. "Official Journal of The European Union." Accessed March 21, 2020. https://eur-lex.europa.eu/LexUriServ/LexUriServ.do ?uri=OJ:L:2014:078:FULL:EN:PDF.

Vara, Vauhini. 2014. "Hurt Putin, Hurt Yourself." *The New Yorker*, April 4, 2020. https://www.newyorker.com/business/currency/hurt-putin-hurt.

Varol, Tuğçe. 2013. "The Russian Foreign Energy Policy." *European Scientific Institute*, Accessed March 5, 2020. https://eujournal.org/files/journals/1/books/Tug ceVarol.pdf.

Yafimava, Katja. 2015. "European Energy Security and the Role of Russian Gas: Assessing the Feasibility and the Rationale of Reducing Dependence." *Istituto Affari Internazionali* IAI Working Paper 15: 1–21.

Chapter 8

The Role of Human Capital and Technology in Economic Integration-Growth Nexus[1]

Fatma Didin Sönmez

INTRODUCTION

Technological progress and innovation are the main factors to increase the country's economic growth. Innovation-based policies that invest in research and development activities to generate technology creation offer greater growth potential. Endogenous innovation models include international flows of capital, goods, and knowledge (Grossman and Helpman 1994). Because trade and communication between countries have increased, technology has been disseminated and industrial research has increased. Broadly speaking, the exchange of goods and ideas has increased global interdependence (Ventura 1997). The relationship between growth and international trade, however, is not clear because of the country-specific factors. The existence of open trade and foreign markets does not guarantee success in trade-based economic growth.

The total factor productivity of a country depends on both domestic and foreign technology stock resulting from trade partnerships. Countries that import from the countries having a high level of technology exhibit higher productivity than the countries which import from countries having a low level of technology (Coe and Helpman 1995). Since the knowledge is embedded in the inputs which are imported, the technology level of trade partners is crucial in the diffusion of technology. Also, it is pointed out that a more open developing country with a more skilled labor force benefits more from foreign R&D spillovers (Coe et al., 1997).

The critical point is that there are two obstacles to the diffusion of technology. First, technology-producing countries may not be voluntary to give their innovations to other countries. Second, the domestic capacity of countries

123

may be insufficient to take innovations from technology-producing countries. If technology is a free good for every country, economies need to implement the most effective policies to make domestic resources capable of technology spillover. Additionally, the effects of R&D spillover on the other factors of production should be taken into account. For instance, R&D spillover may urge the cost of production in some countries. Success in technology transfer has been varied, and it has been affected by institutional factors and policies. Thus, even if the technology is accessible for every country through international trade, the benefits of technological change may not be the same for all countries.

Human capital is an important factor that can favor or limit to exploit their growth potential because it determines the ability to absorb knowledge spillovers from abroad. Productivity differences among the countries are explained by technological mismatches (Acemoğlu and Zilibotti 2001). Using the same technology by both developed and less developed countries causes a technological mismatch resulting in productivity differences. Even if the technology is accessible for every country, less developed countries use unskilled workers in tasks performed by skilled workers in developed countries.

The purpose of this study is to analyze the impact of economic integration between developed and developing countries on the rate of economic growth, human capital allocation across sectors, and technological change. The model is expanded on Romer's expanding variety of product model by considering an open economy and including new variables affecting domestic technology accumulation (Romer 1990). There are some other papers in the literature presenting models similar to Romer's version of the economic growth model. Rivera-Batiz and Romer (1991) focus on the integration between countries with similar endowments and technologies. Rivera-Batiz and Xie (1993) analyze the effects of integration for the countries that have different endowments. Frenkel and Trauth (1997) explore the effects of the economic integration of countries that have different time preference rates or productivity parameters of human capital in R&D.

This chapter extends them in a different direction. The model is including a fixed cost of using foreign technology which is available for everybody. Also, it is important to say that since this study does not include imitation, it is crucially different from North-South models of growth explaining the effect of trade between developing and developed countries. This study uses the two-country model of technological change with the expansionary variety of production. The model suggests that integration changes the allocation of human capital and technological activities, and human capital is the most important factor to benefit from integration. Thus, the chapter is developed on the basic question of how developing countries can benefit from foreign technological knowledge flow available with integration. If the level of foreign technology is relatively higher than the level of domestic technology, knowledge produced by foreign technology leads to technological progress. However, it is important to note that human capital devoted to the research sector should have minimum requirements to use foreign technology and the share of this type of human capital is crucial. As in the other papers, integration makes foreign technology as completely available, but in this study, using this technology is not costless. Developing countries that have not human capital skilled enough to use developed countries' technology have to pay a fixed cost such as training costs.

The rest of this study contains three sections. Section 2 presents the model of Rivera-Batiz and Xie (1993) as a benchmark case and analyzes the steady-state behavior of the economy. Section 3 describes the model in which using technology requires a fixed cost and presents the steady-state analysis. It compares two different models and shows how fixed cost paid by developing country affects the human capital allocation and economic growth rate. Section 4 concludes the chapter.

THE EXPANDING VARIETY OF PRODUCT MODEL

The model with an expanding variety of products builds on Romer's model of endogenous growth (Romer 1990). Consider the economic integration of the two countries. Each country has one final good which is not tradable for the foreign country and three factors of production; human capital, unskilled labor, and intermediate goods. There are two possible uses of the final good: producing intermediate goods and producing consumption goods. It is assumed that the manufacturing sector uses the same technology for both types of final goods. Moreover, intermediate goods are assumed to be non-durable for simplicity.

In the model, technological advance comes from a sector that produces ideas. In this model, knowledge enters production in two different ways. A new design allows the production of new intermediate input. Also, a new design increases the total stock of knowledge and productivity of human capital. If the firm owns a new idea, it has some property rights to produce new durables but not over its use in research.

Intermediate goods are tradable and technological flow across the countries is allowed. There is an asymmetry between the knowledge stocks of two different countries. Also, the sources of knowledge processes are different. Since both countries have distinct knowledge stocks, there is no redundancy in this model. Thus, in contrast to the closed economy model, a country may increase research activities leading higher growth rate with the research activities of other countries.

Another assumption for simplicity is that there is no labor mobility across the countries. While the research sector uses only human capital, the manufacturing sector uses both human capital and unskilled labor. Also, aggregate unskilled labor and total human capital are constant.

Following the previous studies (Rivera-Batiz and Romer, 1991; Rivera-Batiz and Xie, 1993), the Cobb–Douglas production function is

$$Y\left(H_Y, L_u, x, m\right) = H_Y^\alpha L_u^\beta \left[\int_0^N x_i^{1-\alpha-\beta} di + \int_0^{N^*} m_i^{1-\alpha-\beta} di \right] \quad (8.1),$$

where Y is the final domestic output. H_Y and L_u denote human capital devoted to the final good sector and unskilled labor, respectively. Output also depends on domestically produced nondurable goods, x_i, and imported nondurable goods, m_i. Asterisks represent the variables for a foreign country. N denotes the most recently invented goods in the country, and it gives the number of available types of intermediate goods. Since technological progress takes the form of expansions in the number of available intermediate goods, new designs lead to more differentiated goods and thus higher productivity in the final good sector. It is also assumed that the foreign country has the same production technology.

The model includes knowledge-driven specification of R&D. Thus, accumulation of new designs is provided by the human capital and existing stock of knowledge determined by both domestic and foreign research sectors. Profit-seeking private R&D sector producing new designs is crucial for growth. Since the exchange of technological knowledge is available between two countries and using all available knowledge stock is costless, in the domestic research sector, the production function of new designs is

$$\dot{N} = \delta H_R \left(N + N^* \right) \quad (8.2),$$

where δ is a constant productivity parameter and H_R denotes human capital devoted to the research sector. Equation (8.2) implies that an increase in human capital in the research sector leads to an increase in the rate of production of new designs and the greater total stock of knowledge as in Romer's model. It also infers that higher knowledge stock leads to higher productivity in the research sector. Hence, the technology stock of partner in the integration is very important. But still, it is possible to say that integration leads to a higher growth rate in both countries.

Since $N^* \neq N$ such that $N^* / N \equiv \lambda$, the growth rate of technology in the domestic country is as the following,

$$\frac{\dot{N}}{N} = g = \delta H_R \left(1 + \lambda\right) \tag{8.3}$$

It is assumed that the home country is the developing country and the foreign country is the developed country, so $\lambda > 1$.

2.1 Market Structure

In the model, intermediate goods are produced by a monopolist who buys a patent from an R&D enterprise and produces intermediate goods for final good manufacturers willing to pay a price that is equal to the marginal product of domestic intermediate good. If a manufacturer is able to pay the patent price which is a kind of fixed cost, it will be a monopolist and get a monopoly rent.

Since both countries have identical mark-up parameters, the price of the intermediate good is identical in these two countries $p = p^*$. The total demand for domestic intermediate good, X, is the summation of domestic and foreign demand. Assuming equal endowment for unskilled labor in each country, first-order conditions and mark-up price, $p = 1/\left(1 - \alpha - \beta\right)$, yield the total demand for domestic intermediate goods as,

$$X = \left(1 - \alpha - \beta\right)^{2/(\alpha+\beta)} H_Y^{\alpha/(\alpha+\beta)} \left[1 + \gamma^{\alpha/(\alpha+\beta)}\right] L_u^{\beta/(\alpha+\beta)} \tag{8.4},$$

where $\gamma \equiv H_Y^* / H_Y$ and $\gamma < 1$. Thus, total demand for domestic intermediate goods depends on human capital allocation in both domestic and foreign countries.

Since the opportunity cost of producing one unit of intermediate good is one unit of consumption good which is sold at unit price, the profit of intermediate good producer is

$$\pi = \left(\alpha + \beta\right)\left(1 - \alpha - \beta\right)^{2-\alpha-\beta/(\alpha+\beta)} H_Y^{\alpha/(\alpha+\beta)} \left[1 + \gamma^{\alpha/(u+\beta)}\right] L_u^{\beta/(\alpha+\beta)} \tag{8.5}$$

Since $1 + \gamma^{\alpha/(\alpha+\beta)} > 1$, integration leads to higher profit because of higher demand.

Monopolist buying a patent to produce intermediate good maximizes the present value of its profit. Symmetry assumption allows us to write a common value of all patents. If the patent price is less than the value of the firm, an infinite amount of resources would be devoted to R&D, and if the patent price is higher than the value of the firm, there would be no incentives to use resources for R&D (Barro and Sala-I Martin, 2004). In the equilibrium, firms are willing to pay the patent price for design, P_N, if the following equality holds

$$P_N = V(0) = \int_0^\infty \frac{(\alpha + \beta)}{(1 - \alpha - \beta)} X e^{-\bar{r}t} dt \tag{8.6}$$

Differentiating the free entry condition with respect to time obtains,

$$r = \frac{\pi}{V} + \frac{\dot{V}}{V} \tag{8.7}$$

This is the key arbitrage condition of the model with expanding variety as it is derived by the previous studies. Therefore, the R&D rate of return which is interpreted as the interest rate is the summation of profit rate and rate of the capital gain or loss from change in the value of the firm.

2.2 Labor Market

Labor market equilibrium requires full employment of unskilled labor and human capital. Assuming a competitive labor market, human capital in the research sector is paid at the same wage as in the final good sector. Wage is determined by using the marginal product of human capitals in both sectors. Thus, the wages in each sector are

$$W_{H_Y} = \alpha H_Y^{\alpha-1} L_u^\beta \left[N \left(x^{1-\alpha-\beta} + \lambda m^{1-\alpha-\beta} \right) \right] \tag{8.8}$$

$$W_{H_R} = P_N N \left[\delta (1 + \lambda) \right] \tag{8.9}$$

Wages in both sectors should be the same to get the equilibrium for the human capital market and make both sectors active. Substituting the demand function of intermediate goods imported from abroad into equation (8.8) and equalization of the wages in the research sector and final good sector yield P_N as

$$P_N = \alpha (1 - \alpha - \beta)^{2(1-\alpha-\beta)/(\alpha+\beta)} H_Y^{-\beta/(\alpha+\beta)} L_u^{\beta/(\alpha+\beta)} \frac{1}{\delta} \tag{8.10}$$

Since integration increases productivity in both sectors by $(1 + \lambda)$, in the model patent price depends on just human capital allocation as in the case of the closed economy but not on the technology stock.

2.3 Households

A representative infinitely lived household chooses optimal consumption. The preferences of each identical individual are demonstrated by the utility function which has discounted constant elasticity preferences as the following,

$$U\left[C(.)\right] = \int_0^\infty e^{-\rho t} \frac{C(t)^{1-\sigma} - 1}{1-\sigma} dt \qquad (8.11),$$

where $\sigma > 0$ is the inverse of the intertemporal elasticity of substitution, C is consumption and ρ is the rate of time discount. At each point in time, the budget constraint for the representative household is

$$\dot{a} = ar + w - c \qquad (8.12),$$

where a, w and r denote existing assets, income and world interest rate, respectively. It is assumed that domestic and foreign claims on financial assets are perfect substitutes, and thus each country has the same interest rate. Therefore, equation (8.12) implies that the change in the stock of real assets held by the household is equal to the difference between the current flow of earnings and current consumption.

The equilibrium for the financial market also requires equality between the total value of the security held by the households and the total value of security issued by the firms. Assuming trade balance which gives zero foreign debt, thus

$$aL = NV \qquad (8.13),$$

where V is the stock market value of each firm which is equal to the present value of the firms' profit.

The household chooses an optimal path for consumption to maximize equation (8.11) subject to equation (8.12). The intertemporal optimization condition is as the following,

$$r_p = \sigma \frac{\dot{C}}{C} + \rho \qquad (8.14)$$

Equation (8.14) implies that an increase in interest rate leads to a higher incentive for consumption in the future.

2.4 Steady-state Analysis

In balanced growth equilibrium, the production and profits of the firms are constant over time. Using profit function in equation (8.5) and patent price in equation (8.10), the interest rate at the steady state is

$$r_t = \frac{\pi}{P_N} = \Lambda^{-1}\left(1 + \gamma^{\alpha/(\alpha+\beta)}\right)\delta H_Y \qquad (8.15),$$

where $\Lambda = \dfrac{\alpha}{(\alpha+\beta)(1-\alpha-\beta)}$.

Thus, the human capital devoted to the final good sector is

$$H_Y = \Lambda \frac{1}{\left(1+\gamma^{\alpha/(\alpha+\beta)}\right)\delta} r_t \qquad (8.16)$$

A higher interest rate leads to a lower discounted present value of profit which equals to patent price. Since a decrease in patent price brings a decline in the marginal product of human capital in the research sector, the economy has more human capital working in the manufacturing sector and less human capital working in the research sector in the case of the higher interest rate. Thus, interest rate is negatively related to the growth rate of technology.

The domestic economy's human capital devoted to the final good sector decreases by $\left(1+\gamma^{\alpha/(\alpha+\beta)}\right)$ after integration because of the market size effect. This means that economy has more human capital working in the research sector after integration than it has before. This is because an increase in market size raises profits leading to higher patent price. An increase in patent price which corresponds to an increase in the marginal product of human capital employed in the research sector leads to a higher wage for them. Thus, integration induces a shift of human capital toward the research sector. Integration also changes the foreign country's human capital allocation by increasing human capital in the research sector by $\left(1+\gamma^{-\alpha/(\alpha+\beta)}\right)$. The technology equilibrium gives

$$r_t = \frac{\delta}{\Lambda}\left(1+\gamma^{\alpha/(\alpha+\beta)}\right)\left(H-H_R\right) \qquad (8.17)$$

Since, under balanced growth, consumption, production, and technical knowledge grow at the same constant rate, equations (8.3) and (8.14) obtain,

$$r_p = \rho + \sigma\delta H_R\left(1+\lambda\right) \qquad (8.18)$$

Thus, the balanced growth rate for the domestic economy specified with the knowledge-driven model is determined by the intersection of equations (8.17) and (8.18). As it is mentioned before, the market size effect leads to more human capital in the research sector, but an increase in human capital employed in the research sector and productivity effects coming from a high level of available technology stock induce a higher steady-state growth rate which, in turn, increases the interest rate. Since the interest rate is negatively related to the number of human capital in the research sector, the primary effect is partially reversed (Frenkel and Trauth, 1997).

Equations (8.3) and (8.18) give the steady-state level of growth rate as,

$$g = \frac{\left[\frac{\delta}{\Lambda}\left(1 + \gamma^{\alpha/(\alpha+\beta)}\right)\right]H - \rho}{\frac{1}{\Lambda}\frac{1 + \gamma^{\alpha/(\alpha+\beta)}}{1 + \lambda} + \sigma} \tag{8.19}$$

Similarly, the growth rate of the foreign country is

$$g^* = \frac{\left[\frac{\delta^*}{\Lambda}\left(1 + \gamma^{-\alpha/(\alpha+\beta)}\right)\right]H^* - \rho}{\frac{1}{\Lambda}\frac{1 + \gamma^{-\alpha/(\alpha+\beta)}}{1 + \lambda^{-1}} + \sigma} \tag{8.20}$$

Equations (8.19) and (8.20) imply that market size effect is larger in the foreign country than in the domestic country. On the other hand, productivity effect coming from greater technology stock available with integration is higher in the domestic research sector than in the foreign research sector.

EFFECTS OF INTEGRATION WITH COSTLY TECHNOLOGY

The model in this study uses the same definition of technology as it is in the model presented in section 2. Technology is a public good that is free for everybody. It is free to take it, but it is not free to use in this section.

Imagine that a developing country integrated with a developed country that has higher technology stock than it has. Since the developing country's human capital is not skilled enough to use this technology, it needs to pay a fixed cost. Since this fixed cost is a kind of training cost to make human capital capable of using new technology stock produced by the developed country, it is inserted into the model in the unit of human capital. Thus, this is a kind of fixed cost that is not paid in cash. The economy pays this cost by losing some working hours of human capital employed in the research sector.

Although the model in this study is structurally very similar to the model of Rivera-Batiz and Xie (1993), it uses the idea that using technology is not costless and fixed cost paid by developing country affects human capital allocations and growth rates of both countries after integration. Thus, the effect of integration on growth is determined not only by human capital allocation and technology stock, but it is also determined by the capability of human capital to use all available technology stock. Countries should invest in R&D at least to make the research sector capable to use foreign technology that is available with integration. It emphasizes the idea that policies should consider not only the amount of human capital, but quality of human capital is also crucial.

This model produces different theoretical results in the study of growth and integration nexus. It is possible to say that integration may decrease the growth rate of the economy by slowing down the growth rate of technology, because positive growth effects of integration may be reversed by the cost of technology available with integration. As in the other papers, it is concluded that because of the market size effect, integration induces human capital employed in the manufacturing sector to shift toward research sector producing technology. However, the model also suggests that integration may lead to a decrease in human capital in the research sector. Human capital allocation is determined by the market size effect, the domestic human capital ability which determines the level of the fixed cost required and the number of researchers and it is ambiguous in this kind of model. Thus, this study suggests that integration may lead to a higher cost than its benefit.

Additionally, unlike the previous studies, patent price depends not only on human capital allocation; it also depends on the growth rate of both countries. This is because if fixed cost is very high, there is a possibility that the growth rate of patent price might be negatively related to the growth rate of human capital devoted to the research sector. Thus, the relationship between the growth rate of human capital in the research sector and the growth rate of technology is conditional.

If The Country Pays the Fixed Cost

Since the developing country has not human capital skilled enough to use the developed country's technology, it has to pay a fixed cost in the unit of human capital. The technology stock available with integration is not costless anymore in this section. Technological change is

$$\dot{N}(t) = \delta\big(H_R(t) - \phi\big)\big(N(t) + N^*(t)\big) \tag{8.21}$$

Equation (8.21) and the expression $N^*(t)/N(t) \equiv \lambda(t)$ obtain the growth rate of technology as

$$\frac{\dot{N}(t)}{N(t)} = g(t) = \delta\big(H_R(t) - \phi\big)\big(1 + \lambda(t)\big) \tag{8.22}$$

If the quality of human capital is very low comparing to foreign human capital, they need to spend a lot of time to make them capable to use foreign technology instead of producing. Thus, higher fixed cost means less human capital working actively to produce technology. Integration may decrease the growth rate of technology if the economy pays a very high fixed cost and productivity and market size effects which are discussed in section 2 are not high enough to compensate for this fixed cost.

To make both sectors active, human capitals in both sectors are paid at the same wage. Since the research sector has total revenue that equals the total cost of technological change, the wage equations derived in section 2 and the definition of technological growth rate yield,

$$P_N(t) = \frac{1}{\dfrac{\dot{N}(t)}{N(t)}} \alpha\big(1 + \lambda(t)\big)\big(1 - \alpha - \beta\big)^{2(1-\alpha-\beta)/(\alpha+\beta)} \tag{8.23},$$

$$\big(1 - s\big)^{\beta/(\alpha+\beta)} s^{\alpha/(\alpha+\beta)} \big(1 - u(t)\big)^{-\beta/(\alpha+\beta)} u(t) L$$

where s is the fraction of human capital in total population and u is the fraction of human capital devoted to the research sector in total human capital. Since fixed cost is in the model now, patent price does not depend on only human capital allocation as it is discussed in section 2, but it also depends on the growth rate of technology and productivity effect of integration. A higher growth rate decreases the average cost of human capital which, in turn, decreases the patent price. On the other hand, higher foreign knowledge stock generates higher productivity in the domestic research sector leading to higher wage and thus higher patent price.

At the steady state, key arbitrage condition yields,

$$r_t = \frac{\pi(t)}{P_N(t)} = \frac{(\alpha+\beta)(1-\alpha-\beta)}{\alpha} \frac{1-u(t)}{u(t)} \frac{\left(1 + \gamma(t)^{\alpha/(\alpha+\beta)}\right)}{\big(1+\lambda(t)\big)} \frac{\dot{N}(t)}{N(t)} \tag{8.24}$$

The profit rate is increased by the market size effect and the growth rate of technology while it is decreased by the productivity effect.

Thus, technology equilibrium gives,

$$r_t = \Lambda^{-1}\delta\left(1+\gamma(t)^{\alpha/(\alpha+\beta)}\right)(H-H_R)\frac{(H_R-\phi)}{H_R} \qquad (8.25)$$

As it is discussed in section 2, because of the market size effect, integration induces human capital employed in the manufacturing sector to shift toward the research sector by $1+\gamma^{\alpha/(\alpha+\beta)}$ which is greater than 1. In the model including fixed cost, the effect of integration on the allocation of human capital is reduced by the ratio of human capital employed in the research sector to human capital working actively to produce technology. This suggests that integration may lead to a decrease in human capital in the research sector. Human capital allocation determined by market size effect, domestic human capital ability and number of researchers is ambiguous in the model.

If the Country Cannot Pay the Fixed Cost

Suppose that the developing country has not enough human capital employed in the research sector to pay a high level of fixed cost. After integration, it uses just domestic technology, while the developed country uses all available technology. Thus, the production function of new designs in the domestic country is

$$\dot{N} = \delta H_R N \qquad (8.26)$$

In this case, the integration creates a productivity effect in the research sector of a foreign country but not in the domestic county. Even if taking foreign technology is free for every country, using this technology is very expensive for the domestic country that is not able to pay it.

As it is derived in the previous section, equalization of wage in the manufacturing sector to wage in the research sector yields the patent price. Since integration increases productivity just in the manufacturing sector by $(1+\lambda)$, now patent price depends on human capital allocation and also the ratio of knowledge stocks of both countries. Human capital devoted to the final good sector at the steady state is

$$H_Y = \Lambda\frac{(1+\lambda)}{\left(1+\gamma^{\alpha/(\alpha+\beta)}\right)\delta}r_t \qquad (8.27)$$

While the market size effect decreases human capital employed in the manufacturing sector, productivity effect increases human capital employed in the manufacturing sector. Since $\gamma < 1$ and $\lambda > 1$, integration induces human capital to shift toward the manufacturing sector.

Thus, the technology equilibrium is given as

$$r_t = \frac{\delta}{\Lambda} \frac{\left(1 + \gamma^{\alpha/(\alpha+\beta)}\right)}{(1+\lambda)} (H - H_R) \tag{8.28}$$

3.3 Allocations of Human Capital with Different Models

Equation (8.25) gives r_t curve for the country which can pay the fixed cost and uses all available technology. Equation (8.28) gives r_t curve for the country which has not enough human capital in the research sector to pay the fixed cost and uses only domestic technology stock in its research sector. Figure 8.1 presents these two curves and compares them with the curve under autarky. The thin line represents the case of autarky. The thick lines represent the case of integration with the fixed cost. Since the

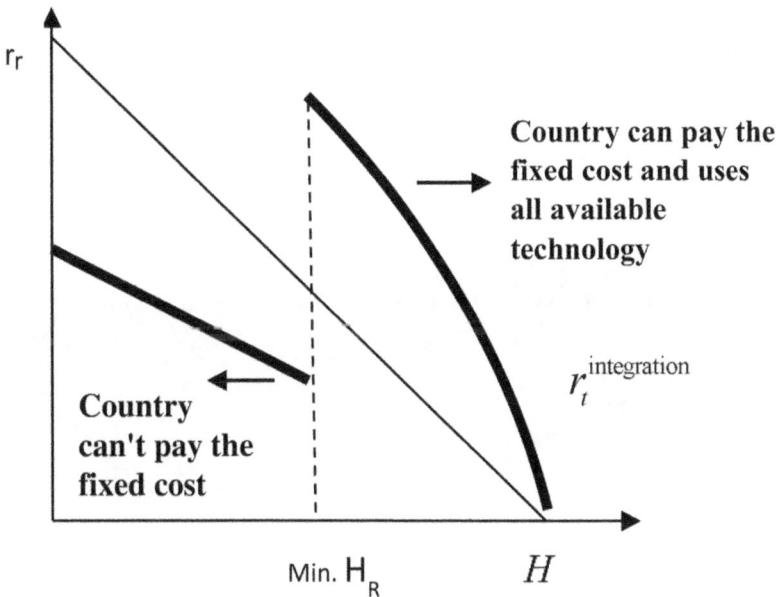

Figure 8.1 **Autarky and Integration Leading to More Human Capital in the Research Sector.** *Source*: Created by the author based on the model derived.

economy needs to have the minimum amount of human capital employed in the research sector to use foreign technology, below this minimum level, equation (8.28) is used to drive the relationship between the interest rate and human capital allocation. If the economy has human capital above this threshold level, this relationship is determined by equation (8.25). Assuming that the market size effect is larger than the effect of adaptation cost, human capital in the research sector is higher in the case of integration than in the case of autarky (figure 8.1).

There is a possibility that the economy may have less human capital in the research sector after integration, even if the economy can afford the fixed cost and use foreign technology. If expansion in the market with integration leads to shifting less human capital than the fraction of human capital actively producing technology in total human capital devoted to producing technology, for a given level of interest rate economy has more human capital in the manufacturing sector than it has under autarky. Figure 8.2 illustrates this case and shows how r_t curve shifts to left.

After integration, how much r_t curve shifts to left depends on market size effect and fixed cost. Figure 8.3 demonstrates the case in which $(1+\lambda) < H_R / (H_R - \phi)$, thus economy has a larger negative effect on human capital allocation to the research sector.

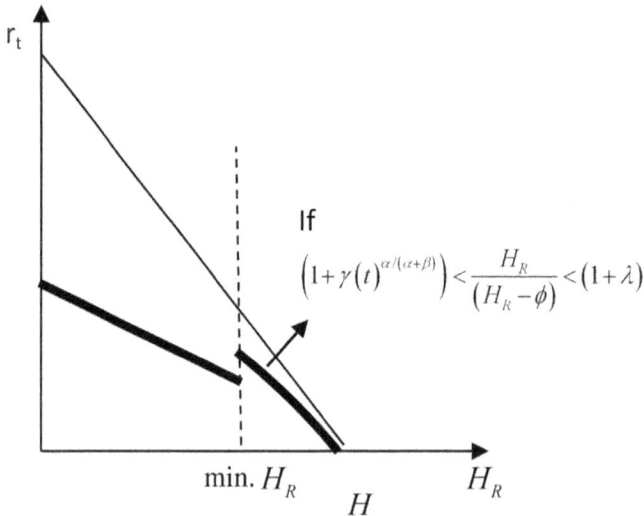

If
$$\left(1+\gamma(t)^{\alpha/(\alpha+\beta)}\right) < \frac{H_R}{(H_R-\phi)} < (1+\lambda)$$

Figure 8.2 Autarky and Integration Leading to Less Human Capital in the Research Sector. *Source*: Created by the author based on the model derived.

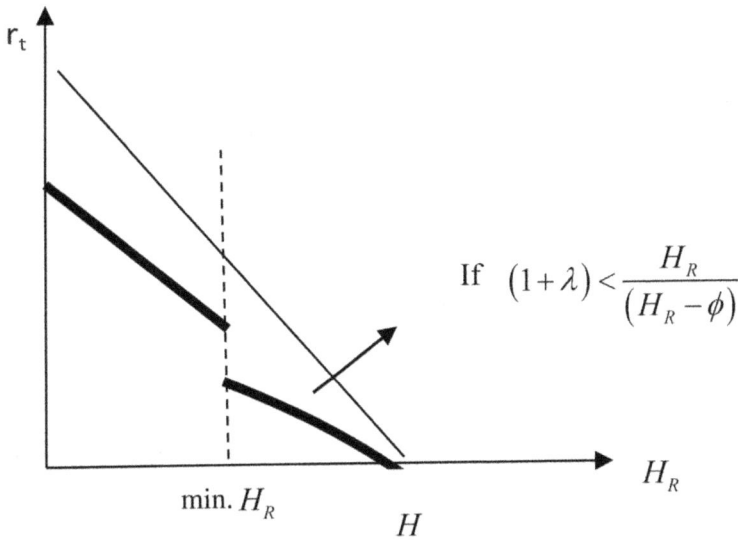

Figure 8.3 Market Size Effect Reduced More by Fixed Cost. *Source*: Created by the author based on the model derived.

Steady-State Level of Growth Rate

Consider a developing country that has enough human capital in the research sector to use foreign technology. Also, suppose that the foreign country has human capital skilled enough for using all available technology, and thus, it does not pay any fixed training cost,

Since r_t should be equal to r_p from equation (8.14) derived in section 2 and consumption grows at the same rate of technological growth at the steady state,

$$g = \frac{\dfrac{\delta}{\Lambda}\left(1+\gamma^{\alpha/(\alpha+\beta)}\right)(H-\phi)\dfrac{(H_R-\phi)}{H_R}-\rho}{\dfrac{1}{\Lambda}\dfrac{1+\gamma^{\alpha/(\alpha+\beta)}}{1+\lambda}\dfrac{(H_R-\phi)}{H_R}+\sigma} \tag{8.29}$$

Equation (8.29) shows the equilibrium growth rate of the developing country which has enough human capital in the research sector to use costly foreign technology. It implies that the effect of integration on economic growth is ambiguous.

Also, the equilibrium growth rate for the developing country which does not have enough human capital in the research sector to use foreign technology is,

$$
g = \frac{\dfrac{\delta H}{\Lambda} \dfrac{\left(1 + \gamma^{\alpha/(\alpha+\beta)}\right)}{(1+\lambda)} - \rho}{\dfrac{1}{\Lambda} \dfrac{\left(1 + \gamma^{\alpha/(\alpha+\beta)}\right)}{(1+\lambda)} + \sigma}
\tag{8.30}
$$

If the developing country cannot afford the fixed cost, it cannot use foreign technology. However, it is importing foreign intermediate goods which lead to higher productivity in the manufacturing sector by more differentiated products. Higher productivity in the manufacturing sector decreases the effects of expanding in market size.

CONCLUSION

The model mentions that even if foreign countries producing technology are voluntary to give their innovations, the domestic capacity of countries may be insufficient to use them. This idea is represented by inserting a fixed cost into the model. If the human capital is not capable of using foreign technology, it will take time to adapt its human capital to foreign technology. Low-quality human capital brings a high level of fixed cost corresponding to more time in training. Thus, human capital working actively in the research sector may decrease after integration.

This idea produces different results for the nexus between economic growth and integration. It is possible to say that integration may decrease the growth rate of the economy by slowing down the growth rate of technology, and positive growth effects of integration may be reversed by the cost of technology available with integration.

As in the other studies, integration induces human capital employed in the manufacturing sector to shift toward research sector producing technology because of the market size effect. However, in the model with a fixed cost, the effect of integration on the allocation of human capital is reduced by the ratio of human capital employed in the research sector to human capital working actively to produce technology. The model suggests that integration may lead to a decrease in human capital in the research sector. Human capital allocation is determined by the market size effect, the domestic human capital ability which determines the level of fixed cost required and the number of researchers. It is ambiguous in this kind of model, and the results are conditional.

Also, the foreign country's human capital and knowledge stock are important for the integration-growth nexus. The model shows that integration with a more developed country does not always mean a higher growth rate. Domestic country capacity in terms of human capital and knowledge stock needs to be sufficient to use all technology available with integration. If the domestic capacity is not enough and the economy pays a high level of fixed cost, economic integration may lead to a higher cost than its benefit.

To understand the main idea summarized above, this study exercises different types of countries. First of all, consider a developing country that has not enough human capital employed in the research sector to pay the fixed cost required for using foreign technology. Thus, this country cannot use foreign technology available with integration. In this kind of integration, while the market size effect decreases human capital employed in the manufacturing sector, the productivity effect increases human capital employed in the manufacturing sector. Since the model suggests that the productivity effect is higher than the market size effect, integration induces human capital to shift toward the manufacturing sector. Less human capital in the research sector means a lower growth rate of technology and thus lower economic growth.

Second, suppose that economy has human capital above the minimum level which is required to pay the fixed cost. Even if foreign technology is also available in the domestic research sector, it is not possible to say that integration always leads to an increase in economic growth. The model demonstrates that if expansion in the market with integration leads to shifting less human capital than the fraction of human capital actively producing technology in total human capital devoted to producing technology, for a given level of interest rate economy has more human capital in the manufacturing sector than it has under autarky. Thus, the model shows that every integration does not induce human capital toward the research sector producing technology. Reduction in human capital working in the research sector depends on market size effect, productivity effect, and fixed cost of integration. In this sense, the effects of integration on human capital allocation and economic growth are ambiguous. The effect of integration varies across countries that are differentiated in terms of their human capital and knowledge stock.

These two different exercises discussed above give some results to develop policies for economic growth. The first exercise produces a result that countries should invest in R&D at least to make the research sector capable to use foreign technology which is available with integration. In other words, if the country does not have enough research and development activity before integration, it will not benefit from integration in terms of economic growth. The second exercise emphasizes the idea that policies should consider not only the amount of human capital, but quality of human capital is also crucial. The model includes the fixed cost as an exogenous variable which is given to make the model simple. However, it is important to say that low-quality human capital needs a high level of fixed cost. The model suggests that if the country does not have human capital skilled enough to use foreign technology produced by the developed country, integration may not lead to higher economic growth.

In this study, unlike the first model without cost, patent price depends not only on human capital allocation; it also depends on the growth rate of both countries. Mathematically, it provides that if fixed cost is very high, there is a possibility that the growth rate of patent price might be negatively related to the growth rate of human capital devoted to the research sector. Therefore, the relationship between the growth rate of human capital in the research sector and the growth rate of technology is conditional.

In short, high adaptation costs in the research sector resulting from less capable human capital and low knowledge stock reduce the production of domestic technology and knowledge. This makes developing countries dependent on high-tech imported intermediate goods. Many developing countries use human capital mostly for the manufacturing sector instead of research and innovations. Economic integration is deepening by importing intermediate goods, but this is decreasing even more human capital working in the research sector. In order to overcome this problem, the developing country needs to invest in the research sector to increase its capacity and make the foreign knowledge and technology accumulation available at a low level of cost.

NOTE

1. This chapter is extracted from author's doctorate dissertation entitled "Integration and Growth: The Role of Human Capital and Technology."

REFERENCES

Acemoglu, D. and Zilibotti, F., 2001. Productivity Differences. *The Quarterly Journal of Economics* 116, no. 2: 563–606.
Barro, R. and Sala-i-Martin, X., 2004. *Economic Growth*. London: MIT Press, pp. 293–294.
Coe, D. and Helpman, E., 1995. International R&D spillovers. *European Economic Review* 39, no. 5: 859–887.
Coe, D., Helpman, E. and Hoffmaister, A., 1997. North-South R & D Spillovers. *The Economic Journal* 107, no. 440: 134–149.

Frenkel, M. and Trauth, T., 1997. Growth Effects of Integration Among Unequal Countries. *Global Finance Journal* 8(1): 113–128.

Grossman, G. and Helpman, E., 1994. Endogenous Innovation in the Theory of Growth. *Journal of Economic Perspectives* 8, no. 1: 23–44.

Rivera-Batiz, L. and Romer, P., 1991. Economic Integration and Endogenous Growth. *The Quarterly Journal of Economics* 106, no. 2: 531–555.

Rivera-Batiz, L. and Xie, D., 1993. Integration Among Unequals. *Regional Science and Urban Economics* 23, no. 3: 337–354.

Romer, P., 1990. Endogenous Technological Change. *Journal of Political Economy* 98, no. 5:71–102.

Ventura, J.,1997. Growth and Interdependence. *Quarterly Journal of Economics* 112: 57–84.

Chapter 9

Dynamics of University-Industry Knowledge Transfer in a Global Economy

Çağla Özgören

INTRODUCTION

Over recent decades, shifting paradigms through the introduction of neoliberal policies, have led universities to focus on revenue generation from industry engagement, the so-called third mission, in addition to research and teaching missions. The role and mission of universities have evolved toward being more responsible not only to meet the educational need of wider society but also to foster innovation through knowledge transfer (KT) mechanisms from university to industry to gain a competitive advantage in a global economy (Audretsch, Lehmann and Wright 2014). More specifically, as a prerequisite of the knowledge-based economy, this new role questioned the universities' market impact and their role in regional and national economic growth, as well as their importance in terms of creation of public value such as advancing life standards in the areas of health, education, leisure, safety, among others (Bozeman, Rimes, and Youtie 2015), which could be achieved through effective KT mechanisms from universities to industry and vice versa.

In this line, there is a growing, but the heterogeneous body of work in the area of knowledge exchange (KE) mechanisms between the university and industry. One strand of this literature is concerned with the determinants for the effectiveness of technology transfer. This strand aims to unpack characteristics of the industry—such as emergent or mature (e.g., Bodas-Freitas, Marques, and eSilva 2013b), characteristics of a firm—such as size, technology openness (e.g., Bodas-Freitas, Geuna, and Rosi 2013a), research orientation of universities (e.g., Hewitt-Dundas, Gkypali, and Roper 2012), the existence of university policies and procedures (e.g., Caldera and Debande 2010), geographical proximity between university and industry partners (e.g.,

Brostrom 2010), governance of intermediary organizations (Siegel, Waldman and Link 2003), as well as the role of third-party funding (e.g., Bolli and Somogyi, 2011) in this process. Another strand of this literature relies on the motivations for academic entrepreneurship (e.g., Arque-Castells et al. 2016). On the other hand, numerous studies also demonstrate outcomes of effective technology transfer in terms of regional or national innovation systems (e.g., Cowan and Zinovyeva 2013), acknowledging its importance in creating a "knowledge-based society," and bestowing competitive advantage (e.g., Audretsch, Lehmann, and Wright 2014).

Although current scholarship provides insights on the different aspects of this subject, we have a fragmented understanding of the main motives, success, and outcomes of the knowledge interaction between university and industry. Some review articles aggregate the body of work on university-industry relations (e.g., Perkmann et al. 2013; Perkmann, Salandra, and Tartari 2021; Skute et al. 2019). For example, covering 2011 onward, the most updated review is conducted by Perkmann, Salandra, and Tartari (2021). They provide a systematic review of the antecedents of academic engagement and its consequences on scientists' research productivity and research agenda. Another systematic review on university-industry relations is conducted by Skute et al. (2019), who systematically cluster papers on this topic through conducting the quantitative bibliometric analysis of 435 peer-reviewed articles published from 2011 to 2016. They provide six clusters of papers in the university-industry relations: ecosystem perspective, social relation perspective, academic entrepreneurship perspective, distance perspective, interaction process and KT perspective, policy implications on university engagement perspective. These works are crucial in gaining better insights on the comprehensive view and enhancing the current state of knowledge in the field of university-industry relations, however, lack of providing insights on firm-level drivers of effective technology transfer, and broader level consequences, which is complemented in this work.

Drawing on a critical review of peer-reviewed articles on university-industry relations from 2010 to 2020, this chapter undertakes a broader view of scholarship on university-industry relations through integrating firm-level drivers and the broader level consequences of effective technology transfer, which are neglected in the previous works. Documenting the literature on the antecedents that lead firms to engage with universities and broader level impact of effective KT is cardinal in piecing together a two-pronged aspect of university-industry relations, which is complemented in this study.

In doing so, I seek to provide a not only comprehensive and integrative view on the subject through unpacking dynamics of KT mechanisms in university-industry relations, with a particular focus on macro-, meso-, and micro-level drivers for academic engagement involving perspectives on both academia and industry, but also delineate the impact of technology transfer for firms' innovativeness, regional and national economic growth, and society at large. In doing so, this book chapter contributes to the ongoing conversation on KT mechanisms through mapping a multilayered picture of KE mechanisms and providing avenues for future KE research.

The rest of this book chapter is organized as follows: Section 2 provides an overview of KE channels. This is followed by the review process section. Subsequent six subsections discuss relevant scholarly work on macro, meso, and micro drivers of KE, as well as implications of KE for the firm and regional/national development. Macro-level drivers of university-industry relations are mainly related to the regulative and normative technology transfer mechanisms at national and regional levels and industry-specific regulations and norms. These are discussed under the subsection 4.1. Meso-level drivers of technology transfer are associated with university-related drivers such as university characterizations and support, and intermediary organizations such as technology transfer offices (TTOs), incubators, accelerators, and science parks, as well as firm-level drivers, which are other prongs of KE mechanism. These are pertinent to subsections 4.2., 4.3., 4.4. Last, micro-level determinants are mainly related to the motivations of academics in engaging with industry and discussed in the subsection 4.5. On the other hand, subsection 4.6. discusses the consequences of effective KE. Section 5 concludes.

KNOWLEDGE EXCHANGE CHANNELS

The literature on university-industry relations is broad, since there are a variety of ways in which universities collaborate with industry partners and engage in KE activities. These could be achieved through formal or informal channels. Numerous studies have focused on formal channels such as contract research, consulting (e.g., D' Este and Patel 2007), licensing of university patents, spin-offs (e.g., Muscio, Quaglione, and Ramaciotti 2016). However, less attention has been paid to informal channels including joint projects between universities and industry such as joint student supervision, external teaching, use of nonacademic literature and participation in private seminars, a personal contract between academic and industry partners or secondment (Alexander et al. 2020; Lorio, Labory, and Rentocchini 2017).

Informal and formal channels are interconnected (Azagra-Caro et al. 2017; Landry et al. 2010), as informal activities play a crucial role in facilitating formal relations. For example, in their longitudinal study of highly cited university patent, Azagra-Caro et al. (2017, 473) show that the *"knowledge embodied in a patent can be related to informal channels of knowledge transfer such as recruitment of researchers and recent graduates, attendance at conferences, collaboration with migrant graduates, and personal contacts between students and inventors.*" Their work is crucial in terms of bringing new insights on the role of temporally unfolding, the dynamic relationship among formal and informal KE channels for achieving local economic impact.

Similarly, employing a competency approach and linking a variety of KE channels and relational and transactional modes of governance, Alexander et al. (2020) argue that secondments, student placement, joint conferences, and networking are related to "boundary spanning competency" and relational mode of governance; while patenting, licensing practices and spin-off creation are attached to "patent and entrepreneurial policy competency" and transactional mode of governance. They suggest context-specific KT choices for universities. University capabilities, priorities, departmental resources and at the project level, required training for particular KT practices are determinants for the choice of relational or transactional mode of governance (Alexander et al. 2020). Given this backdrop, this book chapter covers both formal and informal KE channels as part of university-industry collaborations, with a particular emphasis on macro-, meso-, and micro-level drivers and outcomes of these collaborations for regional and national-level innovativeness.

REVIEW PROCESS

Adopting the scope reviewing approach, which has a broader "scope" than the systematic review process (Munn et al. 2018), this book chapter provides a systematic review of the journals with the highest article counts on the subject over the past ten years and critical search for the highly cited papers. Following the relevant literature on the scope reviewing, I first performed a manual search of the journals with the highest article counts on the university-industry relations over the past ten years (from 2010 to 2020), which are *Research Policy and Journal of Technology Transfer* as noted by scholars (Perkmann, Salandra, and Tartari 2021; Skute et al. 2019). This procedure yielded 397 (86 papers from Research Policy, 311 papers from The Journal of Technology Transfer) results. Subsequently, I conducted an extensive search in the titles and abstracts of published, peer-reviewed articles held by the bibliographical database service EBSCO, using a series of keywords including "university-industry," "technology transfer," "knowledge transfer," "intermediary organization." This procedure resulted in additional 85 results. However, twenty-four of them were excluded, since these were overlapping with the previous research.

Overall, out of 421 papers, some of the papers were discarded based on several criteria. Placing particular focus on informal and formal KT channels and antecedents and outcomes of the technology transfer process, papers out of this focus were eliminated. For example, the papers dealing with the technology transfer metrics and measures, later phases of particular knowledge channels such as spin-off growth, spin-off progeny, internationalization of spin-offs were out of this scope, since my particular focus was on active KE between universities and industry partners. Additionally, empirically weak, practitioner-focused papers, and special issue introductions were all eliminated. Overall, this procedure yielded 180 articles for the evaluation of the state of current knowledge.

STRANDS OF LITERATURE ON
KNOWLEDGE EXCHANGE

There are two main strands of literature on the university-industry relations: drivers and outcomes of the university-industry relationship. While the former literature mainly focuses on the KT and knowledge spillovers from universities and public research organizations to industry, with a particular focus on drivers of the effectiveness of this process; the latter unpack the impact of the KT mechanisms on the university research performance, firm innovativeness, regional, and national innovation systems and economic growth.

National and Regional Context as a
Driver for Knowledge Exchange

Anchored in regulative, normative and cognitive components (Scott 2008), institutional contexts shape the nature of university-industry involvement. Regulative components are mainly related to the governmental legislations such as federal technology transfer law and policy and university Intellectual Property (IP) policies (Hayter and Rooksby 2016). Importantly, the introduction of Bayh-Dole Act in the United States, which is the most influential legal arrangement that granted IP ownership from public-funding agencies to universities and fostered commercialization of university research (Rasmussen 2008, 506). Region-specific Intellectual Property Rights (IPR) enforcement or other governmental instruments to support commercialization of university research (Rasmussen 2008), as well as industrial agreements and standards (Bruton et al. 2010) also shape boundary conditions for universities and industry partners. For example, Kafourous et al. (2019) examine region-specific IPR enforcement, international openness, and quality of university and research institutions as a condition, which could affect outcomes of academic collaborations and firms' innovativeness in the Chinese context. Contrary to the United States and European countries, the role of institutional forces such as relations with ministries or local government play more critical role in facilitating platforms on university-industry relations in developing and catching up countries such as China (e.g., Hong and Su 2013) or Korea (e.g., Eom and Lee 2010). On the other hand, normative components mainly derive from supporting mechanisms of university-industry involvement such as the existence of business incubators and the availability of venture capitals (Qiu, Liu, and Gao 2017), technical tools such as performance evaluations and control mechanisms or national culture. For example, Iacobucci and Micozzi (2015) conclude that lack of business incubators, venture capital firms, and other business services supporting the local entrepreneurial ecosystem in the majority of Italian provinces hinder long-term growth and potential impact of spin-offs for the local development. Casper (2013) articulates how regional universities in the San Francisco area are much more successful in commercialization outputs (e.g., twice as many patents and three times spun-out), through having larger and more cohesive inventor networks in the biotechnology industry in this area, compared to Los Angeles California regional universities, whereby known with lack of social inventor network. They illuminate that dense social network enables universities in San Francisco area to embed in a community whereby academics and industrialists have a higher level of connectivity through a variety of bidirectional channels, rather than directional knowledge flow from university to industry. Other than the role of regional quality, norms of open science also shape university-industry KT mechanisms and commercialization outputs, as shown by Walsh and Huang (2014), in their study comparing the US and Japanese contexts. The choice of participation in open science and the underlying rationale for the participation differ in these contexts. For example, while in the US context, patents are regarded as a means to acquire venture capital or licensing income, which are directly linked to commercialization, they are mainly seen as a means for collaboration and demonstrating scientific productivity in Japan (Walsh and Huang 2014).

These works also draw attention to the role of region-specific idiosyncrasies affecting technology transfer (Casper 2013; Fini et al. 2011; Kafourous et al. 2019; Qiu, Liu, and Gao 2017). Qiu, Liu, and Gao (2017, 1307) show that in the least developed regions of China, whereby characterized as low level of economic development and insufficient business services (such as lack of business incubators and venture capital), domestic collaborations are beneficial in meeting demands of the local context, and, thus increasing local firms' innovation, while international academic collaborations harmed firms' innovativeness in these least developed regions. Because *"the absorptive capacity of local firms is insufficient to recognize, assimilate and use the knowledge from university research.*" Their findings are striking in putting forward the role of regional infrastructure including regional economic development (beyond university sources) in determining the effectiveness of different types of KT channels (domestic versus international academic collaborations).

Related to regional context, a large number of studies have verified the effect on geographical proximity between university and industry partners in facilitating collective learning and benefits from the collaborations (e.g., Bishop, D'Este and Neely 2011; Brostrom 2010; Mowery and Ziedonis 2015). Even this geographical localization may determine the type of KT channel. For example, Mowery and Ziedonis (2015) find that market-mediated channels such as licensing (in particular exclusive licensing) are more localized geographically than the knowledge spillovers such as patent citations. Because "exclusive licenced inventions" involve more uncertainties and challenges that require more technology-specific and relational complementary assets such as obtaining tacit knowledge, which is more likely to be achieved by geographical proximity. Brostrom (2010) shows that geographical distance is a critical factor for the interaction of R&D activities, in particular for short-term R&D projects, rather than long term. In sum, geographical proximity matters in the flow of knowledge across different partners through a variety of KT channels that spur the learning process through effective social networking and interaction.

University-Level Drivers of Knowledge Transfer

Most attention has been devoted to the university-level drivers of effective KT. While one strand of the literature argues the importance of the university-linked characterizations for the effectiveness of KT, the other strand focuses on the role of the intermediary organizations in this process. The main focus of the first strand is centered on internal-university rules such as regulations on policies and monitory incentives (Muscio, Quaglione, and Ramaciotti 2016), established university policies and procedures about IPR regimes (Caldera and Debande 2010; Kenney and Patton 2011; Halilem et al. 2017), existence of science park affiliated to a given university (Caldera and Debande 2010), status of the university (Kenney and Patton 2011), institutional orientation of the university (Bishop, D'Este, and Neely 2011; Hewitt-Dundas, Gkypali, and Roper 2012; Sengupta and Ray 2017), entrepreneurial mission orientation of the university (Zhao, Brostrom, and Cai 2020), university capabilities (Rasmussen and Borch 2010), university resources in terms of human, financial, and physical (Scuelke-Leech 2013), strategic priority and planning supporting KT (Horner et al. 2019), existence and longevity of educational programs in life science and biotechnology (Kato and Odagiri 2012) in building effective KT.

More specifically, in their study interrogating the role of rules and policies in the creation of academic spin-offs in the Italian context, Muscio, Quaglione, and Ramaciotti (2016) show that clear and specific internal-university rules related to general procedures of technology transfer and rules regulating monitory incentives have a fundamental effect on the creation of academic spin-offs. They argue that the creation of academic spin-offs is a rational response to university rules in this area. Strikingly, they also show that if rules cause restriction of revenues obtained from the spin-off, this might hamper initiatives on spin-offs. Caldera and Debande (2010) provide similar findings in their study conducted in Spain, demonstrating how clear and specific internal-university rules on the teaching, research and "third mission" of the academics are impactful in increases in R&D contracts, licenses, or spin-off creation. Designing the right incentives and crafting clear royalty sharing policies, granting a higher share of licensing royalties to the inventor, and sharing the risk between different parties strongly affects licensing income (Caldera and Debande, 2010). On the other hand, in their survey conducted in Portuguese and Spanish contexts, Argue-Castells et al. (2016) find conflicting evidence. They find that majority of inventors consider royalty sharing as not remarkable in fostering their efforts. It is argued that a potential reason for that is that intermediary organizations may highly focus on regional development and entrepreneurship rather than the commercialization of inventions and licensing activities in these contexts.

Indeed, one of the discussions about the commercialization process of academic inventions is on how to allocate rights and responsibilities for the inventions. In their study, drawing attention to the importance of the inventor control-centric policies and procedures, Kenney and Patton (2011) draw on data from 515 spin-offs generated from 6 universities located in the United States and Canada and confirm that inventor ownership, rather than university ownership regime has a great influence in generating spin-offs. More specifically, Halilem et al. (2017) note the role of different types of IPR regimes on inventors' behaviors, and in contrary to the most literature, find that control rights (obligation to disclose and option to commercialize) and sharing of income between the university and the academic inventors, rather than invention ownership regime, motivates academic inventors to engage with KT in Canada.

Complementing this body of work, Rasmussen and Borch (2010) suggest that university capabilities that are anchored in bottom-up initiatives and embedded in multiple levels within the university or outside the university is more important than top-down policies and university procedures in the spin-off creation process. Comparing four venture creation processes longitudinally in the Norwegian context, they propose three main capabilities: opening new paths of action, balancing *academic and commercial interest*, and *integrating new resources*. While *"opening new paths of action,"* which is related to acting outside the box, is informal in nature and matters most in the initial phase of venture creation, competency in *"balancing academic and commercial interest"* becomes more crucial in launching the business. Last, *"integrating new resources"* becomes crucial merit after launching the business.

Furthermore, institutional orientation of the university (either research or teaching) matters in the choice of strategic priorities and planning, and drives nature and type technology transfer channels (Hewitt-Dundas, Gkypali, and Roper 2012; Sengupta and Ray 2017). For example, Hewitt-Dundas, Gkypali, and Roper (2012) show that while research-oriented universities are more likely to focus on the development and exploitation of IP and maximizing the return on research through TTOs, in low research-oriented ones, industry involvement is achieved through vocational training ethos. This is in line with the findings of Horner et al. (2019), who draw on data from 115 UK universities and discuss that there is no "one fits all" approach. They demonstrate that it is the alignment of strategic priorities and strategic planning with support for technology transfer, which is fundamental for the effectiveness of the technology. These findings confirm that bigger facilities and better resources do not always result in effective university-industry involvement.

Innovation Intermediaries

The second stream of university-related research focuses on the role of intermediary organizations including incubators, TTOs, and technology licensing offices in increasing the effectiveness of KT. Serving to the "third mission" of universities, these units act as interface between academia and industry. In particular, in parallel with the introduction of paradigmatic shifts in the higher education field and across the globe, the strategic importance of these units or organizations has been recognized well, in particular, in the developed world. For example, Perkmann and Schildt (2015) show how the boundary organization, Structural Genomics Consortium, which was established to create a platform that bridge university and industry partners in the pharmaceutical industry, resolved the tensions that firms face. This is achieved through the implementation of open data initiatives through ensuring the anonymity of parties` information to minimizing the risk of adverse use of this information by competitors and resolving goal conflicts of different parties (industry and university partners).

TTOs are critical boundary organizations or units established within or outside the universities, serving as interface between different parts. TTO characteristics such as size, the industrial background of staff, scale of TTO activities leading to effective technology transfer have been extensively studied (Caldera and Debande 2010; Conti and Gaule 2011; Sengupta and Ray 2017; Siegel, Waldman and Link 2003; Van Looy et al. 2011). In their study comparing the licensing activities and revenues from licensing in US TTOs and European counterparts, Conti and Gaule (2011) demonstrate that industry experience of TTO staff matter in negotiating the financial clauses of licensing contracts, which result in increases in licensing revenues in US TTOs. Caldera and Debande (2010) find that size and experience differ based on the type of technology transfer activities. While larger and more experienced TTOs are more likely to generate higher contractual research, these characterizations matter less for licensing and creation of spin-offs. In their longitudinal study of 404 spin-off from 64 STEM universities in Italy, Fini et al. (2011) evidence that the existence of TTO and participation in Italian the network of technology transfer (NETVAL) contributes spin-off creation rate. Horner et al. (2019) show that the scale of TTO support determines technology transfer effectiveness.

Furthermore, Hewitt-Dundas, Gkypali, and Roper (2012) find that the scale and scope of TTOs differ, based on a strategic priority of the universities (research or teaching orientation) in the UK context. TTOs in high research-oriented universities are more likely to engage with licensing contracts and academic spin-offs. However, TTOs in low research-oriented universities are more likely to respond to the needs of the regional area in providing *"professional teaching, user-driven research and problem-solving with local and regional companies"* (Hewitt-Dundas, Gkypali, and Roper 2012, 273) and have a profound contribution for regional economic development through human resources agenda. In sum, it is the alignment of capabilities and strategic priorities of the university and TTO capabilities that matter for effectiveness rather than governance or characterizations of TTOs, as outlined above.

Last but not least, scholars draw attention to the lack of institutional infrastructure supporting intermediary organizations in emerging and transition economies (Belitski, Aginskaja, and Marozau 2019; Barletta et al. 2016). Belitski, Aginskaja, and Marozau (2019) draw attention to the limited function of TTOs in their legal and resource ability in transition economies, as they do not find any positive relationship between commercialization of university research and the existence of TTOs, TTO awareness, and the number of contracts signed via a TTO. The situation is similar in the Argentinean context. In their study surveying 314 Argentine ICT research groups, Barletta et al. (2016) find that lack of intermediary organizations in Argentina leads to the disentanglement of university and industry partners. Arque-Castells et al. (2016) also claim that TTOs in Portuguese and Spanish contexts are lack of commercial orientation vision, which result in insufficiencies in licensing revenue, while they are mainly focused on regional development through university spin-offs.

Firm-Linked Drivers of Knowledge Transfer

Firms are inclined to collaborate with universities through consulting services, contract research, or informal channels that broaden and enhance absorptive capacity and develop innovative capacities (Cattaneo, Meoli, and Vismali 2015). Considered the firm-level antecedents of effective KT, firm characteristics such as size, age (Yu and Lee 2017), absorptive capacity, and technology openness (Bodas-Freitas, Geuna and Rosi 2013a), firms' R&D commitments (Bishop, D'Este and Neely 2011), prior experience with university collaboration, firms' social capital (Bruneel, D'Este and Salter 2010), prior experience in collaborative research, trust to partner and breadth of interaction (Steinmo and Rasmussen 2018), sectoral differences (Lee and Miozzo 2019), exploration and exploitation orientation of firms (Yu and Lee 2017), among others, determine nature of the interaction between university and industry.

First, the characteristics of the firm determine the way that firms interact with universities. Bodas-Freitas, Marques, and eSilva (2013b) show that larger firms are likely to employ an institutional mode of governance in their relations with universities, in which formal relationships are established through contracting with the institutional agency, which requires a higher degree of bureaucracy, share of resources with other collaborators and continuous commitment of researcher, and are likely to be afforded by larger firms. While small firms choose the personal mode of governance that requires contracting with an expert to solve a particular problem and grants a higher degree of control to the firms (Bodas-Freitas et al., 2013a). Additionally, firms having a higher degree of absorptive capacity are likely to benefit from basic research, which would be achieved through continuous involvement with the researcher, and leads firms to collaborate with universities through the institutional mode of governance. Moreover, the technological openness of firms is another characterization that renders firms more competent in identifying key technological and market issues, and less relied on institutional university support. Hence, technologically open firms are likely to choose personal mode of governance (Bodas-Freitas, Marques, and eSilva 2013b).

Firm age and orientation are other crucial drivers of KE. As firms age, inertia appears as an obstacle to innovative capability. So, older firms may need to collaborate with universities to increase innovativeness through acquiring tacit knowledge (Yu and Lee 2017). On the other hand, drawing on data from 542 firms in the manufacturing industry in Korea, Yu and Lee (2017) show that exploration-oriented firms are likely to benefit from collaboration with research organizations in increasing innovativeness, compared to exploitative-oriented ones. Because firms employing exploration perspective are likely to concentrate on research and development (are in search of newness), think outside the box and pursue longer-term benefits of collaborations. Linked to this, Cattaneo, Meoli, and Vismali (2015, 410) note that: "*affiliation with a prestigious university is expected to increase the technological capabilities and network opportunities of affiliated firms and to provide more dynamic and mobile human capital.*" More specifically, Bishop, D'Este, and Neely (2011) discuss that explorative and exploitative benefits could be reaped from university collaborations based on firm characteristics including continuous R&D commitment, as well as geographically closeness to the university partner and research quality of university partner. Accordingly, proximity to university partners are crucial for firms' developing "exploitative learning" and "problem-solving" benefits from universities, which is referred to as "demand-pull contribution" from universities. Firms, which are continuously committed to R&D and collaborated with university partners excelling in research are likely to attain the required skills and competency to increase their commercial output. This refers to "science push contributions" from universities (Bishop, D'Este and Neely 2011).

Considered the sectoral difference in firms' inclination to KE with universities, Lee and Miozzo (2019) draw attention to the heterogeneity of knowledge-intensive business services (KIBS) firms in their approach to university collaborations. According to their evidence, science-based KIBS, in particular, highly customized service providers such as firms specializing in marketing, recruitment or IP, are more likely to collaborate with universities, with the purpose of innovation. Because these firms serve as knowledge facilitators or intermediaries by sharing their commercial expertise with universities. More specifically, scholars provide an example of an IP group, which is expert in the commercialization of science in the UK and collaborate long term with many universities across the globe, absorb knowledge from these universities through benefiting "executive research, legal support and corporate finance advice" (Lee and Miozzo 2019, 1644).

Micro-Level Drivers of Knowledge Transfer

The micro aspect of KE among university and industry partners is mainly centered on issues including motivations of academics in engaging with the industry at the individual level and inventor team compositions at the group level. Accordingly, gender (Abreu and Grinevich 2017), seniority, career status, publication productivity (Haeussler and Colyvas 2011), departmental peer effect (Moog et al. 2015; Tartari, Perkmann and Salter 2014), social capital (Aldridge and Audretsch 2011), financial incentives (Arque-Castells et al. 2016), among others, have appeared as vital drivers of KT. More specifically, although it is argued that seniority and age bring social capital and experience in accessing industry partners and achieving higher commercialization outputs (Stephan et al. 2007), this assumption is not pertinent in some works (e.g., Haeussler and Colyvas, 2011). Recent debates are on how entrepreneurial competency and proclivity of graduate students and early career scholars in commercial engagement result in successful commercial outputs (e.g., Bercovitz and Feldman 2008), which requires more interrogation.

Gender and disciplinary differences appear as essential in the way that academics interact with industry partners through resources available. The difference in gender stems from women's participation in science rates and their positions at the seniority levels that affect the breadth and depth of commercial engagement (Abreu and Grinevich 2017). Evidence shows that women are likely to engage in commerce through consulting activities, rather than establishing a company (Haeussler and Colyvas 2011, Tartari and Salter 2015). Tartari and Salter (2015) add joint research projects as an important channel preferred by women academics. Cardinally, it is the university-driven proactive practices such as equality-mandated human resources practices that matter in supporting women for industrial involvement (Tartari and Salter 2015). Additionally, scholars have shown that disciplinary differences also matter in the TT process. While academics in social sciences and humanities (SSH) are more likely to be more relational and collaborative in responding needs of society, focusing on consultancy and contract research, rather than other transactional ways of engagement, as documented by Olmos-Penuela, Castro-Martinez, and D'Este (2014) in their study covering eighty-three research groups from SSH departments in Spain.

Production productivity is another aspect of this process. The underlying rationale is that academics who publish more are likely to have greater sources such as implications of research that are transferable to industry context and reputation that render academics more visible in the eyes of industry partners as well (Haeussler and Colyvas 2011). Particular evidence is on positive the relationship between publication frequency and number of patents (Grimm and Jaenicke 2015; Meyer, 2006). These findings suggest that academic works and commercial activities may complement each other (Perkmann et al. 2013). Another driver of commercial engagement is peer effect (Moog et al. 2015; Tartari, Perkmann, and Salter 2014). In their survey of 1,371 UK scientists, Tartari, Perkmann, and Salter (2014, 1200) find that departmental peers have a great influence on academics' decisions in involvement with industry. In particular, this peer influence is greater among lower-performing junior academics, since the social comparison mechanism allows "*individuals to derive self-worth by comparing themselves with similar contexts and competing with them for professional status and achievement.*"

Academic engagement is also driven by the social capital of academics, which is mainly measured with linkages to private industry that increase the propensity of a scientist to become an entrepreneur (e.g., Aldrich and

Audretsch 2011; Colyvas and Powell 2006; Haeussler and Colyvas 2011). In particular, in this regard, diversity of inventor teams or research groups, such as the composition of teams from multiple institutions (focal university, other research institution, and/or industry) matter in the success of commercialization process. Importantly, the presence of prior social ties supporting links with external team members positively influences commercial outcomes (Bercovitz and Feldman 2011).

Dynamics on Outcomes of Effective Knowledge Transfer

Encroachment of neoliberal ideology across the globe in the 1990s facilitated marketization of higher education fields that obliged universities to demonstrate their economic and societal impact to a greater extent (Fallis, 2004), which is achieved through engaged university and effective technology transfer from university to industry. Scholars draw attention to the different criteria for effective technology transfer (see Bozeman, Rimes, and Youtie 2015), which are of (a) out the door aspect (if the technology is transferred or not), (b) market impact, economic development aspect (commercial success, regional and national economic growth), (c) political reward aspect (enhancing political support), (d) opportunity cost aspect, (e) scientific and technical human capital aspect, as well as (f) public value aspect. Most attention has been given to the market impact and economic development aspect, with a particular focus on effective technology transfer in terms of regional or national innovation systems (e.g., Cowan and Zinovyeva 2013), acknowledging its importance in creating a "knowledge-based society," and gaining competitive advantage in a global economy (e.g., Audretsch, Lehmann, and Wright 2014). These include, for example, the impact of basic research and university-industry involvement on firms' overall innovativeness (e.g., Dornbusch and Neuhausler 2015; Leten, Landoni and van Looy 2014; Yu and Lee 2017; Tang et al. 2020), in particular, the introduction of market novelties such as product innovation (Hewitt-Dundas et al., 2019; Higon 2016; Toole 2012), process innovation (Maietta 2016), and creation of original knowledge and original patents (Guerzoni et al. 2014), as well as regional development and competitiveness (Caree, Malva and Santarelli 2014; Guerrero et al. 2014; Lehman and Menter 2016) or national economy (Roessner et al. 2013).

In their study conducted in 5,606 Spanish manufacturing firms, Higon (2016) illuminates that combining external and internal research is crucial for being a pioneer in the sector. While internal basic research is crucial in developing absorptive capacity and gaining relevant competency or benefiting economies of scale or scope that leads to being a pioneer in the market, collaboration with universities enhance the propensity of being the pioneer in new product developments. Moreover, firms that collaborate with universities in their region are more likely to bring incremental product innovations, while collaboration with cross-regional universities producing higher quality research is more likely to result in radical innovations, as shown by Tang et al. (2020) in their study drawn from 166 manufacturing firms in China. The underlying rationale is that while proximity is related to *"commonalities in local context and institutional framework,"* diverge institutional contexts are more likely to be associated with a variety of knowledge networks and a greater level of absorptive capacity that result in radical product innovations (Tang et al. 2020). Lehman and Menter (2016) use panel data set from 1998 to 2012 in twenty regions varying in competitiveness and wealth in Germany and show the reciprocal relationship between regional wealth, which is measured by GPA per capita, and university-industry relations as measured by the amount of funds provided by the industry. They show that entrepreneurial activities, in particular, the creation of new ventures foster regional economic developments in an almost three-year time lag, while increases in regional wealth impact on the research funds in the next period. Caree, Malva, and Santarelli (2014) provide empirical evidence from Italy and show that new entrepreneurial ventures that are produced from scientific knowledge contribute to regional economic growth.

In addition to the market and economic impact of university-industry engagement and KT mechanisms, the public value aspect, which is mainly pertinent to advancing life standards in the areas of health, education, leisure, safety, among others (Bozeman, Rimes, and Youtie 2015) appears as crucial impact. Iacobucci and Micozzi (2015), based on 290 academic spin-offs in Italy, concluded that although the economic impact of academic spin-offs is not observed in Italian provinces, their role in academics in creating and enhancing technology clusters is monitored.

CONCLUSION

Based on a critical review on university-industry relations, this book chapter provides an overview of studies on university-industry KT channels from a multilayered perspective, with a particular focus on macro-, meso-, and micro-level drivers of this process as well as outcomes in terms of firms' innovativeness and regional and national economy. Relying on extensive literature search, this work contributes to the KE literature by providing an updated state of knowledge in the field and piecing together a two-pronged aspect of university-industry relations.

This book chapter is limited to multilevel drivers of effective KT from university and firm perspective, as well as broader level consequences. The scholar work on university-industry relations and KT is vast. Some of the literature focuses on technology transfer metrics and measures, incubators, and science parks, and others focus on later phases of particular knowledge channels such as spin-off growth, spin-off progeny, internationalization of spin-offs, which are excluded from the scope of this work.

The increasing emphasis on university-industry involvement through a variety of KT channels has created new research opportunities in some key areas. First, the majority of studies on university-industry relations are conducted in the United States, United Kingdom, and European contexts. However, technology transfer mechanisms in the emerging market contexts, whereby known with weak national innovation systems and limited development capacity (Arocena and Sutz 2010) fundamentally differ from the developed world and require more interrogation. As noted by Walsh and Huang (2014), *there is a need for a more nuanced and institutionally contextualized analysis of public researchers' participation in proprietary science* (Walsh and Huang 2014).

Second, what remains unknown is the technology transfer in a global economy (Audretsch, Lehmann, and Wright 2014; Wright 2014). We have a limited understanding of the role of institutional interventions in achieving university-industry collaborations (except Hong and Su 2013). I would suggest more exploration of the role of government, national-level policies, programs or the role of other supporting organizations in creating an effective entrepreneurial ecosystem that enhances the capacity of firms in gaining competitive advantage in a global economy, in particular, in emerging market contexts. As noted by Audretsch, Lehmann and Wright (2014), *"not all emerging economies have developed at the same rate . . .* while some of them entail more established institutional infrastructure in developing entrepreneurial capacity than other emerging economies. Hence, studies focusing on the cross-comparative understanding of policies and programs supporting or hampering KT initiatives from different emerging market contexts would be an important step in achieving more effective mechanisms in similar contexts.

Importantly, in addition to top-down policies, bottom-up practices were undertaken by academics at the micro-level, as well as intermediary organizations or universities at the meso-level becomes more critical in ensuring effective KT in emerging market contexts. These practices may include influencing policies at a broader level through, for example, lobbying with other agencies to facilitate interaction among different parts of KT or bringing new field-shaping norms, among others. Studies unearthing these bottom-up dynamics would be a valuable contribution to the field.

Third, another potential research avenue that I propose would be to unpack the multilayered nature of KT mechanisms by revealing the interdependency among macro-meso and micro-level determinants of KT. Importantly, cognitive components are mainly related to the cognitive scripts, schemas, and behaviors of individuals (Scott 2008) that may be driven by broader institutional context dynamics including regulative and normative components of institutions. In particular, studies linking micro and macro-level dynamics through unpacking, for example, how cognitive schemes of academics or industrialists in their approach to KT channels differ in different institutional contexts would be a valuable contribution.

Furthermore, the interaction between determinants at different levels such as regional idiosyncrasies and university-level support mechanisms on the KT would provide new insights on the literature placed intersection of regional innovation systems and academic collaborations, as noted by scholars (e.g., Fini et al. 2011; Casper 2013). For example, Fini et al. (2011) contend that if significant contributions offered by regional support mechanisms in the creation of academic spin-offs, universities' additional contribution might not spur additional spin-off creation in the Italian context. As noted by Casper (2013), it is required to consider both internal-university factors such as resource endowments and external factors including quality of the regional area in a better understanding of effective commercialization outputs. Therefore, empirical evidence on the multilevel explanation of effective KT mechanisms would be the cardinal contribution.

REFERENCES

Abreu, Maria and Vadim Grinevich. 2017. "Gender patterns in academic entrepreneurship." *The Journal of Technology Transfer* 42: 763–794.

Aldridge, T. Taylor, and David Audretsch, 2011. "The Bayh-Dole act and scientist entrepreneurship." *Research Policy* 40, no. 8: 1058–1067.

Alexander, A., D. P. Martin, C. Manolchev, and K. Miller. 2020. "University–industry collaboration: Using meta-rules to overcome barriers to knowledge transfer." *The Journal of Technology Transfer* 45: 371–392. https://doi.org/10.1007/s10961-018-9685-1

Arocena, Rodrigo, and Judith Sutz 2010. "Weak knowledge demand in the South: learning divides and innovation policy." *Science and Public Policy* 37, no. 8: 571–582. https://doi.org/10.3152/030234210X12767691861137

Arque-Castells, Pere, Rui M. Cartaxo, Jose Garcia-Quevedo, and Manuel M. Godinho. 2016. "Royalty sharing, effort and invention in universities: Evidence from Portugal and Spain." *Research Policy* 45, no. 9: 1858–1872.

Audretsch, B. David, Erik E. Lehmann, and Mike Wright. 2014. "Technology transfer in a global economy." *The Journal of Technology Transfer* 39: 301–312. https://doi.org/10.1007/s10961-012-9283-6.

Azagra-Caro, M. Joaquin, Anabel Fernandez-Mesa, and Nicolas Robinson Garcia. 2017. 'Getting out of the closet': Scientific authorship of literary fiction and knowledge transfer." *The Journal of Technology Transfer* 45: 56–85. https://doi.org/10.1007/s10961-018-9672-6.

Barletta, Florencia, Gabriel Yoguel, Mariano Pereira, and Sergio Rodrigues. 2016. "Exploring scientific productivity and transfer activities: Evidence from Argentinean ICT research groups." *Research Policy* 46, no. 8: 1361–1369.

Belitski, Maksim, Anna Aginskaja, and Radzivon Marozau. 2019. "Commercializing university research in transition economies: Technology transfer offices or direct industrial funding?" *Research Policy* 48, no. 3: 601–615.

Bercovitz, Janet, and Maryann Feldman, 2011. "The mechanisms of collaboration in inventive teams: Composition, social networks, and geography." *Research Policy* 40, no. 1: 81–93.

Bercovitz, Janet, and Maryann Feldman. 2008. "Academic entrepreneurs: Organizational change at the individual level." *Organization Science* 19, no. 1: 69–89.

Bishop, Kate, Pablo D`Este, and Andy Neely. 2011. "Gaining from interactions with universities: Multiple methods for nurturing absorptive capacity." *Research Policy* 40, no. 1: 30–40.

Bodas Freitas, I. Maria, Rosane A. Marques, and Evando M. D. e Silva. 2013b. "University–industry collaboration and innovation in emergent and mature industries in new industrialized countries." *Research Policy* 42, no. 2: 443–453.

Bodas-Freitas, I. Maria, Aldo Geuna, and Federica Rosi. 2013a. "Finding the right partners: Institutional and personal modes of governance of university–industry interactions." *Research Policy* 42, no. 1: 50–62.

Bolli, Thomas, and Frank Somogyi. 2011. "Do competitively acquired funds induce universities to increase productivity?" *Research Policy* 40, no. 1: 136–147.

Bozeman, Barry, Heather Rimes, and Jan Youtie. 2015. "The evolving state-of-the-art in technology transfer research: Revisiting the contingent effectiveness model." *Research Policy* 44, no. 1: 34–49.

Brostrom, Anders. 2010. "Working with distant researchers-distance and content in university–industry interaction." *Research Policy* 39, no. 10: 1311–1320.

Bruneel, Johan, Pablo D`Este, and Ammon Salter, A. 2010. "Investigating the factors that diminish the barriers to university–industry collaboration." *Research Policy* 39, no. 7: 858–868.

Bruton, Garry D., Igor Filatotchev, Salim Chahine, and Mike Wright. 2010. "Governance, ownership structure, and performance of IPO firms: the impact of different types of private equity investors and institutional environments." *Strategic Management Journal* 31, no. 5: 491–509.

Caldera, Aida, and Olivier Debande. 2010. "Performance of Spanish universities in technology transfer: An empirical analysis." *Research Policy* 39, no. 9: 1160–1173.

Caree, Martin, Antonio Della Malva, and Enrico Santarelli. 2014. The contribution of universities to growth: empirical evidence for Italy. *The Journal of Technology Transfer* 39: 393–414.

Casper, Steven. 2013. "The spill-over theory reversed: The impact of regional economies on the commercialization of university science." *Research Policy* 42, no. 8: 1313–1324.

Cattaneo, Mattia, Michele Meoli, and Silvio Vismara. 2015. "Cross-border M&As of biotech firms affiliated with internationalized universities." *The Journal of Technology Transfer* 40: 409–433.

Colyvas, A. Jeanette, and Powell, W. Walter. 2006. "Roads to institutionalization: the remaking of boundaries between public and private science." *Research in Organizational Behavior* 27: 305–353.

Conti, Annamaria, and Patrick Gaule. 2011. "Is the US outperforming Europe in university technology licensing? A new perspective on the European Paradox." *Research Policy* 40, no. 1: 123–135.

Cowan, Robin, and Natalia Zinovyeva. 2013. "University effects on regional innovation." *Research Policy* 42, no. 3: 788–800.

D'Este, Pablo, and Parimal Patel, P. 2007. "University–industry linkages in the UK: what are the factors underlying the variety of interactions with industry?" *Research Policy* 36, no. 9: 1295–1313.

Dornbusch, Friedrich, and Peter Neuhausler. 2015. Composition of inventor teams and technological progress – The role of collaboration between academia and industry. *Research Policy* 44, no. 7: 1360–1375.

Eom, Boo-Young, and Keun Lee. 2010. Determinants of industry–academy linkages and, their impact on firm performance: The case of Korea as a latecomer in knowledge industrialization. *Research Policy* 39, no. 5: 625–639.

Fallis, G. 2004. *Postsecondary Review: Higher Expectations for Higher Education. Government of Ontario.* The Mission of the University: Ontario.

Fini, Riccardo. Rosa Grimaldi, Simone Santoni, and Maurizio Sobrero. 2011. "Complements or substitutes? The role of universities and local context in supporting the creation of academic spin-offs." *Research Policy* 40, no. 8: 1113–1127.

Grimm, Heike, M., and Johannes Jaenicke. 2015. "Testing the causal relationship between academic patenting and scientific publishing in Germany: Crowding-out or reinforcement?" *The Journal of Technology Transfer* 40: 512–535.

Guerrero, Maribel, David Urbano, James Cunningham, and Damien Organ. 2014. Entrepreneurial universities in two European regions: a case study comparison. *The Journal of Technology Transfer* 39: 415–434.

Guerzoni, Marco, T. Taylor Aldridge, David D. Audretsch, and Sameeksha Desai. 2014. "A new industry creation and originality: Insight from the funding sources of university patents." *Research Policy* 43, no. 10: 1697–1706.

Haeussler, Carolin, and Jeannette A. Colyvas. 2011. "Breaking the Ivory Tower: Academic Entrepreneurship in the Life Sciences in UK and Germany." *Research Policy* 40, no. 1: 41–54.

Halilem, Norrin, Nabil Amara, Julia Olmos-Penuela, and Muhammad Mohiuddin. 2017. "To Own, or not to Own? A multilevel analysis of intellectual property right policies on academic entrepreneurship." *Research Policy* 46, no. 8: 1479–1489.

Hayter, Cristopher, S., and Jacob H. Rooksby. 2016. "A legal perspective on university technology transfer." *The Journal of Technology Transfer* 41: 270–289.

Hewitt-Dundas, Nola, Areti Gkypali, and Stephen Roper. 2012. "Research intensity and knowledge transfer activity in UK universities." *Research Policy* 41, no. 2: 262–275.

Hewitt-Dundas, Nola, Areti Gkypali, and Stephen Roper. 2019. "Does learning from prior collaboration help firms to overcome the 'two- worlds' paradox in university-business collaboration?" *Research Policy* 41, no. 2: 1310–1322.

162   *Çağla Özgören*

Higon, A. Dolores. 2016. "In-house versus external basic research and first-to-market innovations." *Research Policy* 45, no. 4: 816–829.

Hong, Wei, and Yu-Sung Su. 2013. "The effect of institutional proximity in non-local university–industry collaborations: An analysis based on Chinese patent data." *Research Policy* 42, no. 2: 454–464.

Horner, Sam, Dilani Jayawarna, Benito Giordano, and Oswald Jones. 2019. "Strategic choice in universities: Managerial agency and effective technology transfer." *Research Policy* 48, no. 5: 1297–1309.

Iacobucci, Donato, and Alessandra Micozzi. 2015. How to evaluate the impact of academic spin-offs on local development: an empirical analysis of the Italian case. *The Journal of Technology Transfer* 40: 434–452.

Kafourous, Mario, Chengqi Wang, Panagiotis Piperopoulos, and Mingshen Zhang. 2019. "Academic collaborations and firm innovation in China: The role of region-specific institutions." *Research Policy* 44, no. 3: 803–817.

Kato, Masatoshi, and Hiroyuki Odagiri. 2012. "Development of university life-science programs and university–industry joint research in Japan." *Research Policy* 41, no. 5: 939–952.

Kenney, Martin, and Donald Patton. 2011. "Does inventor ownership encourage university research-derived entrepreneurship? A six-university comparison." *Research Policy* 40, no. 8: 1100–1112.

Landry, Rejean, Malek Saihi, Nabil Amara, and Mathieu Ouimet. 2010. "Evidence on how academics manage their portfolio of knowledge transfer activities." *Research Policy* 39, no. 10: 1387–1403.

Lee, Hsing-fen, and Marcela Miozzo. 2019. "Which types of knowledge-intensive business services firms collaborate with universities for innovation?" *Research Policy* 48, no. 7: 1633–1646.

Lehman, Erik, E., and Matthias Menter. 2016. University-industry collaboration and regional wealth. *The Journal of Technology Transfer* 41: 1284–1307.

Leten, Bart, Paolo Landoni, Bart van Looy. 2014. "Science or graduates: How do firms benefit from the proximity of universities?" *Research Policy* 43, no. 8: 1398–1412.

Lorio, Roberto, Sandrine Labory, Francesco Rentocchini. 2017. "The importance of pro-social behaviour for the breadth and depth of knowledge transfer activities: An analysis of Italian academic scientists." *Research Policy* 46, no. 2: 497–509.

Maietta, W. Ornella. 2016. "Determinants of university–firm R&D collaboration and its impact on innovation: A perspective from a low-tech industry." *Research Policy* 44, no. 7: 1341–1359.

Meyer, Martin. 2006. "Are patenting scientists the better scholars? An exploratory comparison of inventor-authors with their non-inventing peers in nano-science and technology." *Research Policy* 35, no. 10: 1646–1662.

Moog, Petra, Arndt Werner, Stefan Houweling, Uschi Backes-Gellner. 2015. "The impact of skills, working time allocation and peer effects on the entrepreneurial intentions of scientists." *The Journal of Technology Transfer* 40: 493–511.

Mowery, C. David, and Arvids A. Ziedonis. 2015. "Markets versus spillovers in outflows of university research." *Research Policy* 44, no. 1: 50–66.

Munn, Zuchary, Micah D. J. Peters, Cindy Stern, Catalin Tufanaru, Alexa McArthur and Edoardo Aromataris. 2018. Systematic review or scoping review? Guidance for authors when choosing between a systematic review or scope review approach. *MC Med Res Methodology* 18, no. 143: 1–7. https://doi.org/10.1186/s12874 -018-0611-x.

Muscio, Alessandro, Davide Quaglione, and Laura Ramaciotti. 2016. "The effects of university rules on spinoff creation: The case of academia in Italy." *Research Policy* 45, no. 7: 1386–1396.

Olmos-Penuela, Julia, Elena Castro-Martinez, and Pablo D`Este. 2014. "Knowledge transfer activities in social sciences and humanities: Explaining the interactions of research groups with non-academic agents." *Research Policy* 43, no. 4: 696–706.

Perkmann, Markus, and Henri Schildt. 2015. "Open data partnerships between firms and universities: The role of boundary organizations." *Research Policy* 44, no. 5: 1133–1143.

Perkmann, Markus, Rosella Salandra, Valentina Tartari. 2021. "Academic engagement: A review of the literature 2011–2019." *Research Policy* 50.

Perkmann, Markus, Valentina Tartari, Maureen McKelvey, Erkko Autio, Anders Brostrom, Pablo D`Este, Ricardo Fini, Aldo Geuna, Rose Grimaldi, Alan Hughes, Stefan Krabel, Michael Kitson, Patrick Llerena, Francesco Lissoni, Ammon Salter, and Maurizio Sobrero. 2013. "Academic engagement and commercialisation: A review of the literature on university–industry relations." *Research Policy* 42, no. 2: 423–442.

Qiu, Shumin, Xielin Liu, and Taishan Gao. 2017. "Do emerging countries prefer local knowledge or distant knowledge? Spillover effect of university collaborations on local firms." *Research Policy* 46, no. 7: 1299–1311.

Rasmussen, Einar, and Odd Jarl Borch. 2010. "University capabilities in facilitating entrepreneurship: A longitudinal study of spin-off ventures at mid-range universities." *Research Policy* 39, no. 5: 602–612.

Rasmussen, Einar. 2008. "Government instruments to support the commercialization of university research: lessons from Canada." *Technovation* 28 (August): 506–517.

Roessner, David, Jennifer Bond, Sumiye Okubo, and Mark Planting. 2013. "The economic impact of licensed commercialized inventions originating in university research." *Research Policy* 42, no. 1: 23–34.

Scott, W. Richard. 2008. Institutions and Organizations, 2nd edition. Thousand Oaks, CA: Sage.

Scuelke-Leech, Beth-Anne. 2013. "Resources and research: An empirical study of the influence of departmental research resources on individual STEM researchers involvement with industry." *Research Policy* 42, no. 9: 1667–1678.

Sengupta, Abhijit, and Amit S. Ray. 2017. "University research and knowledge transfer: A dynamic view of ambidexterity in British universities." *Research Policy* 46, no. 5: 881–897.

Siegel, Donald S., David Waldman, Albert Link. 2003. "Assessing the impact of organizational practices on the productivity of university technology transfer offices: An exploratory study." *Research Policy* 32, no. 1: 27–48.

Skute, Igor, Kasia Zalewska-Kurek, Isabella Hatak, and Petra de Weerd-Nederhof. 2019. "Mapping the field: a bibliometric analysis of the literature on university–industry collaborations." *The Journal of Technology Transfer* 44:916–947.

Steinmo, Marianne and Einar Rasmussen. 2018. "The interplay of cognitive and relational social capital dimensions in university-industry collaboration: Overcoming the experience barrier." *Research Policy* 47, no. 10: 1964–1974.

Stephan, Paula, E., Shiferaw Gurmu, Albert Sumell, and Grant Black. 2007. "Who's patenting in the university? Evidence from the survey of earned doctorates." *Economics of Innovation and New Technology* 16: 71–99.

Tang, Yongli, Kazuyuki Motohashi, Xinyue Hu, and Angeles Montoro-Sanchez. 2020. "University industry interaction and product innovation performance of Guangdong manufacturing firms: the roles of regional proximity and research quality of universities." *The Journal of Technology Transfer* 45: 578–618. https://doi.org/10.1007/s10961-019-09715-2

Tartari, Valentina, and Ammon Salter, 2015. "The engagement gap: Exploring gender differences in University – Industry collaboration activities." *Research Policy* 44, no. 6: 1176–1191.

Tartari, Valentina, Markus Perkmann, Ammon Salter. 2014. "In good company: The influence of peers on industry engagement by academic scientists." *Research Policy* 43, no. 7: 1189–1203.

Toole, A. Andrew. 2012. "The impact of public basic research on industrial innovation: Evidence from the pharmaceutical industry." *Research Policy* 41, no. 1: 1–12.

Van Looy, Bart, Paola Landoni, Julie Callaert, Bruno van Pottelsberghe, Eleftherios Sapsalis, and Koenraad Debackere. 2011. "Entrepreneurial effectiveness of European universities: an empirical assessment of antecedents and trade-offs." *Research Policy* 40: 553–564.

Walsh, John. P., and Hsini Huang. 2014. "Local context, academic entrepreneurship and open science: Publication secrecy and commercial activity among Japanese and US scientists." *Research Policy* 43, no. 2: 245–260.

Wright, Michael. 2014. "Academic entrepreneurship, technology transfer and society: Where next?" *Journal of Technology Transfer* 39: 322–334.

Yu, Gun Jea, and Joonkyum Lee. 2017. "When should a firm collaborate with research organizations for innovation performance? The moderating role of innovation orientation, size, and age." *The Journal of Technology Transfer* 42: 1451–1465.

Zhao, Zhiyan, Anders Brostrom, and Jianfeng Cai. 2020. Promoting academic engagement: university context and individual characteristics. *The Journal of Technology Transfer* 45: 304–337.

Chapter 10

Artificial Intelligence Technologies, the Impact to Economic Growth, the Global Economy, and Future Professions

Yusuf Kurtoğlu

INTRODUCTION

The human brain can produce "result" due to innate thinking ability. Is it possible the machines carry out "thinking ability" realized by the human brain? This question is accepted as the major basis behind improving artificial intelligence (AI) technologies. Thinking machines try to reach the level of the human brain's thinking and deciding ability.

Computers are machines developed engineering design together with the combination of the software engineering products such as semiconductors, operating systems, processors, internal and external data recording systems memories, etc., and hardware engineering parts such as glass and frame, display equipment, keyboard, mouse, connecting cables, etc. Computers as machines can calculate, either can imitate human speeches and behaviors; thereby, the difference from the human is the thinking ability. The computer processor process the required data from the entered data according to the process content loaded in the program. The data is processed following the codes defined in the algorithm, and computers are provided to perform the intended functions.

The basis of computer engineering is based on Alan Turing's article "Computing Machine and Intelligence." Turing practiced a test about imitation game, known as the "Turing Test" (Koyuncu 2015). The question is whether machines should think. If the machine replies to the test questions as a human participant and convinces the examiner, then we should say the machine should think. Thereby, AI is considered as conditionally required data input into the machine.

The robots used in many fields in the economy today are computer-equipped, human-looking machines. In the past two decades, the application of the internet and digital technologies makes it possible to collect and availability of big data including images for economic agents. This allowed utilizing the application of creative digital technologies on big data analysis such as machine learning (ML) algorithms. Prediction task of ML for the future that infers from the past experiences, improvements in artificial neural networks (ANNs), and deep learning (DL) techniques makes possible further solutions for complicated problems in business and economic sectors. These technologies are considered as part of the AI. Thereby, AI technologies' functions are becoming a requirement for big data processing and improvements in competitive power at sectors in the economy.

AI technologies have advanced rapidly over the past several years. Application of AI makes fundamental change and development in different economic activities such as productivity, competing for power, employment, and economic growth. As machines display ever-more sophisticated cognitive capabilities, generate new efficiencies, and yield cost savings substantially, these development occur through profound impact developments in technology and innovations.

On the other hand, AI is a more common term, dealing with more generic problems of developing a system to imitate the computational, processing, and analytic power of the human mind. It is an umbrella that encompasses other fields such as image processing, sound recognition, neural networks (NN), and much more. ML and DL are also part of this umbrella and are subsets of AI.

Despite such developments to process the given data through learning and predicting human capacity has superiority compared to the machines in terms of solving a complicated problem. For example, compared to the human brain, AI-containing machines lack adaptivity in terms of learning new and undefined processes. Besides, the computers are also unable to process existing knowledge that it serves for other undefined purposes.

The purposes of this study first give adequate detailed explanations to the researchers, about AI technologies, second inform applications of these technologies into the sectors, impacts on the world trade and economy due to significant impact on economic activities, and within the framework of growth theories, develop a model to examine the relationship between AI and economic growth. Then, effects on employment, wages, and future professions.

The rest of the study is organized as follows. In the second section, AI, ML, DL, ANNs are analyzed, respectively; section 3 presents the application of AI in economic sectors, the global trade, the world economy, effects on productivity, and examine AI as a production factor, the effects on employment, wages and the future professions supposed to be created by AI technologies. In the last section, the concluding remarks are reviewed.

ARTIFICIAL INTELLIGENCE: MACHINE LEARNING, DEEP LEARNING, ARTIFICIAL NEURAL NETWORKS

Intelligence should be defined as being able to understand the relations between feelings and objects, having thinking ability, analyze the complex problems, solving the problem, collect the proper data, learn and solve it, then reach a result and apply. AI, as the name suggests, could be interpreted as setting up a model and applying it by imitating human talent and behaviors into the machines. The major purpose of AI is to generate machines that could be possible to realize works that require human intelligence, thereby, maintaining a system that provides the needs which require natural intelligence (Yılmaz 2019, 1–5; Egor 2018).

While AI is such technology that works similar to human behavior, ML algorithms analyze and search the problems more effectively via detailed big data. ML is one of the most influential and powerful technologies in today's world that uses data and answers to discover the rules behind a problem.

AI (the 1950s) as a broader concept comprises some other major technologies such as ML (1980s), DL (2010s), and NN, ML is a subset of AI, and DL is a subset of ML. Mentioned technologies, relationships between them, and the impact on AIs functioning the process is examined in detail below sections.

Artificial intelligence

AI is defined as the abilities which belong to human that are analyzed and provided by machines such as think, reasoning, perceiving objective realities, investigate and derive the result. Accordingly, the basis and operating functions such as thinking, acting, and problem-solving abilities of AI function are similar to that realized by the human brain. But the human brain has additional functions realized simultaneously as sensation, control the internal organs, emotions, actions.

Through AI applications, each cognitive activity could be exercised by artificial systems with higher success levels. Once a machine by learning complete the tasks that depended upon a series of defined rules then solve problems called AI. AI is neither a human mind exerciser nor has public psychology machine program.

AI-based machines execute either general tasks or could perform some specific tasks within a limited sophistication. AI technologies are used to predict a certain task and when this type of prediction is automated, more accurate results should be reached on that specified decision task compare to human performed decision tasks (Say 2019, 83; Taddy 2018; Yiğit 2011; Banger 2018, 37; Agrawal et al. 2019, 8). AI as general-purpose technology trained and perform to solve a defined subject in a specified area. That it has the ability of learning and preparing solution across multiple domains (Andersen 2018).

Some certain indications of AI given at Yılmaz' study of 2019 (Yılmaz 2019, 5–7, 13) as such;

    i. Learning and understanding via experience
    ii. Gaining experience with learning through repetition
    iii. While imitating the human brain use algorithmic thinking
    iv. Quick and succeeded adaptation to surprising conditions
    v. Subtracting a meaning from complicated and opposite messages
    vi. Understand and use of knowledge
    vii. Having the ability to think, guess, decide, and judge
    viii. Cope with particular conditions
    ix. Easier transfer of knowledge between machines
    x. Same reactions against the same problem
    xi. Practical reporting and documenting of saved knowledge

Autonomous robots should be indicated as one of the most common application forms of AI which is developed learning by themselves through the implications of AI technologies. They're not acting throughout the order of what they learned rather first learning then thinking and deciding for the proper way of acting. The robots collaborate with both of the other robots and the responsible people at the same working place (Apilioğulları 2018, 24–25).

Machine Learning and Methods

ML is empowered computer systems and a subset field of AI that has been learning ability from experiences as a general-purpose technology. The definition of ML is given as the study of computer algorithms that allow computer programs to automatically improve through experience, and designed to be applied to datasets, mainly focus on prediction, classification, and grouping tasks (Iriondo 2019, Athey 2018).[1]

ML system developed for first, recognizing and learning from past experiences then maintaining algorithms that making predictions for the future possible new events. Algorithms change and update the output as the new inputs are entered. ML techniques facilitating with big data loaded algorithms use for the realization of AI. Big data analysis allows rising learning ability of machines without programming throughout algorithms about the processed information. ML predicts defined tasks by using computers to reach reliable decision and result. After related data and variables entered into the computer about determined problem, algorithms predict the proper solutions. In ML computer;

  i. first, learn the features of an event by experiencing, sampling, finding, seeing, or instruction
 ii. then decide and
iii. produce a proper solution for similar events that not meet previously.

The realization of the learning is provided by the correlation between the sample inputs and the outputs to reveal the knowledge of the data. The major objective of the learning process is to find and apply the most convenient variables as the input. To do this, the learning methods of ML algorithms require to improve. For example, for an adaptive speed control system in autonomous cars, the required prospective inputs should be the legal speed limit, traffic conditions, speeds of nearby vehicles, weather and road conditions, etc. Internet search engines' operating systems process via ML techniques as well. Missing words of any searching activity correct by the ML algorithms system itself without any programming. Given the necessary inputs, we could expect to get the most convenient output with the application of the cruise control system in cars. Thereby, for the desired output finding facilitation of optimum inputs plays a major role in the ML methods. When the algorithmic solutions resulted in undesired, it could be possible to change the way of the learning process of algorithms. Thereby, as the decision-making process altered, the mistakes related to the decision should be eased and reached more proper decisions and solutions. This kind of correction practice could be sufficed by giving the differences of the object compared to other objects. For the proper decision, key elements of the systems are the input values. The ML process works also through "visual learner algorithms" that produce the expected output by using proper inputs. To realize this, we need to instruct each input which output is supposed to produce. This instruction process is comprised of technical operation that is repeated thousands of times until to clarify what we search as the desired output (Banger 2018, 38, Yılmaz 2019, 42–45, Bilgin 2018, 13–14, Elmas 2018, 95–96, Yiğit 2011, 14).

Learning types of ML explaining (Yılmaz 2019, 43) as,

  i. Programming: works with ordered statements for achieving the requirements,
 ii. Memorizing: rewarding and achieved proper result or otherwise giving a penalty after the decision,

iii. Statistical: defining the proper relations statically against reaction for the decision,
iv. Sampling: generalizing the system through counseling,
 v. New knowledge: without consultancy modeling, the system supposed to learn by itself

In an ML model, it would need to perform additional steps, such as already-mentioned extraction of the features of given data. For example, if we use an ML model and use a car as an input, it's required that first of all need to program the unique features of a car (shape, size, windows, wheels, etc.) into the algorithm.

While the methods of ML explaining as supervised, unsupervised, semi-supervised, and reinforcement learnings, major steps of ML assignment realization given at the same study (Bilgin 2018, 14–15) as below;

  i. To get a better learning experience from ML, collecting "the big raw data" related to the previous periods from various sources such as databases, websites, etc.,
 ii. Preparing the data,
iii. Training a model: for creating the model choosing the appropriate algorithm and for representing the data it is choosing process of the appropriate model,
iv. Evaluating the model by testing the model developed at the previous stage and registering the test results,
 v. Improving the performance through bigger data collections and pretreatment of the data for creating the model.

Deep Learning

DL is a technique for realizing the ML, and it's a subset of ML that has developed in the early past decade. The word "deep" refers to the layer numbers that have a lot, and DL works with the use of algorithms. DL algorithms are facilitated in a similar way to the human brain functions and imitate it. It's a kind of ML that algorithm is shaped as NN. For instance, ANNs a kind of algorithms that try to imitate the way of human brain decision-taking process. DL algorithms are more developed compared to ML that they realize the data automatically for the classification of prediction models. Between two neuron networks, through common warning messages, simultaneous activation of neurons occurs.

DL process depends upon the models that are inspired by neurons simple but multilayered and large NN. In such a proceeding structure, DL learning is updating itself realized through analyzed big data that provided to the algorithm as an input (Taddy 2018, 6, Elmas 2018, 98). A variety of data make algorithms learn and produce a proper solution. Deep neural network (DNN) model since having a multilayer structure and billions of parameters, by using a high number of variables is realizing the image identification of the object by combining a lot of information such as the shape of the image, color, design, environment. After taking the data, it's learning how to solve the problem. Later, it prepares and gives proper solutions faster for similar conditions.

DNN's basic steps of image processing designated by Elmas (2018, 150) as;

  i. Education: train with the labeled images of thousands of different people for classification of DL networks
 ii. Entry: shows a picture for recognition to pre-trained network
iii. Input layer: at this layer preserves simple shapes such as edges that are very relevant to the picture, the rest is discarded
 iv. Inter (hidden) layers: at these layers preserves more complicated shapes such as hand, arm, foot, head; the rest is discarded
  v. Output layer: at this layer are available very complicated shapes that can be identified as different people
 vi. Exist: according to its training, the network makes the most likely prediction about what the object is

In DL, the machine will ensure that a convenient output is available even if it encounters a different input than the previous one. An implication that could be realized as the border in an ANN that explains whether the message will be passed or ended. Therefore, ANNs learn by adjusting the weights of neurons, after that new connections reinforced and unused nerve track dies. The features revealed from DL that the algorithm could be the peculiarities sometimes we had recognized, and sometimes not recognized.

Unfavorable network fluctuations reflect the success of fails of decision-making mechanism. Whereas loss functions bigger; it explains that the network does not work well. Otherwise, networks make small errors. Actually, ANN is trained by adjusting the weights and biases of each neuron to realize a smaller loss function.

In the case of a DL model, it would recognize all the unique characteristics of a car by itself and make correct predictions. Thereby, DL models don't need the feature extraction process differently from ML.

Artificial Neural Networks

ANNs make an effort to imitate through modeling biological neurons in the human brain. A human brain incorporates billions of neurons and makes an effort to imitate through modeling biological neurons in the human brain. A human brain incorporates billions of neurons and trillions of connections between them.

Biological neurons function as an interconnected set of nerve cells or as information-processing parts of the human brain. Neurons in the brain can change the nature and with the connections to other neurons respond to the events that occur through senses. The neurons are nerve cells connected with links between brain cells and other organs and muscles of the human body that each link has its own numerical weight. Interacting neural cells estimated 60 million in the human brain. Learning functions do perform through repeated actions of neurons' weights. Thereby, the brain can learn. The strength of connections between neurons determines the power of problem-solving computations. ANNs are collections of nodes that are interconnected—inspired by the huge network of neurons as in the human brain. ANNs are considered as one of the most known applicable ways of the existing ML techniques that enable a computer to learn from the observational data such as speech, image, and video data. ANNs try to maintain the computer to gain the ability of recognition and prediction by learning, and consist of excessively interconnected processors, that is, known as neurons. Compared to biological neurons and the brain they have both fewer connections and smaller in terms of number. Knowledge is taken by the sense organs and sent to the central neural system in which the signal allocates the knowledge to the related organs after interpretation and produces reaction signals. ANNs consist of cells that are structurally similar to biological cells and those cells by working simultaneously realize complicated proceedings that imitate and model these biological neural systems. Artificial neurons are simple compared to biological neurons but imitate four basic functions of the biological neurons: inputs, weighted parameters, calculation activity, and exit functions. Similar to the human neural system, they have a structure of ability to treat and interpret the distributed data. They form plurality of aggregation numerous processing elements. Nodes settle like layers in the network. Knowledge spreads from the first layer to the following ones. Signs at the last layer are network exits. In the case of feedback or repeated networks, at least one node has a return connection (Yılmaz 2019, 61–62, 64; Elmas 2018, 51, Negnevitsky 2005, 166; Coppin 2004, 293, Taddy 2018, 5).

Basic patterns of NN facilitate fast training and computation. The model has linear combinations of inputs that are passed through nonlinear activation functions called nodes or, about the human brain, neurons. A linear function give that multiple layers of an NN are equivalent to one function. But nonlinear functions are introduced to make the network carry out a nearly complex function. Proper working requirements of an ANN explained in Negnevitsky'

2005 (Negnevitsky 2005, 167–168, 212), and (Yiğit 2011, 19, 22–24) studies are as follows:

First of all, the number of neurons required to be activated, and way of connection to be settled;

i. between neurons to form a network. Each neuron' has weighted links connected with the other neurons through signals,
ii. As the second step, we require to choose the most convenient algorithm,
iii. Then, train the NN by initiating and updating the weights of the network from training sets.

ANNs consist of a collection of artificial neurons that have connections that allow signals to be transmitted between neurons. The receiving neuron further sends signals to all the other neurons forward after processing. The network during training also adjusts itself to improve future predictions (Negnevitsky 2005, 167–168, 212, Yiğit 2011, 19, 22–24).

An ANN can only learn how to solve a new problem by analyzing old samples of the same problem that it learned with old knowledge. Learning is the basic integrated part of the ANNs. ANNs are apparatus that learn by itself without any requirement of an algorithm (Elmas 2018).

ANNs designed as tandem multilayers consist of multilayers with hundreds of perceptions-neurons in each layer. The output of each layer is input for the following layer.

The first ranking layer is the input layer and the last layer is called the output layer. Except for the first layer, each layer consists of a series of neural cell. Each cell in the layer takes each signal that comes from the previous layers as an input. The first layer consists of a series of numbers that act as code to explain the output by determining the detailed specifications. First, the number contained in each neural cell multiply with its weighted share at the layer, and second, some of the multiplications belong to all cells in the layer taken. Then this sum is sent to the following hidden layer as the output of the layer.

A set of circle nodes that is called a "layer" has different weighted sums of the same inputs. A weighted combination of inputs in each layer transfers to the following layer in the network as output. The weights of the inputs in layers are updated during network training. To solve the complex problems, nodes in the layers are used (Taddy 2018, 8–10).

The weights are modified to bring the network input/output behavior into a certain compatible line order. Each neuron computes its function according to a given input and numerical weights. The weight of a neuron either defines the strength of NN or realizes the learning situation through repeated adjustments. In the multiplier network, there is more than one weight for each input, and these are contributing to multiple outputs (Say 2019, 99–100).

Functions of multilayer perception with two layers should be explained as the following;

i. Input layer: accept input signals and distribute to all neurons in the hidden layer, and rarely contain computable neurons, thereby, doesn't process inputs. When the input signal exceeds a certain level, a chemical reaction happens in a neuron and sends the signal—the output to connect the other neuron.
ii. Hidden layers: reveal the peculiarity of neurons that represent by the weight of the neurons, and determine the desired output by the layer itself. Both continuous and discontinuous functions of the input signals can be represented in two hidden layers.
iii. Output layer: gets output signals from the hidden layer and prepares the output of the entire NN (Coppin 2004, 293, 299–302, Negnevitsky 2005, 175–176).

Learning is an integral part of ANN and is defined as the observation for persistent renewals or concluding attainments of education activities. Rules of learning activities could be given under three headlines: supervised-active learning, unsupervised (self-organized) learning, and reinforcement learning;

i. In active learning, NN learns with an external supervisor by preparing a training set for the network.
ii. In self-organized learning, first, NNs take different input patterns and discover several features, then learn to classify and decomposing the inputs. This way of learning is similar to the neuro-biological organization of the human brain.
iii. Reinforcement learning (Elmas 2019, 51, Negnevitsky 2005, 176–201).

While computers store the knowledge at a specified section, ANNs spread it into the cells in the network and are stored in the cells. The network decides and chooses the best output among the inputs. Features of the problem are determined by using digital data. Then by learning the problem and realizing the ML, ANNs are able to take a reliable decision against similar situations. The problem learning ability of ANNs improves by using selected convenient samples. After learning the problem, ANNs can produce meaningful output even if there is missing data.

The NN's training process works as follows:

i. get a serial of possible inputs,
ii. calculate the respective outputs by learning which output is supposed to produce for any input,

iii. calculate the performance: by giving a large number of input-output data into the network,

iv. pass the errors to the previous layer to adjust its parameters (and repeat for every layer in the network),

v. repeat for every series of possible inputs until the performance will get good enough,

vi. after completion of the learning process, quite likely expect correct solutions for not only the inputs calculated but also the other inputs previously not seen ever.

Since all ANNs' have neurons, connections, and transfer functions, there have been similarities among different architectures, structures, or neuron networks. Thereby, the facilitation of ANNs allows finding solutions against the conditions not experienced before through making calculations with numerical data and learning the problem by using samples given to the system (Yılmaz 2019, 65–68, Elmas 2018, 29, 34, 73, Say 2019, 101–102).

Additional hidden layers between the input and output layers are called as DNNs; they can solve more properly detailed and complex nonlinear connections.

Artificial Intelligence Applications

As the financial and commercial implications of AI are developing at the world level, some specific initiatives and researches are arising at the world level. For example, a recent collaboration between major information and retail service companies such as Google, DeepMind, Microsoft, IBM, Facebook, and Amazon comprises an "Artificial Intelligence Partnership" on behalf of mankind and society. The major aim of this initiative is to serve the public for awareness and improving the understanding of what is AI and search for the best implications of AI technologies. On the other hand, Stuart Russell, a computer science professor at California University, predicts that the machines' abilities and efficiencies supposed exceeded to the level of humans (Schwab 2019, 170–171).

One of the major reasons for AI applications arise due to the complementary effect between decision task and prediction tasks. Without any decision, even a prediction taken just as timely and correctly has no value itself in terms of creating a net return from economic activities. Thereby, applying AI, economic agents should benefit from the right combination of prediction and decision tasks. Because of correct predictions and decisions with the application of automated machines, it reduces uncertainty compared to humans and increases relative returns to machines versus labor. Data scientists and AI professionals are more involved in the decision-making process as they are the ones leading the process of change within the organization. AI applications by facilitating ANNs mostly used such sectors as financial affairs, engineering, medical science. There are also some others as recognition of voice, handwriting, fingerprint, plaque, electrical sign, and weather broadcasting, autonomous vehicle control, diagnosis, analysis, and interpretations in biomedical and medical fields, flying simulation and automated pilot applications, automated road track, according to the road conditions driving analysis, evaluating of credit applications and customer analysis, signal and image processing, target selecting, production process control, duration analysis, quality control, robotics, word recognition, and language translation, image and data confrontation, and telecommunication applications, retina scanning and face match (Agrawal et al. 2019; Yılmaz 2019, 65–66; Elmas, 2018, 38–39).

These days, DNNs are effectively implemented in image, video, and language processing and content improvements. For instance, it's possible sweeping the images from noisy platforms, crystallize, and enlarging the pictures without altering the original images. Within the context of image processing activities, it is possible to determine the speed and direction of video objects. Through voice and object recognition processes, face and any place recognition (Elmas 2018, 152, 153). In Softtech's 2019 report, further details on image processing technologies are explained as biometric and face recognition, sensitivity analysis, behavior observation, object realization, recognition from appearance, security, and video follow-up (Softect 2019, 41–43).

Application areas of ML and ANNs as a practical form of ML can be summarized as below:

  i. robots, sensors, production process control, quality control, assembly line monitoring, elevator control systems;
 ii. financial transactions: credit controls and risk assessments, stock markets—algorithmic transactions (fuzzy expert systems);
iii. health services—cancer detection, heart-attack-related problems, diagnosis, surgery, visualization;
 iv. analyze of drug side effects, etc.;
  v. prepare personnel marketing plans and solutions by understanding and learning human behaviors for individualistic consumer demands, private product suggestions, and stock analysis;
 vi. avoid fraudulent perceptions—determine legal and illegal transactions;
vii. suggestions on online marketing and sale operations;
viii. internet search engines;
 ix. automated translations—natural language processing;
  x. self-driving cars to manage control—autonomous cars;
 xi. weather forecasting;

xii. face, picture-image, speech-voice recognition;

xiii. aviation and space engineering;

xiv. military science;

xv. chemical engineering;

xvi. environmental and nuclear sciences;

xvii.   protecting data security;

xviii.   prevent from faultily personnel decisions;

xix. other sectors: trade, manufacturing, agriculture (crop yield analysis), telecommunication, electronics, insurance, education, electricity, transportation, human resource vocational evaluations, etc. (Yiğit 2011, 35–61; Bilgin 2018, 31–34; Agrawal et al. 2018).

Achieved positive contributions originated from the implications of AI technologies are indicated in the White House report on the aggregate productivity growth, changes in the skills demanded by the job market, including greater demand for higher-level technical skills. According to the report, while the major achievements of past automation were being productivity gains, current automation applications have the same. The real subject should be how to eliminate the weakness of the technological improvement toward low- and middle-income groups in the society and unemployment conditions. Therefore, policy implications supposed to provide AI's economic returns shared equally at beneficial of all society in order to get sustainable income level (White House Report 2016).

HOW IS AI RESHAPING THE GLOBAL TRADE AND THE WORLD ECONOMY, AND HOW AI IS PLACED AS A PRODUCTION FACTOR

How is AI Reshaping the Global Trade and the World Economy?

Major developments improve the contribution of AI technologies to economic activities. Fast improvements in computing power and capacity. Graphics processing units (GPUs) today reached 40–80 times faster power compared to the fastest GPUs available in 2013. Cloud computing systems enable lower costs for computing and storage services. Within this context, international data availability that feeding the algorithms needed to produce new aspects estimated to reach one trillion gigabytes by 2025. DL techniques and large-scale NN increase the accuracy of prediction and classification. In addition, faster increased digitization due to Covid-19 pandemic in the years of 2020 and expectedly in 2021 is supposed to raise the job automation process that robots replace workers facilitated by AI technologies.

As it is estimated, AI-related activities could add to the world gross domestic production (GDP) as much as $15.7 trillion, and $13 trillion by 2030, as it's estimated by ranking at the World Economic Forum (WEF) study and according to the Mc Kinsey Discussion Paper. This should drive as it is expressed at WEF paper, by the contribution of 40% in productivity, and 60% in consumption (McKinsey 2018).

While herein in this study AI is considered as a significant driver of global trade and economic growth, a detailed analysis could be seen also at a recent study with respect to the AI technologies and firms, economic growth, market structure, sectoral differences, and organizational considerations within firms (Aghion et al. 2017).

AI impacts on sectors and the sector's most convenient AI applicable areas and major innovative impacts of AI onto the related sectors are stated below. Healthcare, diagnosis, early identification of various diseases, accurate and detailed imaging diagnosis (radiology, pathology), automotive: autonomous and semi-autonomous driving, engine monitoring and predictability, autonomous driving. Financial services: personalized financial choices, crypto currencies, attainable transactions. Retail: personalized consumer goods, predictable customer preferences, stock and marketing management. Technology: communication and entertainment marketing new searches, archiving, customized content improvements, personalized. Manufacturing: close control on production process, better management of value chain, flexible production on customer desire. Energy timely grid control and infrastructure maintenance, exact measurement of production and consumption values. Transport and logistic: improving autonomous vehicles, efficient traffic operations and security regulations both in and inter-city transport network security (Pricewaterhouse Coopers, 2017).

AI and Productivity Increases

With the AI use, some of the inadequacies in the traditional economy can be eliminated. To increase efficiency in the economy, AI contributes to fulfill the market participants' requirements such as data availability and analysis, reduction of market search discrepancies, find reliable partners (Milgrom and Tadelis 2018).

AI contributes to economic growth, through increasing productivity, better management of production units, and expansion of trade opportunities through digital platforms (Globalization Partners 2020, 8–9). Within this context, herein an enhanced analysis gives first AI components and second explains AI GDP growth contribution of different features of AI applications. As the general interpretation, AI technologies are constituted by skilled human, algorithms, ML, DL, and ANNs. Comprising of principal components of AI factor change aim and plan of the business activities. While first two variable of AI factor skilled human and algorithms are used generally at any AI implementation, adopting other components, ML, DL, ANNs vary with the requirements of sectoral activities. In case of AI growth, contribution to the GDP could be explained via contributions of three different below quite detailed reviewed activities: productivity increases, management improvement, and trade expansion.

Productivity Increases

AI is already applicable to different sectors and can have a significant impact in areas such as *marketing and sales, supply chains, and trade, manufacturing, health, education, etc.* The size of this contribution varies with the countries that have had some specific factors such as innovation capacity, human capital sources, availability of information technologies, data capacity, and internet users' share in total population.

As the AI technologies automate repetitive tasks via *displacement and replacement effects*, it reduces labor cost and ensures an increase in productivity. AI system also provides accurate and efficient predictions both of *smart manufacturing* and effective use of capacities. As a result, AI increases *productivity* growth that should allow to raise *economic growth* and opportunities for international trade as well.

According to McKinsey's The State of AI in 2020 Survey that responses taken from 1.151 AI adopted firms and organizations at different sectors and regions in the world in 2019, AI adopted and use ratio given as ranging from 15% to 24% within specified business functions at highest five sectors of "product and/or service developments, service operations, marketing and sales, risk modeling and analytics, and manufacturing." Within the ratio of the same business sectors, revenue increases due to adoption of AI raised by ranging from least 5% up to higher 10%.

Management Improvement

AI contributes better management possibilities through centrally controlled system between different production units those are far away from each other. With the AI applications, also warehouses, logistic, marketing, sales activities should be managed better.

Trade Expansion Effect

Automating *trade* operations by facilitating AI technologies contribute to widen their operations internationally. AI-created translation facilities enhance communication, negotiation, and cooperation that positively contribute to trade expansion. AI systems can also respond to predict the changes in demand structure, country-specific market conditions, then adapt the production process at real time. Thereby, save redundant labor and inventory costs.

AI as a Production Factor

Once realized as a certain rise in productivity, economic growth, and national income will be the result of adopting AI technologies. This case indicates; in terms of economic growth theory, AI suppose to function as a production factor. For empirically support to this assumption required more reliable data in longer range of time. Thereby, it should be the subject of growth research studies in the future.

When we consider AI technologies through labor automation and innovation, it contributes to cost saving, and productivity growth which has accelerated and intensified the natural forces of market competition. First, adopting AI technologies create both labor augmenting capabilities and human capital replacement effect as machines take over certain jobs, resulting in a rise in labor productivity. Second, while automation saves labor-wage costs, preventative maintenance on machines and equipment takes longer time of durability of the physical capital-fixed assets.

As a result, while factor endowment intensity at production function changes on behalf of technology factor (AI), it changes the expense of labor and capital factors. That is, AI technologies create substitution effect, and then realize factor augmenting effect onto the other production factors, capital, and labor as well. This also contributes to an additional productivity improvement in the economic sectors. The augmenting effect generates a new situation on the production structure in which factor endowment of production process change on behalf of technology that is AI. Thereafter, AI becomes a production factor.

The contribution of variables in this equation change accordingly to the adaptation ratio of AI technologies into the production process. As in Cockburn et al. 2018 (12–15, 23), policy implications that encourage competition, data sharing, and openness are likely to be an important determinant of economic growth through not only job displacement and create new tasks but also reduced marginal R&D search cost by substituting skilled personnel toward fixed cost investment application in AI technologies.

If it's assumed that using ratio of AI at a variety of business activities raised against to the other production factors capital and labor, factor endowment could be changed on behalf of AI factor. Since, AI creates additional productivity in related industry, possible to gain competitive power, rise market share and market value of the firm. Adopting AI as a production factor requires improved proper algorithms to meet the needs of industry' current and new applications planned in the future.

How AI Technologies Effect Employment Structure and Wages

A recent study of WEF gives some data about AI technologies' job creation and GDP contributions. The study expresses that the technology created millions of jobs and now comprised 10% of US GDP. According to the article, at Price Water House (PWC)'s Annual Global CEO Survey, 63% of CEOs believe AI will have a larger impact than the internet (World Economic Forum 2020).

AI technologies are supposed to create more new jobs than it automates. By 2025, while AI-related technologies will create ninety-seven million new jobs, such as data analysts, AI, ML specialists, IoT specialists, software and applications, and developers, eighty-five million jobs as accounting, bookkeeping, and payroll clerks, administrative and executive secretaries, etc. should decrease. While low digital skills requiring activities and repetitive jobs decline, there will be a rise in nonrepetitive activities and jobs that require high digital skills by 2030. Thereby, such shifts in employment structure change the wage incomes on behalf of the latter group of works as well (McKinsey Discussion Paper 2018, 6, 7).

AI and Future Professions

Whereas inventions, as it is explained in the endogenous economic growth theory, created by the human brain throughout R&D and innovation process knowledge are considered as a production factor that contributes to the economic growth attempts (Kurtoğlu 2010, 2016a; 2016b), facilitating of human brain-imitated AI technologies spreading to every sector of the economic and social affairs. Thereby, AI is considering an innovation like electricity, the internet, and others. Then the discussions are going on how it affects the workforce and employment level in the economies. How employees will adjust to new working conditions in which industrial robots and digital technologies such as AI display some of the workforces and create new tasks? AI, automation, and robots in industries and effects on growth, labor share, wages, and productivity-related issues are discussed and analyzed in some of the recent studies of Acemoğlu and Restrepo 2016–2019. Within the framework of the task-based model (Acemoğlu and Restrepo 2016), and market forces ensured stability in economic growth, the direction of technological change explained with the impact of relative factor prices. For instance, the cheaper long-run rental rate of capital relative to wages indicated an accelerating effect for automation. Thereby, different technological changes should have a different impact on production factors, that is, capital and labor. The authors search how AI-related automation effects production and working conditions. They reach the result that use of AI creates new tasks and new skill requirements for labour. Thereby, labour could be employed more productive and possibly achieving some more gains in terms of economical and social aspects (Acemoğlu and Restrepo 2018, 2019a).

Beyond these, effects of AI, automation, and digital technologies on economic sectors, including replacement and reinstatement of labor, emerging of new professions through creating new tasks, and way of doing business activities in each sector is supposed to change in next decades, Herein, in this section, several "future professions" creating by AI implications that indicated in a recent report dealing in Stillman's search (Inc., 2017) are given as data detective, data processing promoter, ethical sourcing officer, AI business development manager, master of edge computing, walker/talker, fitness commitment counsellor, AI-assisted health care technician, cybercity analyst, genomic portfolio director, man-machine teaming manager, financial wellness coach, digital tailor, chief trust officer, quantum machine-learning analyst, virtual store assistant, personal data broker, personal memory manager, augmented-reality journey builder, highway controller, genetic diversity officer (Stillman, 2017).

CONCLUSION

Economic agents and governments are seen as realizing the impacts of AI technologies on the skill level of the workforce, structural change in professions, and the way of doing business soon. The digital transformation allows widening the use of smart machines and AI in the next three decades. While only a minority of jobs supposed to be affected and would be disappeared, the majority of jobs and tasks should remain and would need humans to work together with the contribution of one of the AI technologies that analyze big data. It is predicted that the improvement of digitalization was supposed to hire adequate qualified human and create "New Collar" workforce. "New Collar" jobs should necessitate not only adaptation to the new technologies, software applications but also work together with the smart machines such as robots contained with the AI technologies. While AI is supposed to require interdisciplinary searchers, it should combine different subjects on studies of economics, big data analysis, and ML technologies; using these technologies allow us to reach more accurate results on specified decision tasks compared to the human workforce providing tasks. Autonomous robots should be indicated as one of the most common application forms of AI which is developed learning by themselves through the implications of AI technologies. They're by ranking: learn, think, and decide for the most convenient solution. The robots collaborate with the other robots and the responsible process managers.

AI technologies and robots operated by these technologies will change the way of doing business and is expected to open new business areas and professions. Cloud computing platforms as part of digital transformation, for instance, providing both hardware and big data and adapting these facilities to the ML techniques provide solutions for users of the platforms. ML techniques with the correlation between the most convenient sample inputs and the outputs reveal the knowledge of the data. To realize the process, first learning, then thinking, and deciding for achieving the proper way of acting.

DL working process as part of the AI technologies functionalize through the models consisted of multilayered neurons and large NN. In such a proceeding structure, DL algorithm updates itself by utilizing the big data provided as an input.

The network consisted of ANNs that build up as the more developed technique of AI applications, during training stages, adjusts itself to improve future predictions. An ANN can only learn by itself without any requirement of an algorithm on how to solve an unknown situation not familiar previously by analyzing old samples of the same problem. Thereby, learning is the basic integrated part of the ANNs.

By the contribution of achieving faster developments in computer capacities, availability of big data, and DL techniques, remarkable gains should be expected at the global output and trade volume by advancing the use of AI technologies. The process as a result of changing factor endowment on behalf of technology, AI substitute labor with displacement and replacement effects and become a production factor. Future professions supposed to be created via AI technologies are ever-increasing and expected to continue to verify the next decades.

NOTE

1. See Athey 2018 for Broader Predictions About the Impact of Machine Learning on Economics.

REFERENCES

Acemoğlu, D. and P. Restrepo. 2016. "The Race Between Machine and Man: Implications of Technology for Growth, Factor Shares and Employment." NBER Working Paper 22252, National Bureau of Economic Research, Cambridge, MA.

Acemoğlu, D. and P. Restrepo. 2018a. "Artificial Intelligence, Automation and Works" NBER Working Paper 24196, National Bureau of Economic Research, Cambridge, MA.

Acemoğlu, D. and P. Restrepo. 2018b. "Democraphics and Automation" NBER Working Paper 24421, National Bureau of Economic Research, Cambridge, MA.

Acemoğlu, D. and P. Restrepo. 2019a. "The Working Kind of AI? Artificial Intelligence and The Future of Labor Demand" NBER Working Paper 25682, National Bureau of Economic Research, Cambridge, MA.

Acemoğlu, D. and P. Restrepo. 2019b. "Automation and New Tasks: How Technology Displaces and Reinstates Labor" NBER Working Paper 25684, National Bureau of Economic Research, Cambridge, MA.

Aghion, P., B. F. Jones, and Charles I. Jones. 2017. "Artificial Intelligence and Economic Growth," NBER Working Paper 23928, National Bureau of Economic Research, Cambridge, MA.

Agrawal, A. K., J. S. Gans and A. Goldfarb. 2018. "Economic Policy for Artificial Intelligence," NBER Working Paper Series, 24690, NBER Working Paper 23928, National Bureau of Economic Research, Cambridge, MA.

Agrawal, A., J. S. Gans and A. Goldfarb. 2019. "Artificial Intelligence: The Ambiguous Labor Market Impact of Automating Prediction," NBER Working Paper Series, 25619, National Bureau of Economic Research, Cambridge, MA.

Andersen, M. L. 2018. "Current Trends in Deep Learning." Accessed October 12, 2020. https://knowitlabs.no/current-trends-in-deep-learning-85e378dc813.

Apilioğulları, Lütfi. 2018. *Dijital Dönüşümüm Yol Haritası Endüstri 4.0 Değişimin Değiştirdikleri*. İstanbul: Aura Kitapları.

Athey, Susan. 2018. "The Impact of Machine Learning on Economics." Accessed October 07, 2020. https://www.gsb.stanford.edu/sites/default/files/publication-pdf/atheyimpactmlecon. pdf.

Banger, Gürcan. 2018. *Endüstri 4.0 Uygulama ve Dönüşüm Rehberi*. Eskişehir: Dorlion Yayınları.

Bilgin, Metin. 2018. "Makine Öğrenmesi," In. Atınç Yılmaz, İstanbul: Papatya Yayıncılık Eğitim Eğitim Bilgisayar Sistemleri.

Cockburn, I. M., R. Henderson and S. Stern. 2018. "The Impact of Artificial Intelligence on Innovation," NBER Working Paper, 24449, NBER Working Paper Series, 25619, National Bureau of Economic Research, Cambridge, MA.

Coppin, Ben. 2004. *Artificial Intelligence Illuminated*. Canada: Jones and Bartlett Learning.

Egor, Dexhib. 2018. "What is Intelligence?." Accessed October 7, 2020. https://to wardsdatascience.com/what-is-intelligence-a69cbd8bb1b4.

Elmas, Çetin. 2018. *Yapay Zeka Uygulamaları*. Ankara: Seçkin Yayıncılık.

Globalization Partners. 2020. "The Impact of AI on Global Expansion." Accessed 08 January 2020. https://ourworld.unu.edu/en/artificial-intelligence-and-global-go vernance-a-thought-leadership-and-engagement-platform.

Iriondo, Roberto. 2019. "Machine Learning (ML) vs. Artificial Intelligence (AI) Crucial." Accessed October 05, 2020. https://medium.com/datadriveninvestor/di fferences-between-ai-and-machine-learning-and-why-it-matters-1255b182fc6.

Koyuncu, Merve. 2015. "Çağdaş Zihin Felsefesinde Yapay Zeka Tartışmaları – Turing Testi ve Yansımaları." Master diss., Çukurova Üniversitesi, Sosyal Bilimler Enstitüsü.

Kurtoğlu, Y. 2010. Process and Product Innovations: A Theoretical Approach. *International Journal of Business and Management*, 2 (2): 89–101.

Kurtoğlu, Y. 2016a. The Knowledge Factor, the Components and the Innovations. *International Review of Management and Business Research*, 5 (1): 214–222.

Kurtoğlu, Y. 2016b. Knowledge Input as a Production Factor and the Competing Power. *International Journal of Arts and Humanities*, 2 (2): 7–18.

McKinsey & Company. 2020. "McKinsey Analytics," The State of AI in 2020. Accessed December 4, 2020. https://www.mckinsey.com/business-functions/m ckinsey-analytics/our-insights/global-survey- the-state-of-ai-in-2020.

McKinsey&Company. 2018. "Notes From The AI Frontier, Modeling the Impact of AI on the World Economy." Accessed October 18, 2020. https://www.mckinsey .com/featured-insights/artificial-intelligence/notes-from-the-ai-frontier-modeling -the-impact-of-ai-on-the-world-economy.

Milgrom, Paul R. and Steve Tadelis .2018. "How Artificial Intelligence and Machine Learning Can Impact Market Design." Nber Working Paper, National Bureau of Economic Research, Cambridge, MA.

Negnevitsky, Michael. 2005. *Artificial Intelligence -A Guide to Intelligent Systems*. England: Pearson Education Limited.

Pricewaterhouse Coopers (Pwc). 2017. "Sizing the prize what's the real value of AI for your business and how can you capitalise?" Accessed October 14, 2020. https ://www.pwc.com/gx/en/issues/analytics/assets/pwc-ai-analysis-sizing-the-prize-re port.pdf.

Say, Cem. 2019. *50 Soruda Yapay Zeka*. İstanbul: Bilim ve Gelecek Kitaplığı.

Schwab, Klaus and Nicholas Davis. 2019. *Dördüncü Sanayi Devrimini Şekillendirmek*. Translated by Nadir Özata. İstanbul: Optimist Yayın Grubu.

Softtech. 2019. "Softtech 2019 Teknoloji Raporu," Accesses October 10, 2020. https ://softtech.com.tr/2019-teknoloji-raporu/.

Stillman, Jessica. 2017. "21 Future Jobs the Robots Are Actually Creating." Accessed October 18, 2020. https://www.inc.com/jessica-stillman//21-future-jpbs-robots-are -actually-creating.html.

Taddy, Matt. 2018. "The Technological Element of Artificial Intelligence," National Bureau of Economic Research Working Paper 24301, National Bureau of Economic Research, Cambridge, MA.

White House Report. 2016. "Artificial Intelligence, Automation, and the Economy." Accessed October 20, 2020 .https://obamawhitehouse.archives.gov/sites/whiteho use.gov/files/docu- ments/Artificial-Intelligence-Automation-Economy.PDF_.

World Economic Forum (WEF). 2020. The Article Written as Part of the "The Jobs Reset Summit Headed Don't Fear AI. It Will Lead to Long -Term Job Growth." October 5, 2020.

Yiğit, Pakize. 2011. "Yapay Sinir Ağları ve Kredi Taleplerinin Değerlendirilmesi Üzerine Bir Uygulama," Master Diss., Istanbul University Social Sciences Institute.

Yılmaz, Atınç. 2019. *Yapay Zeka*. İstanbul:İnkilap Kitabevi.

Index

About the Contributors

Altuğ Günar, who completed the PhD program of the Department of European Union at Istanbul University Institute of Social Sciences in 2017, started to work as an assistant professor at Bandırma Onyedi Eylül University in 2018. He has a large number of works, including articles, book chapters, book, and book editors in the field of the European Union. His main research areas are the European Union, International Relations and Economics, and Schumpeterian Economics. Today, he is the vice dean at Bandırma Onyedi Eylül University in the Faculty of Economics and Administrative Sciences, director of the Mediterranean Policy Applications and Research Center, and lecturer in the department of International Relations. His most recent book is entitled "Creative Destruction, Crisis and European Union: The 2008 Crisis within the Framework of the Schumpeterian Approach European Union and Globalization" and "Future of The European Union Integration: A Failure or A Success? Future Expectations."

Omca Altın graduated from the Izmir University of Economics, Department of International Relations in English and the European Union, and completed her master's and doctorate degrees in the European Union Department of Istanbul University. Omca ALTIN, who has various academic studies and project support in the field of the European Union, is an assistant professor at Kastamonu University, Faculty of Economic and Administrative Sciences, Department of International Relations as a lecturer. She also works as a Head of the Department of European Union Law.

İlhan Aras is an associate professor at the Department of International Relations at Nevsehir Haci Bektas Veli University. He completed his PhD at the Department of European Union Studies at Istanbul University in 2014.

His research interests are European studies and China. He is the author of numerous studies on European Union.

Kaan Çelikok received a BA in Labor Economics and Industrial Relations from Istanbul University in 2012 and an MA in Economic Policy from Istanbul University in 2014. He completed the Postgraduate Program Master of European Studies at the University of Vienna in 2014, where he was an award holder of the Jean Monnet Scholarship. He received his PhD in European Union in the Institute of Graduate Studies in Social Sciences from Istanbul University. During his doctoral studies, he was a doctoral fellow at the Institute of Political Science at Heidelberg University, Germany, in 2017, where he was awarded a scholarship by the DAAD (German Academic Exchange Service). He works as an assistant professor at the Department of Foreign Trade, Bandırma Onyedi Eylül University, Bandırma Vocational School since 2020. His academic fields of interests include industrial economy, competition policy, and transport economy.

Fatma Didin Sönmez received a BSc. in Economics and Management from the University of London and Istanbul Bilgi University in 2001 and an MA in Economics from Marmara University in 2004. She was a visiting scholar at Duke University in 2006. She received her PhD in Economics from Marmara University in 2008. She has been at Istanbul Bilgi University since 2001 and taken on different responsibilities in the Department of Economics and Faculty of Business, including the coordination and quality management of the University of London International Programs and the BİLGİ-Liverpool dual degree programs. She worked as vice head of department between 2012 and 2015, vice dean of Business Faculty between 2014 and 2017, and adviser to rector between 2015 and 2018. She is teaching at graduate and undergraduate programs. Her academic fields of interests include economic growth, economic development, and economic integration

Yusuf Kurtoğlu has got a doctorate diploma in Economics from Gazi University in 2004 and got an associate professor degree in August 2018. He has eight articles presented at the international congresses that seven of them published in international journals and published three books between 2006 and 2019. He has attended his official working life at the Ministry of Finance in 1979 and since 1984 he has been working as a treasury expert for Undersecretariat of Treasury in Ankara. In the meantime, Yusuf Kurtoğlu has worked as a department chief between 1996 and 2000 at the same Undersecretariat and as deputy Economics and commercial counselor and as Economics Counsellor for Turkish Embassy in Athens-Greece between 1991 and 1995. He is teaching/taught the courses "Knowledge, Technology and Innovation Economics," and "Public Administration," at Baskent University, and "Turkey's Economic Developments" at Hacettepe University in Ankara.

Çağla Özgören is an assistant professor in the Business Administration Department at Yeditepe University, Turkey. She obtained a PhD degree in Strategy, Innovation, and Entrepreneurship from Southampton Business School, UK. Her research investigates institutional and organizational change process from process-relational and multidimensional perspective in the field of higher education, knowledge exchange, and sharing economy. Her research lies in the intersection of organization theory (institutional theory), strategy (response strategies to complexities), and entrepreneurship (entrepreneurial logic and social entrepreneurship). Her current research projects explore the role and effectiveness of intermediary organizations in university-industry relations. Her work has been published in the Small Business Economics: An Entrepreneurship Journal, Cambridge Journal of Regions, Economy and Society, among others. Research projects that she has been working on were funded by British Council, British Academy and Newton Fund.

Cem Saatçioğlu is a professor at the Department of Economics, Istanbul University Faculty of Economics, where he teaches microeconomics and macroeconomics. He has previously worked with different aspects of monetary policy, fiscal policy, transport economy, and sports economics. He holds a PhD in Economics from Istanbul University. He has many publications both in national and in international journals.

Rüya Ataklı Yavuz is an assistant professor in the Department of Economics at Çanakkale Onsekiz Mart University, Çanakkale. She finished the undergraduate program at the Economics Department of Balıkesir University in 2008 and her master program at Economics Department Çanakkale Onsekiz Mart University in 2011. Received PhD from the Economics Department Çanakkale Onsekiz Mart University in 2016. Areas of research: international economics and economic development, economic history, Turkish economy.

Prof. Dr. Süreyya Yiğit is a professor of Politics and International Relations at the School of Politics and Diplomacy at New Vision University, Tbilisi, Georgia. Professor Yiğit's research interests include Post-Soviet Eurasian transition, energy security, and British politics. His most recent book is entitled "Mongolia-European Union Relations."

Samet Zenginoğlu completed his bachelor's degree in International Relations at Kocaeli University, his master's degree in the Department of International Relations at Akdeniz University, and his doctorate in the European Union Studies program at Süleyman Demirel University. Samet Zenginoğlu is still working at Adıyaman University. His main research areas of the European Union constitute the Turkey-European Union relations and European history.

www.ingramcontent.com/pod-product-compliance
Lightning Source LLC
Chambersburg PA
CBHW022314280326
41932CB00010B/1094